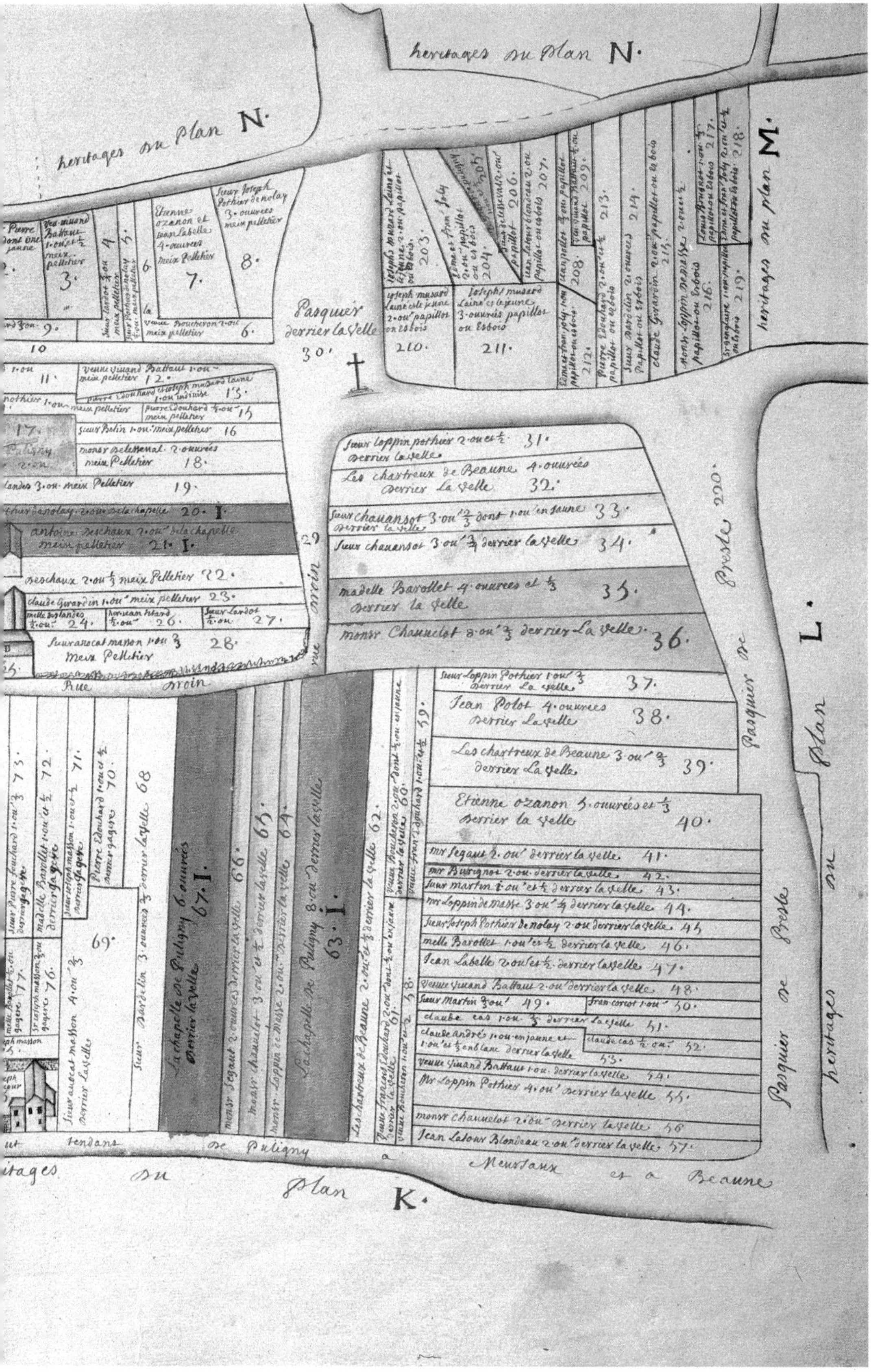

heritages du Plan N.
heritages du Plan N.
heritages du Plan M.
Pasquier derrier la Velle 30.
Sieur Joseph Pothier de nolay 3. ouvrees meix pelletier 8.
Etienne ozanon et Jean Labelle 4. ouvrees meix pelletier 7.
Sieur Belin 1. ou. meix pelletier 16
monsr delessenal 2. ouvrées meix pelletier 18.
antoine deschaux 2. ou. de la chapelle meix pelletier 21. I.
deschaux 2. ou 1/3 meix pelletier 22.
claude Girardin 1. ou. meix pelletier 23.
Sieur Lardot 1/2 ou. 27.
Sieur avocat masson 1. ou 2/3 meix pelletier 28.
Rue Droin
Sieur Loppin pothier 2. ou. et 1/2 derrier la Velle 31.
Les chartreux de Beaune 4. ouvrées derrier La Velle 32.
Sieur chauansot 3. ou. 2/3 dont 1. ou. en jaune derrier la velle 33.
Sieur chauansot 3. ou. 1/3 derrier la velle 34.
madelle Barollet 4. ouvrees et 1/3 derrier la velle 35.
monsr Chauuelot 8. ou. 2/3 derrier La velle 36.
Sieur Loppin Pothier 1. ou. 2/3 derrier La Velle 37.
Jean Polot 4. ouvrees derrier La velle 38.
Les chartreux de Beaune 3. ou. 2/3 derrier La velle 39.
Etienne ozanon 5. ouvrées et 1/3 derrier la velle 40.
Mr Segaut 2. ou. derrier la velle 41.
Mr Busignot 2. ou. derrier la velle 42.
Jean Labelle 2. ou. et 1/2 derrier la velle 47.
Veuve Viuand Battaut 2. ou. derrier la velle 48.
Mr Loppin Pothier 4. ou. derrier la velle 55.
monsr Chauuelot 2. ou. derrier la velle 56
Jean Latour Blondeau 2. ou. derrier la velle 57.
Lachapelle de Puligny 6. ouvrees derrier la velle 67. I.
Lachapelle de Puligny 8. ou. derrier la velle 63. I.
Pasquier de Pyeste 220.
Pasquier de Pyeste
heritages du Plan L.
Chemin tendant de Puligny a Meursaux et a Beaune
heritages du Plan K.

Also by Simon Loftus

A Pike in the Basement
Anatomy of the Wine Trade

Puligny-Montrachet

Journal of a Village in Burgundy

Puligny-Montrachet

Journal of a Village in Burgundy

Simon Loftus

Alfred A. Knopf
New York
1993

This Is a Borzoi Book
Published by Alfred A. Knopf, Inc.

Copyright © 1992 by Simon Loftus
Endpaper maps copyright © 1992 by Jacques Legrand SA

Originally published in Great Britain by Ebury Press, London, in 1992.

Library of Congress Cataloging-in-Publication Data
Loftus, Simon.
    Puligny-Montrachet: journal of a village in Burgundy/by
Simon Loftus.—1st Amer. ed.
        p. cm
    Includes index.
    ISBN 0-679-41814-8
    1. Wine and wine making—France—Puligny-Montrachet. 2. Puligny-
Montrachet (France)—History. I. Title.
TP553.L58   1993
641.2'2'09444—dc20   92-54786
                                        CIP

Manufactured in the United States of America

First American Edition

for Vincent Leflaive

While the earth remaineth, seed time and

harvest, and cold and heat, and summer

and winter, and day and night shall not

cease.

GENESIS, 8:22

Contents

Acknowledgements

My thanks to the people of Puligny. Over the past few years they have grown used to me snooping around the village and prying into their affairs, with a curiosity which must have seemed insatiable. All of those mentioned in the book contributed, directly or indirectly, to its shape and content and many were generous with their time and help. To list everyone here would be invidious because I should certainly miss out some whose comments or suggestions are incorporated in the text, but I must single out a few who contributed more than their fair share to my labours.

This book is dedicated with inexpressible affection, respect and gratitude to Vincent Leflaive. His conversation first provoked my interest in Puligny and he has continued to sustain me by sharing his memories, opening bottles of wonderful wines and extending to me the generous hospitality of his domaine. I have come to think of him as an honorary uncle, a position that he must fill in the hearts of many.

His real nephew, Olivier Leflaive, has also been patient and helpful to a quite extraordinary degree. Without his constant assistance, in innumerable ways, I could not have completed my self-appointed task.

Jean-Louis Alexandre, bookbinder and sceptic, provided a great deal of historical information based on his own extensive researches and introduced me to the Terrier de la Seigneurie de Puligny. I hope that one day he will finally publish the definitive history of the village. The practicalities of my visits to Puligny were made easier by the efficient hospitality of the Hôtel Le Montrachet (Suzanne and Thierry Gazagnes and their predecessor Christine Collet) and by the willingness of Ellen Cartsonis to sort out all manner of small but vital arrangements. Aubert and Pamela de Villaine nourished me, encouraged me and at a critical stage in this book's evolution provided me with a quiet haven in Burgundy where I could write. My secretary Susannah Collings typed and retyped the manuscript and made useful criticisms as the work progressed. To all of them, many thanks.

I have relied very little on other published works, hence no bibliography, but there are two which proved helpful. One is a small pamphlet, *Puligny-Montrachet et son vignoble* by Henri Cannard, and the other a much more substantial book, simply entitled *Montrachet,* by Jean-François Bazin. This proved a mine of useful, entertaining and very occasionally misleading information. The French edition was published in 1988 as part of the series Le Grand Bernard des Vins de France and the English edition appeared under the Longman imprint in 1990.

Finally, to my wife Irène and daughter Hana my thanks for their forbearance. Writing books is a pastime that requires heroic tolerance by the rest of the family, particularly when the project proves as demanding as this did in terms of time and concentration. I hope that the result, full of faults though it is, justifies their patience and that of my long-suffering publishers.

Simon Loftus
October 1991

Introduction

A Village in Burgundy

Puligny is quiet except for the barking of dogs behind the closed gates of stone houses and the gentle susurration of fermenting wine, audible only in the imagination. There is no sign of life in the square with the pollarded chestnut trees or in the other, more open Place which is centred on an ugly war memorial. The village has a third square, actually a small triangle – an intersection – which was formerly known as Place de l'Abreuvoir (the watering place) and has recently been rechristened Place de Johannisberg in honour of Puligny's twinned town on the Rhine. The new name is at odds with reality. An old stone cross (1805, the year of Trafalgar) marks the site of the horse pond. It was erected by J. B. Joly, member of a long line of village vignerons, and its shadow nearly reaches an elaborate sundial incised on the gable of the maison Leflaive (name of the village's most prominent family), which bears mute witness to the silence of the passing hours. Windows are shuttered and the streets have the secretive, sleepy air of provincial France.

This stillness is shaken by a distant racket which suddenly becomes deafening as a small Citroën van appears in the Rue de Poiseul, returning from the vineyards. The driver is an old vigneron, black beret on his head, Gauloise Jaune between his lips. His corrugated van seems to be making a tremendous clatter, even for a 2CV, but as it passes I see that the back doors are propped open and a shrivelled crone sits with her legs dangling precariously over the number plate as she clutches the handles of a makeshift wheelbarrow which is bouncing along behind the van. Its iron wheel rears at every rut and the rusty body, made from an old oil-drum, acts as a sounding board to magnify the noise of its passage. The cacophony echoes off the stone walls of the narrow lane and drowns the frenzied barking of awakened dogs.

Above the village the hillside is dotted with such contraptions, mobile braziers to burn the vine prunings, from which plumes of smoke drift into the misty air of a January afternoon. At this time of the year the vineyards seem spread like a map before the eye, a long, distinctive, clearly demarcated patchwork, ranged in a sinuous line across the southern knuckle of the Côte d'Or. It is a sight to lift the heart. Rows of vines, like cross-hatching on an old engraving, delineate the contours. A narrow track, a patch of rocks or a small change in direction of the planting indicates a boundary, separating Champ Gain from La Truffière, Les Pucelles from Clos des Meix. Half-way up the slope, its name chiselled in variant forms on the four or five stone gates which punctuate the remains of an ancient wall, lies the vineyard of Montrachet, the 'stony hill'.

Walking along the ancient road (now a rutted track) which forms the lower boundary of this modest enclosure, it is hard to see why these seven and a half hectares of impoverished soil should be the most precious agricultural land on earth. The minute differences which distinguish Montrachet from its neighbouring vineyards (separated by no more than the width of a track or the thickness of a wall) are scarcely perceptible in themselves but cumulatively crucial. Details of soil and subsoil, drainage, exposure to the sun, shelter from wind and frost, add up to the perfect environment in which to produce the grandest white wine in the world.

Montrachet straddles the boundary which separates the communes of Puligny and Chassagne, and lends its name to both. But the centuries have tended to divide these immediate neighbours, accentuating minor differences into strong distinctions of physical appearance and social structure, evident to the most casual visitor. The brutally simple summary of one local grower contains a good deal of truth: 'Puligny is more bourgeois, Chassagne more peasant.'

Neither village has a café, curious lack, though twenty years ago there were several. You can still read the faded inscription 'Café du Centre' in the Place du Monument at Puligny, but the men no longer stop for a pastis and women gather at the hairdresser, centre of local gossip. 'The people don't want to meet each other, they don't have time, it costs too much money,' is the bitter comment of Monsieur Alexandre, bookbinder and historian of Puligny, son of the former baker. 'The vignerons don't interest themselves much in books. The wine is everything.'

But the noticeboard outside the Mairie reminds us that Puligny is a place of changing moods and aspirations. The hunting season for wild boar and foxes is extended until 28 February; there will be a meal and soirée dansant at the Salle des Fêtes, for the Co-op Scolaire; a vineyard is available on lease and a house is for sale in the Rue de l'Abreuvoir; the banns of marriage are announced between Pernot (Michel Henri) viticulteur of Puligny, and Franchi (Anna Maria) of Meursault; there will be a general assembly of the Syndicat des Vignerons – 'presence indispensable'.

At Chassagne there is a similar mixture of information on the board, together with a request from the mayor that the inhabitants should water the flowers outside their houses and a stern notice on the subject of rabies, 'maladie toujours mortelle'. It instructs anyone faced with a rabid beast to shoot it in the heart, not the head, so that it may afterwards be inspected by the vet.

Such preoccupations of daily life seem far more important than the arrival of another wine buyer, sniffing his way round the cellars like a dog in search of a good bone, but most visitors have their eyes raised to the vineyards and ignore the village. It is worth pausing long enough to experience the texture of rural France: the sudden downpour on 14 July that causes all the dancers in the square to dash for cover under the chestnut trees; the game of boules under those same trees on a sultry summer afternoon; the jambon persillée served by the butcher from Meursault, whose mobile shop is parked in the Place du Monument on Tuesday and Friday mornings; the marvellous range of goods in Madame Bachelet's tiny épicerie; four crows, sitting on a stone hut in the vineyard of Criots-Montrachet.

The horizon of the peasant growers extends as far as the next village: their traditions and habits are rooted in the immediate locality. But they cultivate vines which produce each year such precious grapes that millionaires in London and Tokyo, Paris and New York, vie with one another to secure a tiny allocation of the treasured product. Such consumers, unconcerned to probe beneath the shuttered surface of village life, unwilling to stretch their legs by a walk through the vineyards, miss out on one of the greatest pleasures of wine, its testimony of the place. The taste changes at every moment and is summarized in the sense of smell, so elusive and immediate, which provides us with sudden jumps of memory, recalling the past with greater urgency than any other stimulus. And the scent of those fabulous white burgundies (a mixture of fresh straw and ripe peaches, an earthy intensity underlying the ele-

A small village with a seductive name: Puligny-Montrachet.

Prelude

1 | Fragments of a Social History

'Everything which is past benefits from time.'

VINCENT LEFLAIVE

The Paths and Patterns of Cultivation

The ligaments of the land tell us more about its history than the structure of ancient buildings or monuments. Stringing together the scattered centres of habitation, separating wilderness from cultivation, demarcating property, such tracks and boundaries often convey a sense of organic necessity, suggesting that they have evolved from the almost imperceptible trails of sheep or goats, repetitively following the line of least resistance. These paths are never entirely straight, never arbitrary, and hence have survived unchallenged, defining the rippling landscape with a precision that predates by many centuries the careful contours of modern cartography.

Two narrow lanes wind along the hillside from Meursault to Santenay, through the vineyards of Puligny and Chassagne. The upper one is to my mind the more ancient (I have no evidence for this, other than instinct) and it cleaves Montrachet from Bâtard, thus forming one of the most subtly decisive boundaries in the whole of Burgundy. The other, Le Sentier de Couches, skirts the hills at a slightly lower altitude and separates the Premiers Crus from the simple village appellation of Puligny. Originally a Roman road, according to local historians, this became the route which linked the Duchess of Burgundy's château at Couches with her spiritual home at the Cistercian abbey of Maizières. Bisecting these well-trodden paths is another which climbs abruptly from the plain to the hamlet of Blagny and divides the commune of Puligny from that of Meursault. It is still remembered by its medieval name of Chemin des Moines (Monks Way), honouring those who first made famous the wines of these impoverished slopes.

Until the monks came, Montrachet was what its name suggests, a barren hill, stony and uncultivated. Above the present vineyards are traces of an ancient burial ground and great piles of tumbled stones, the remains of a Gallo-Roman way station guarding the road to the north. This southern bastion of the Côte d'Or protected three neighbouring settlements which originated over fifteen hundred years ago, during the long decline of the Roman empire. Facing the hill across a winding valley which breaks the line of the Côte d'Or, a Roman named Cassius constructed a house of which no trace remains except the name: Chassagne. More Roman remains (fragments of tiles and brickwork, old stones and the headings of ancient wells) have been found around the hamlet of Blagny, high to the north above Montrachet. The name of this tiny settlement is said to be derived from Belenus, a Celtic god of the fields whose feast was celebrated at the beginning of May by the lighting of bonfires, between which cattle were driven for their ritual protection. Some claim that his temple was on the hill and survived until its destruction during the last wave of the Moorish invasions in 732; others that it was on the plain and that Puligny was built on its ruins. The name, Puliagnicus, means house on the water – a designation which may refer to the old cattle pond at the centre of the village but to me suggests that the original settlement was even less well drained than the present commune, which remains the only notable wine village in Burgundy without subterranean cellars (because the water table is so high that every excavation becomes a well).

Two contrasting forces dominated the evolution of medieval Puligny, as in most of rural France. The Church provided continuity, order and the structures of civilization (expressed through the organizational genius of powerful monastic communities). Feudal society, by contrast, was riven by struggles for land and power – between local seigneurs, their ducal overlords and eventually the King. These turbulent upheavals allowed space for individuals to flourish in the cracks of a disintegrating system; the shelters of determined peasants being built, as often as not, from the ruins of their masters' castles. But the demise of one noble family meant the aggrandizement of another, as Burgundy grew increasingly prosperous under its Valois dukes and became during the fourteenth and fifteenth centuries the richest state of medieval Europe.

An appetite for luxury and splendour spread from the court and the castles to the merchants and wealthy lawyers of the towns. And the greatest luxury of this fertile land, increasingly appreciated by all who could afford to drink it, was the wine.

No one knows what medieval burgundy tasted like but it certainly became the most highly esteemed wine of France, thanks in part to the proselytizing enthusiasm of the Valois dukes, who issued edicts to safeguard its quality and who sent gifts of it to popes and kings. But it was the monks, not the feudal lords, who made this reputation possible. They planted the best sites (those hillside suntraps which are now classified as the Grands Crus of the Côte d'Or) and they came to understand winemaking practice through the cumulative experience and observation of generations of contemplative enthusiasts, for whom the ideal of perfection was basic to their monastic calling. It was the monks who first established the fundamentals of viticulture and vinification which remain at the heart of the Burgundian tradition today.

Monastic influence was certainly of great importance to the development of Puligny. By 1094, when the village church was given by its feudal lord to the Abbey of Cluny, Puligny had grown from a tiny cluster of houses to a hamlet of sufficient size to need the care of a priest. But the spiritual influence of the Benedictines from distant Cluny became subordinated in succeeding centuries to the economic dominance of Cistercian monks from the nearby Abbey of Maizières. Situated a few miles east of Puligny, on the plain, this monastery was founded in 1102 and grew increasingly wealthy by endowment from the local seigneurs. Between 1169 and 1179 Maizières was given much of the hilltop of Blagny and by the beginning of the thirteenth century it had acquired the right to the tithes of Puligny itself. In May 1252 the Abbey received the first of several gifts of vines in Montrachaz, from the brothers Pierre and Arnolet de Puligny. So the hill was already planted with vines, if not yet famous.

In order to administer its growing domaine (which eventually extended to fifty hectares of well-sited vineyards in the Côte de Beaune, including eighteen hectares in Blagny and Puligny) the Abbey of Maizières established a dependence at Blagny, building houses, cellars, a cuverie and finally a chapel, opening up a quarry in Chalumeaux and clearing the forest to plant more vines. In 1304 the Abbey deemed it worthwhile to pay for the construction of a tower to house the great clock of

Beaune, in return for the right to sell its wines in the town. Evidently those wines had already achieved sufficient reputation to be a valuable commodity of commerce.

The contribution of Puligny's lords was initially less significant; for them the village was little more than a hesitation (thirty-one households in 1288) on the way to somewhere else. Administrative authority over this hamlet was in any case shared between various local landowners and the de Mypont family who for over four hundred years (until the middle of the fifteenth century) exercised the right of justice. These local grandees took their title from the stronghold of that name which was located a couple of kilometres north-east of the village, commanding the approaches to Beaune, but it was not until Philippe le Hardi, Duke of Burgundy, confiscated half the domaine of the Seigneurs de Mypont in 1388 that Puligny gained much tangible benefit from the pretension of its masters. The abandoned tower of Mypont fell into ruins and was used as a quarry for the villagers to build some of the first stone houses in Puligny, giving a sense of permanence to a settlement which (with the exception of the thirteenth-century church) had until that time been constructed mostly of timber, wattle and daub. Further confiscations brought more of the de Mypont domaine into ducal hands (and eventually, after the death of Charles the Bold, to the crown), but much of Puligny was granted by Duke Philip the Good, in 1448, to a prosperous lawyer from Beaune, Jean Perron. Perron, like his predecessors, adopted the title de Mypont but unlike them he built himself a modestly fortified manor house in the village, Le Vieux Château, and his son Charles added the seigneurial chapel to Puligny's church, where he was buried in 1514.

The Perron de Mypont family remained lords of Puligny until the end of the sixteenth century, took an active part in the management of their estate and may well have done much to establish the main structure of the village as it exists today, but their achievements are largely undocumented because the succession eventually failed. By the beginning of the seventeenth century Puligny was owned by the Jacquots, then it came into the hands of Gaspard d'Amanzé, who regrouped the domaine and finally sold it to the Rigoley family of Dijon in 1685.

For the following hundred years the Rigoleys owned Puligny and treasured it, until all was lost in the Revolution. They tended the vineyards, built and repaired the walls which divide and define the appellations and laid out a formal garden in the grounds of the château, next to its vines and its orchards. And finally they commissioned a record of the village and their domaine, mapping every detail of the complex patchwork of landholdings, the boundaries and pathways – which had evolved with such appropriate intuition over the centuries that they remain almost unaltered to this day.

Mappa Mundi

Le Terrier de la Seigneurie de Puligny et Mypon, a beautiful and utterly enthralling treasure, is preserved in the Mairie at Puligny for the delight of anyone with an inquisitive nose. Compiled between 1741 and 1747, the three enormous leather-bound volumes of this land register comprise one of the earliest, most detailed and most complete surveys of any of the classic vineyard regions of France – and surely the loveliest record ever undertaken for fiscal purposes. Two of the volumes list the name of every landholder, together with details of ownership and tenure for each fraction of an ouvrée* of the vineyards and meadows of Puligny, of every house in the village itself, of every tree: page after page of fascinating information inscribed with the utmost clarity in a boldly elegant copperplate hand, all cross-indexed to the third volume, the book of maps.

Twenty-five hand-drawn double-page spreads, vividly coloured, depict the boundaries of each field and the subdivisions of every vineyard between its various owners. Green strips represent the domaine of the Seigneur himself, Jean-Baptiste Rigoley, for whom this record was made. His holdings of the royal domaine (formerly that of the dukes of Burgundy) are painted blue. Yellow stands for his dependencies, farmed by *censitaires*, or copyholders, who cultivated the land as their own but were obliged to pay taxes to their lord. A deep ecclesiastical pink indicates the endowment of the seigneurial chapel in the church of Puligny and the rest, uncoloured, are the holdings of those who owed no allegiance to the Seigneur. Every patch is numbered (a cross-reference to the other volumes) and neatly inscribed with a note of its area, ownership and appellation.

The detail is extraordinary. You can compare the exactly drawn houses of the village with their counterparts today to discover which remain

---

*1 ouvrée = 428 square metres, approx. one-tenth of an acre.

intact and which have been altered in succeeding centuries. The old horse pond is marked which gave the Place de l'Abreuvoir its name, but which has since been drained and levelled. Its spring appears to have fed the communal washing trough, just down the hill, which was only quite recently converted into a room for receptions and village meetings. Every tree is shown, for each is a landmark. At the junction of the Rue du Château and the Rue de l'Abreuvoir an elm tree is focus and namesake of the tiny Place de l'Orme. Both tree and Place have since disappeared, replaced by a grocer's shop, which is now permanently closed. Another elm is shown outside the village, east of the main road, but this one recalls its traditional sinister significance as the tree of justice, for here was the site of the gallows. A pear tree is marked, to my delight, just to the north of the present-day Cross of Montrachet, in the exact position that a solitary walnut tree stands today, marking the boundary between Grandes Pucelles and Petites Pucelles. But the cross itself has evidently been moved or is a replacement for the one dedicated to St Abdon, which is marked on the eighteenth-century plan. This shrine stood further up the hill than the present cross, beside the track which separates Montrachet from Le Cailleret. Few now remember that this lane was once called Rue du Reposoir (altar of repose) and that the original cross was erected in honour of the saint to whom the growers used to pray for rain.

Back in Puligny itself, it is interesting to note that the southern boundary of the village extended no further than the present Mairie. The Place des Marronniers was a windswept field and the buildings which now house the Domaine Leflaive did not exist. But the Leflaives themselves were already well established in Puligny – Claude Leflaive owned a house on the edge of the Place du Grand Cimetière (now the Place du Monument) which is presently occupied by his direct descendant, Olivier. And he had patches of vines in various appellations. So too did three other families (Carillon, Joly and Meney) which remain prominent in the village today.

The cartography of the vineyards reveals a similar intriguing mixture – of continuity and change. Most of the low-lying land to the east of Puligny was given over to woods and pasture. A patch of pear trees is marked (still there) but none of the vines which nowadays yield modest Bourgogne Blanc. Immediately around the village lie the vineyards of Meix Pelletier, Derrier la Valle, Papillot, Vouettes, Grand Champ and

Boudrières – names which can readily be traced on any modern map of the appellations. But further up the hill the picture is more confusing – some of the most famous designations, familiar now to wine lovers throughout the world, appear to have been the invention of a later generation, anxious to classify what had formerly been a somewhat looser system of local reference. It is clear, in particular, that the present distinction between the Grands Crus of Montrachet, Chevalier and Bâtard did not exist – all was Mont Rachet, the stony hill. But that renowned slope was subdivided by ownership, and the major demarcations of that partition correspond exactly to the modern boundaries of appellation. The Clermont-Montoison family, seigneurs of Chassagne, had by the mid-eighteenth century acquired the heart of the vineyard – including an undivided block of a hundred ouvrées within the boundaries of Puligny. That left none of what was later referred to as Grand Montrachet for the Seigneur de Puligny or anyone else in the village. He had to be content with a couple of strips, totalling fourteen ouvrées, within the present appellation of Chevalier.

Curiously enough, that pattern of tenure has continued until recent times; none of Puligny's most famous vineyard being owned within the village. The Marquis de Laguiche, whose ancestor married into the Clermont-Montoison family, has inherited approximately half their original parcel of Montrachet. Other important holdings belong to Baron Thenard of Santenay and Bouchard Père et Fils of Beaune, but most of the rest is fragmented between various domaines of the Côte d'Or and a few families of Chassagne. The great domaines of Puligny cultivate significant portions of the other Grands Crus – Chevalier, Bâtard and Bienvenues – but it was not until 1991 that one of them, Domaine Leflaive, managed to acquire a few rows of vines in the vineyard which gives the village its renown.

That fame is ancient. If there is one thing above all others which these maps make plain, it is that the *climats* which we treasure today were already highly valued in the mid-eighteenth century, and probably much earlier – otherwise it is inconceivable that so lavish and detailed a survey would have been worth making; because it is, fundamentally, a fiscal document, a record of ownership and rentability, a summary of dues. For the returns to have justified the labour of compilation, the vineyards of Puligny must have been prized by their owners to a quite exceptional degree, long before most other wine-producing regions of the world were mapped or evaluated in any systematic way – or indeed were known at all, outside their immediate locality.

Le Terrier de la Seigneurie de Puligny implies a wider world of wealthy connoisseurship but maps a rural microcosm, narrowly circumscribed in place and time. Such exceedingly close focus endows these plans with the surreal and evocative magic of ancient cosmologies, a fantastical character which suggests that this is the record of a parallel universe, deceptively similar to our own but subtly different. The orientation is unexpected. Instead of north being at the top of the page it is west (the natural viewpoint when looking towards the vineyards from the village) and the edges of every map are inscribed with the stations of the sun's daily journey rather than the points of the modern compass: Couchant (the setting sun, west); Orient (the rising sun, east); Midi (noon); and Septentrion (north, from the seven stars of the constellation Ursa Major). The units of measurement are equally unfamiliar, being those in common usage prior to Napoleon's introduction of the metric system. Area was judged by the amount that a man could work in a day and the measure varied with different types of cultivation: *ouvrée* for vineyards, *arpent* for woods, *soiture* for meadows and *journal* for arable land.

This fascinating sense of a remote but familiar world, the visual splendour of every page and the sheer physical bulk of the three volumes of Le Terrier de Puligny have ensured its survival for two hundred and fifty years. Other land registers of lesser interest were lost or destroyed, used to light fires or eaten by worms, but this one merely went astray, turning up eventually on one of those bookstalls by the Seine in Paris, from which it was rescued and returned to its proper home. The vast pages of thick handmade paper are unstained by any sign of neglect, the colours of the maps are as vivid as when first drawn and the plain leather covers continue to protect their contents as stoutly as ever, having recently been restored by Monsieur Alexandre, bookbinder and historian of Puligny.

Substance, proportion, texture and visual allure; sturdy simplicity and subtle sophistication; the evocation of place and time. This endlessly intriguing marvel satisfies the senses, entrances the intellect and distils a self-contained world for our continuing delight. If you could drink it, this would be the taste of Montrachet.

A Century of Revolutions

Charles Paquelin, vigneron of Chassagne, wrote his diary for 1789 with a heavy heart. Describing the year of the French Revolution as 'the unhappiest year of this century', he noted that it was also a terrible vintage. 'We made scarcely any wine and it was mean stuff which never had any colour.'

Nor were the local nobility of Burgundy immune to the general upheavals. The Marquis Pradier d'Agrain (who had married the heiress of the Rigoley family, seigneurs of Puligny) fled to Switzerland; Charles de la Guiche (husband of the heiress of the Clermont-Montoisons, seigneurs of Chassagne) failed to make his escape and was guillotined. The estates of both were confiscated by the state and for a while even their finest vineyards lay abandoned. In 1792 the procurator of the district of Beaune ordered that the Clermont-Montoison holding of Montrachet (over a hundred ouvrées, in the best part of the vineyard) and Pradier-Rigoley's eight ouvrées in Chevalier should be cultivated by three vignerons of Chassagne in return for half the yield, the other half to belong to the Republic.

As always, the decline of some meant the rise of others. Many of the former *métayers* of the seigneurial estates managed to take over their masters' land, with the result that ownership of the finest vineyards of Burgundy remains highly fragmented to this day. Others found favour with the authorities, as Republic became Empire, and assumed the privileges (sometimes even the titles) of the aristocrats who had been exiled or killed. A typical case is that of the D'Esdhouard family of Puligny. When Jean-Baptiste Rigoley's Terrier de Puligny was compiled in the 1740s the Edouhards (as their name was then spelt) were evidently the most prominent inhabitants after the seigneurs themselves, and they prospered mightily with the rise of Bonaparte. During the succeeding century their newly built château on the edge of the village was enlarged, enclosed by a high wall and used as a place to entertain and influence the great names of the day. They acquired a significant domaine and enjoyed rapid social aggrandizement.

There was another unexpected consequence of the Revolution, more permanent in its effects than the replacement of a hereditary King and landed aristocracy with self-crowned Emperor and his cronies. Famous chefs and their armies of assistants, the cooks of the great aristocratic households, were thrown unemployed on to the streets of Paris. They started restaurants and thereby changed the eating habits of a nation, which had previously known little better by way of public catering than cookshops and taverns. And these revolutionary restaurants created an entirely new market for the finest wines of France.

Burgundy quietly prospered, despite the extraordinary series of political upheavals which characterized French history for the first half of the nineteenth century. The defeat and exile of Napoleon, the Restoration of the monarchy, assassinations both actual and attempted, the Revolution of '48 and finally the establishment of the Second Empire in 1852: such constant turmoil at the centre is in marked contrast to the uneventful repetitiveness of village life. The most notable dates in Puligny's history had purely local significance: the founding of the Confrérie of St Bernard in 1825 (a mutual aid society of vignerons to provide assistance to one another in times of sickness or hardship) and the establishment of the village band in 1846.

Then, just as France was settling down to nearly twenty years of peace and growing prosperity, disaster struck the vineyards with the appearance of *oidium*, which was first noticed in Puligny in 1853. This disease (which attacks the leaves and shoots of the vine, drastically reducing the size of the crop) appears to have spread from England, where it was identified in 1845, but probably originated in America. Effective treatment (dusting the vines with sulphur powder) was discovered fairly quickly but not before many vignerons had been ruined.

Fortunately Puligny was less dependent on the monoculture of the vine than most communities of the Côte d'Or. Much of the low-lying land around the village was pasture, or planted with cereal crops, and it had resources of raw materials which were of use to local industries. An underground quarry at the level of the Premier Cru vineyard La Truffière supplied sand and friable rock (crushed on the spot by a giant millstone) for the manufacture of glass at Chalon-sur-Saone. An opencast quarry higher up the hill at Blagny supplied more sand for use in the Bessemer steel furnaces of Creusot.

The development of such industry was characteristic of the era, which was one of urban improvement, the construction of roads, canals and ports and the expansion of the railway network to most corners of France. The establishment of a major rail depot at Chagny brought hordes of immigrant workers to the region, several of whom settled in Puligny, and the arrival of the iron way provided the vignerons with vastly improved access to their major market, the restaurants of Paris.

Improved communications meant that discriminating wine drinkers became acquainted with diversity (rather than being limited to whatever was produced in their particular locality). To the nineteenth-century mind such variety of any phenomenon was a challenge to describe and classify it. Hence the birth of the wine writer, spiritual cousin of those remarkable naturalists whose illustrated volumes on fauna and flora remain so enthralling today. André Julien in 1816, Dr Denis Morelot in 1825 and Dr Jules Lavalle in 1855 were the first Frenchmen since Father Arnoux in the early eighteenth century to write authoritative descriptions of the vines and wines of Burgundy. Their work was complemented by that of the Agricultural Commission for Beaune, which in 1860 produced a superb map of the Côte d'Or, classifying the major vineyards as Premières, Deuxièmes or Troisièmes Cuvées. But my favourite text is that of Cyrus Redding, whose *History and Description of Modern Wines* was published in London in 1835. It is worth quoting his summary of Puligny's most famous vineyards.

'The situation to the south-west of Meursault, where it joins Puligny, is noted for the delicious wine called Mont-Rachet, of exquisite perfume, and deemed the most perfect white wine of Burgundy, and even of France, rivalling Tokay itself in the opinion of many French connoisseurs. The vine ground of Mont-Rachet is divided into *l'Aîné* Mont-Rachet, *Le Chevalier* Mont-Rachet, and *Le Bâtard* Mont-Rachet. The vineyard of the Chevalier, which is on the higher part of the ground, is a slope of about twelve or fifteen degrees, and contains eighteen hectares. L'Aîné, or the true Mont-Rachet, is but six or seven hectares. The Bâtard is only separated from the two other vineyards by the road which leads from Puligny to Chassagne, and contains twelve hectares. The vineyards have all the same south-eastern aspect, yet the wine from them is so different in quality, that while Mont-Rachet sells for twelve hundred francs the hectolitre, the Chevalier brings but six hundred, and the Bâtard only four hundred. There are two vine grounds near, called the Perrières and Clavoyon, which produce white wines sought after only from their vicinity to Mont-Rachet.'

Redding's description of Montrachet's virtues is a model of succinct clarity: 'It is remarked in good years for its fineness, lightness, bouquet and exquisite delicacy, having spirit without too great dryness, and a luscious taste without cloying.'

Such a literature of wine presupposed an appreciative public eager to learn; these works are evidence of the growing connoisseurship which was bringing increasing prosperity to the region, thanks to the renown of its finest wines. It was to capitalize on this renown that several villages of the Côte d'Or decided to bracket their own names with those of their most famous vineyards: thus Gevrey-Chambertin, Aloxe-Corton, Vosne-Romanée and Chambolle-Musigny. So too with Chassagne and Puligny, places of purely local significance which decided to join their names officially and for ever to that of Montrachet, the tiny segment of a stony hill divided by their communal boundary which was known to emperors and popes, millionaires and charlatans as the source of the finest dry white wine in the world. And thus the bigamous marriage was proclaimed, on 27 November 1879. Puligny became Puligny-Montrachet, inscribed in the register in the presence of witnesses, at the same time as Chassagne took the same partner, for better or for worse, from that day forth.

This moment of apotheosis, long aspired to, coincided with the onset of catastrophe; less than five months earlier, on 1 July 1879, phylloxera had been identified in Puligny. This small yellow insect, inadvertently imported to Europe from the United States, was given the scientific nickname of 'vastatrix'; the devastator. Feeding on the roots of vines, it destroyed them. Within ten years the vineyards of Burgundy were utterly laid waste and it was not until 1889, when replanting began with vines grafted on to phylloxera-resistant American rootstocks, that any hope of recovery was in sight. Replanting took time and the young vines yielded no saleable crop until they were three or four years old, producing wines of real quality only after a decade. In the absence of the genuine article the name of burgundy became debased by fraudulent imitations and the fine wines of Montrachet (on which the newly designated village of Puligny-Montrachet had hoped to base its fame and fortune) became little more than a memory – only a few meagre bottles being produced from the scattering of sickly vines which struggled to survive this terrible affliction.

The effects of phylloxera were as catastrophic for village society as they were for the vine. Deprived of their livelihood, many families were forced off the land in pursuit of menial work in the towns and cities or emigrated to the colonies of North Africa or to the United States. The Revolution a century earlier had dispossessed the grandees; phylloxera ruined the peasants. Between these two calamities the old pattern of Burgundian landownership and cultivation was altered beyond recognition.

The advent of phylloxera reminds me of biblical plagues and parables. Its immediate effects were comparable to those of a cloud of locusts, laying waste the land, but it also marked quite decisively the destruction of ancient certainties. The metamorphosis of Puligny into Puligny-Montrachet was more than a legal nicety; it signalled the end of a sense of self-sufficiency, of the immutability of agricultural rhythms, the changeless appropriateness of the patterns of daily life, which had needed no justification other than conformity to habit and tradition. All of these things, the roots of village society, were being gnawed at by destructive ideologies, imported from the wider world: the imperatives of a market economy, ideals of progress, competition, accumulation, advertisement and change. And like the old, ungrafted, deep-rooted vines destroyed by phylloxera, the rural traditions survived only in modified form, grafted on to imported stock whose roots spread wider but burrowed less vigorously into the subsoil. Puligny was a name; Puligny-Montrachet is an advertisement, implying the dependence of the place on a complex market, extending far beyond the boundaries of the village and its vineyards, the stony hill and the placid meadows of the plain, the rivalry with immediate neighbours. In making this change, Puligny swapped the straightforward cycles of birth and death, bounty and calamity, for the sophisticated anxieties of the modern world.

Changing Identities
By the early years of the twentieth century Puligny had recovered from the onslaught of phylloxera and returned to a state of modest prosperity, but progress was interrupted by a series of calamities. After the glorious harvest of 1906, four disastrous vintages in a row (1907-10), the First World War and then the Great Depression prevented Puligny achieving much sense of stability following the storms of the previous century. Another marvellous vintage in 1934 heralded a brief five years of relative optimism, which was crushed once again by the advent of war.

Despite these vicissitudes, Puligny in the thirties must have been an agreeable place to visit. The old horse pond, still undrained, made the Place de l'Abreuvoir a muddy swamp, but the local blacksmith was as ready to turn his hand to mending a broken motor-car as shoeing his neighbour's plough horse. Four tonneliers vied for business, making wooden casks for the vignerons. Several grocers, two bakers, a butcher and three cafés (one of which boasted a ballroom upstairs) supplied the basic necessities of rural life. And on high days and holidays Monsieur Beaumarchais led the thirty-strong village band in serenades and fanfares, to honour the saints, mourn the dead, commemorate the Revolution and celebrate the wine.

It was the wine which brought the visitors. This was the age of the motor-car, suddenly transformed from the chauffeur-driven transport of the rich to the mass-produced runabout of the middle classes. Families on weekend excursions would turn off the Route Nationale into the village, following their noses to the cellars, keen to buy wine direct from the producers. Other visitors arrived from further afield, men like the great English wine merchant Charles Walter Berry and the Americans Frank Schoonmaker and Frederick Wildman. The latter two, in particular, did more than anyone else at this time to promote the finest burgundies, opening up new markets in the States while insisting on authenticity. All of which encouraged the development of domaine bottling by the best growers, following the example of Joseph Leflaive.

In one form or another the problems of authenticity – of identity – have preoccupied Puligny for much of the past century. The confusion of names is expressed at its most innocent level by Puligny's decision to become Puligny-Montrachet, a ploy which was quite openly intended to give added lustre to wines of lower quality from vineyards which were more or less distant neighbours of the village's most famous Cru. Far more serious was the downright fraud and misrepresentation which was commonplace throughout France for much of the nineteenth century and which reached the proportions of an epidemic after the arrival of phylloxera and the consequent disruption of genuine wine production. The fortunes of many now-famous négociants were founded on the most shameless blending and inventive labelling, which enabled them to build grand establishments and purchase extensive domaines at the expense (and sometimes at the serious risk to health) of the gullible public. As the habits of such corrupt wine traders persisted well into modern times it became evident to the authorities that the problem could be solved only by legislation, but it was not until the eve of the Second World War that the worst of these malpractices were successfully curbed.

Puligny's history during this period is to a very considerable extent that of the long struggle to give legal definition to the wines of its finest vineyards.

It took thirty years, from 1905 until 1935, for the system of Appellation Contrôlée to become fully established and it was even longer before the map of Puligny's vineyards and classifications took final shape. Montrachet itself was defined by the judgement of the Beaune tribunal in 1920, which limited the appellation to the seven and a half hectares which had been traditionally known as Montrachet Aîné or Grand Montrachet, plus half a hectare of parcels from Dent des Chiens (in Chassagne) which were deemed to be of equal quality. This decision was reached in the teeth of vigorous opposition from various local growers and négociants, who had been in the habit of using the famous name to designate wines from Chevalier and Bâtard, Bienvenues and Les Pucelles and other vineyards all the way across the slope to the hill of Blagny. The other Grands and Premiers Crus remained substantially undefined until after the Second World War, and as recently as 1974 a portion of Le Cailleret was authorized to be counted as part of its more prestigious neighbour Chevalier.

It was not until 1927 that the Loi Capus was passed (named after a resolute Minister of Agriculture) which empowered the local tribunals to legislate on the subject of grape varieties. Three years later the 'noble' varieties of Pinot and Chardonnay were recognized as the most appropriate raw materials for the finest burgundy. Until that time it was not uncommon to find Aligoté planted in the Grands Crus of Puligny, or Gamay (which had been outlawed by Philippe le Hardi in 1395) proliferating in the red wine vineyards which then still accounted for over half the village's production. Such grapes made wines which complied with the legal definition of Appellation d'Origine but bore little resemblance to anything that we should now recognize as fine burgundy.

The character of Puligny's wines continued to change after the Second World War, less in response to further legal definitions than as a result of the evolution of modern techniques of viticulture and vinification. The replacement of the horse by the tractor in the 1950s, the arrival of mechanical harvesters in the 1980s, the widescale use of temperature control to regulate the process of fermentation, clonal selection of rootstocks and vine varieties, experiments with cultured yeasts, changing attitudes to the use of oak casks and the introduction of stainless steel – these are only the most significant of innumerable developments which changed step by step the apparently immutable traditions of Burgundian winemaking. And each step meant an alteration, however slight, in the wines themselves.

Parallel to the gradual evolution of legal appellations and the sudden technical revolutions which altered what those designations implied, the identity of the village itself was modified by changes in its population. This was not merely a matter of numbers, of decline from a peak of about twelve hundred inhabitants to the present level of around five hundred, but a more basic if scarcely perceptible alteration in its constituent parts.

Puligny, like most rural communities, is a village of immigrants. This may seem surprising to those who cherish the persistent myth of rustic immobility but it reflects a pattern of local migrations which seems to have been general throughout western Europe for centuries past. The medieval village was not a static community, breeding prejudice and superstition from intermarriage within a tiny genetic pool, but a dynamic organism, in constant flux. Children left to find work, to get married, to flee from justice, to escape the pressures of local rivalries or family feuds. Newcomers arrived for similar reasons, often from far afield. And so it continues today.

There are long-established families in Puligny (Carillon, Leflaive and Joly spring immediately to mind), but most of the present inhabitants (or their fathers or grandfathers) originated elsewhere. Puligny has probably absorbed more such immigrants than neighbouring Chassagne because its villagers are less tied to the land by ownership. In times past the vignerons of Puligny were often smallholders who also grazed a few cows on the meadows below the village and grew vegetables or cereals for the market. Less dependent on the vine than their neighbours to north and south, in Meursault and Chassagne, they were perhaps better protected from the periodic depressions of the wine business, but for this very reason they tended at various points in their history to cling to their vines with less resolution. The vignerons of the nearby villages and the négociants of Beaune managed over the years to acquire considerable segments of Puligny's heritage, with the result that nearly half of its vineyards today belong to outsiders and much of the remainder is divided between a handful of village domaines. So there are a good many landless labourers, rootless individuals whose ambition often takes

In Puligny there are a good many landless labourers. Jean Cosnefroy works for the widow Moroni.

them away, leaving a void, and a house, to be filled by an immigrant.

Some of these have been relatively local; Burgundians from the vicinity who seized a chance to better themselves by working for one of the prosperous domaines of Puligny or by marriage to a village daughter. Others came from Bresse, driven by poverty, or from Poland or Yugoslavia or Spain – refugees from political and economic turmoil. A discreet mezuzah by the door of one village house bears witness to the tragic diaspora of the Jews at the time of Hitler's persecutions. And there were railwaymen, following the lines to the big depot at Chagny and then retiring to the villages nearby. Madame Robaire, the chambermaid, arrived from a tiny hamlet in Chaume, eighty miles to the north, in search of better education for her children. Monsieur Lafond, the present mayor, settled here because the employees of a new Kodak factory in the Côte Chalonnaise had commandeered all the available housing near his work.

This slow but steady influx of newcomers, some of whom have accumulated the wherewithal to buy a few rows of vines, is of critical importance to the wine. The land is a constant; so too the grape varieties (give or take a few clonal variations). But the human factor is fundamental, and variable. Starting with the same raw material, different men make different wine; but within a relatively isolated community, nurturing closed traditions, such differences may be less evident than the family resemblance. In a village like Puligny, by contrast, each new arrival adds a facet, reflecting his own personality and culture, to the collective idea of what is possible, enriching thereby the complexity and potential of its wines.

The winemaking process is an endless series of small but significant decisions and the end product is a summary of all those factors of character, ambition and personality which differentiate the winemakers themselves. Just as wine lovers look for and appreciate the characteristics in wine which suit their own temperament – some preferring power to elegance, richness to lightness, youth to maturity – so too with the winemakers; it is their preferences which largely determine the character of the wine they make. Hence the dramatic difference between, for example, a Bâtard-Montrachet from Domaine Leflaive and one from Domaine Sauzet: superlative wines in quite individual ways. Hence, too, the fact that some tasters claim to perceive a village identity in the wines made in Puligny as opposed to those from neighbouring Chassagne; characteristics which reflect differences of culture as much as variations in soil. The former tend to complexity, the latter to pungency. Puligny, for better or worse, has been afflicted by civilization. Chassagne maintains a stronger, less refined sense of peasant vigour.

For more than two hundred and fifty years wine lovers have claimed that a small stony vineyard, shared by the two villages, produces the greatest dry white wine in the world, but the object of their adoration can never be defined because its character continues to evolve. There is no timeless archetype of Montrachet, no Platonic ideal of Chardonnay's potential. On the contrary: each generation and each enthusiast has a varying perception of its splendours.

2 | The Rivals

The Fraternity of St Vincent

Père Menestrier, curé of Puligny, preached to an unusually large congregation on the morning of Sunday, 22 January, 1989. Grandly ensconced in the choir stalls, the dignitaries of Chassagne and Puligny stared at each other across the chancel while the lesser mortals of both villages crowded the pews and overflowed into the aisles. Everyone had come to church to celebrate the Feast of St Vincent, patron of wine-growers, and everyone had come to the same church (for the first time in living memory) because that of Chassagne was closed for repairs. This temporary rapprochement between the rival villages was signified by the presence in front of the altar of two up-ended wine barrels, one supporting the brightly painted figure of St Bernard, staring upwards in ecstasy at the elaborate little canopy suspended above his head, the other bearing the unadorned oak statue of St Vincent, head modestly bowed and a bunch of grapes clutched in his sturdy hand. The exultant St Bernard represented the wine-growers' confrérie of Puligny; St Vincent that of Chassagne. Between the two saints and closer to the altar was a little tower of freshly baked brioche rings, crowned by a posy of flowers, and beside it was a bottle of wine.

The saints and the tower of brioches had arrived at the church half an hour earlier, borne shoulder-high with banners, to the clamour of celebratory bells. The procession had started from the cellars of Bernard Clerc, on the Place des Marronniers, where everyone had gathered for a glass of wine at ten-thirty and for the cheese gougères which accom-

The saints and the tower of brioches, borne shoulder-high.

pany all Burgundian festivities. It was a bright winter morning, one of those days which encourage a certain amount of stamping of the feet and puffing of steamy breath into the crisp invigorating air. Bernard Clerc, the morning's host, had the expression of an anxious bloodhound as he shepherded the carloads of vignerons from Chassagne to park around the square, but everyone else seemed in brisk good spirits, greeting one another with the amiability of familiar antagonists.

The young men carried the banners, the brioches and the saints, the old followed with their badges of office and the rest clustered behind in a noisy and ragged procession which gathered adherents from the side streets as it headed past the cross which marks the site of the old horse pond, past the post office, past half-open cellars and shuttered houses and emerged in the tiny square in front of the parish church of Notre Dame de l'Assomption.

The village choir, led by the strong voice of old Jean Pascal, greeted the arrival of the confréries with a series of cheerful modern hymns, asking forgiveness, promising to do better, thanking God for the benefits of the earth. The congregation responded with several rousing choruses of Alleluia.

Then the priest began his sermon, taking as his text a verse from the Gospel of St John: 'I am the vine, you the branches.' He reminded his audience that this was not only the Feast of St Vincent but the Sunday of ecumenical unity, dedicated to those separated by different faiths. In that spirit he welcomed to the church for this historic occasion the villagers of both Puligny and Chassagne.

It was a wry and appropriate comment on a rare moment of truce in the long-standing rivalry, bordering on aversion, which has for so long divided these neighbouring communities. As a fat little girl in the front row of the congregation sat whispering to her neighbour, Père Menestrier talked of 'the long civilization of the vine', of 'solidarity' between those who work together (expressed in the two societies of St Bernard and St Vincent, gathered in this church to celebrate the latter's feast day) and about bringing a sense of morality, purpose and Christianity into the daily work in vineyards and cellars. The vignerons sat with an air of rigid self-importance as their métier was thus extolled and they nodded approvingly when the priest referred to the miracle of the feast at Cana, when Jesus changed water into 'good wine, of excellent quality'. Reminding the congregation that Puligny was twinned with the

German village of Johannisberg, thus bringing together and reconciling two nations formerly at war, Père Menestrier returned pointedly to the theme of fraternity, before leading the assembly in a joint recitation of the Creed.

Then he blessed the brioches which were to be shared at the feast to follow, hoping they would be a sign of shared friendship, and consecrated the bread and wine for communion to the accompaniment of a chorus of Hosannahs. The congregation's attention on higher things was briefly interrupted by the sound of clinking and shuffling as everyone reached into their pockets to find money for the collection, but serenity and goodwill were restored with the gesture of friendship: a handshake between the men, a kiss on the cheek among the women. A wobbling fanfare on the trumpet accompanied the communion.

At the conclusion of the mass, the priest read the parish notices, gave thanks to those who had helped with this celebration and announced that Monsieur Amiot invited his confréres of Chassagne to enjoy a glass of wine in his cellars before their feast at the village hall and that Bernard Clerc extended a similar invitation to his confréres of Puligny. The choir sang a hymn of friendship and rejoicing as the congregation poured out of the church, eager for a cigarette and a gossip before the two villages divided for their respective celebrations.

The saints were carried in procession back to the Place des Marronniers, where St Bernard was installed on an up-ended barrel in the cellars of Domaine Clerc, as the centrepiece of a party which began with wine and gougères and continued in one form or another for the rest of the day and much of the night. St Vincent was packed with less ceremony into the boot of a car and the men of Chassagne set off up the hill, without a backward glance at their neighbours.

The inhabitants of both villages have long ago decided that solidarity, reconciliation, fraternity and neighbourly goodwill begin, like charity, at home. And they stick to their principles.

Family Feuds

In the tiny village of Bouzeron, a few kilometres south of Puligny, there are two cafés on adjacent corners of the Place. For reasons which have long since been forgotten by most of their regulars, there was a period of many years when the proprietors of these cafés were not on speaking terms and those who were habitués of one establishment would not be seen dead in the other. Thus was the village divided.

Similar minor differences, so long established as to have grown into instinctive rivalry, separate neighbouring villages in the Côte d'Or. The children of Volnay have traditionally hurled stones at the prosperous 'pommards', and the *métayers* of Nuits St-Georges have a deep-seated aversion to the proud proprietors of Vosne-Romanée. So too with Puligny and Chassagne. Yoked by their resounding surname, the villages are divided by generations (perhaps centuries) of mutual distrust. 'They're like twins, they hate each other,' claims Aubert de Villaine, whose family estate, the Domaine de la Romanée-Conti, makes one of the greatest wines of Montrachet.

Cain and Abel almost, the dark and the light. Chassagne seems to clasp to itself the bitter memory of the time when it was destroyed by the Swiss mercenaries of Louis XI and the inhabitants were burnt in their houses, in vengeance on their lord, Jean de Chalons, Prince d'Orange, who had dared to defy the crown. The nickname 'les mâchurés' (the blackened ones) reminds scholars of those ashes, but the children of Puligny have always taken it to mean 'the unwashed' and taunted their neighbours whenever their hillside well ran dry. The brats from Chassagne, looking down to the lush pastures of their rivals far below, spat back the word 'cochons' in unambiguous contempt.

Puligny, by contrast, survived placidly in the plain; its occasional catastrophes being those of the region as a whole, without the singularity which regularly reinforced the communal vigour of Chassagne. Unlike its rival on the hill, whose stony slopes gave sustenance to nothing but the vine, Puligny enjoyed relative economic equilibrium, based on an agriculture which depended almost as much on cereals and cattle as it did on wine. When times were good, Puligny prospered; when times were hard (a succession of bad vintages or the periodic plagues of the vine), it survived. After the phylloxera the vignerons at least had their pigs.

As the great white wines of Burgundy became more fashionable (and outstripped the reds in price), the vineyards of Puligny were much coveted by outsiders. Rich négociants from Beaune and prosperous producers from Meursault arrived after every funeral to tempt the heirs with a good price, and within the village itself the big domaines gobbled up the smaller ones. Today forty per cent of Puligny's vineyards are owned by outsiders and the old community of peasant proprietors has been replaced by a divided society. Several domaines have prospered mightily in recent years, particularly those which sell their wine in bottle. Larger numbers of much smaller growers (selling by contract to the négoces) have experienced a less dramatic rise in their standard of living and those of them who are *métayers*, sharecroppers, live in fear of dispossession when the term of their lease expires. A mobile population of local immigrants travels to work outside the village and the old, retired and immobile, find it increasingly difficult to supply their daily necessities from the limited resources of the single épicerie, the baker and the travelling butcher.

Chassagne has remained much closer to its origins in terms of social cohesion. Until recently its reputation was almost exclusively for red wines: appetizingly lean expressions of Pinot Noir which had some local renown but were not appreciated on the international markets. So its vineyards had less value to acquisitive outsiders and tended to remain in the village families. These families themselves intermarried to a remarkable extent; trying to sort out the complex cousinage of Bachelet, Ramonet, Gagnard and Delagrange, for example, is sufficient to perplex the most determined genealogist. The result is that 80 per cent of Chassagne's vines are still owned within the village and that the average size of the domaines has remained relatively stable (and generally small). There is a sense of modest well-being, reinforced by the fact that those few who are exceedingly rich continue to live like impoverished peasants. .

Families work together, wives alongside their husbands in the vineyards (unlike Puligny), and there are few employees. This spirit of independence extends to the sale of their wine. Unusually in Burgundy, even small growers like to bottle their own production (there are very few regular contracts with the négociants) and they sell these bottles either direct from their cellars to tourists and restaurateurs or through the village Caveau, a shop which was set up with municipal help to provide a centre for the promotion of Chassagne and its wines. In Puligny they have often talked of establishing a similar venture, but the talk has come to nothing – because the big domaines can easily manage to market their output worldwide (thus achieving international renown without reliance on passing tourists) and the small ones lack the self-confidence, or the energy, to break with négoces to whom they sell their wine in bulk, for immediate cash in hand, after the harvest.

Chassagne's cohesion as a community is expressed in the physical structure of the place. There are few fine houses and no elegant squares; the village seems at the same time densely huddled together and strung out in an ungainly line along the hillside, knotted together like an old rope. But Chassagne can boast an exceptionally splendid Mairie (built in the nineteenth century from the same pink sandstone which is still quarried above the village by its present mayor, Monsieur Gabriel Lardet) and a modern Salle des Fêtes which is twice as big as that at Puligny, and regularly used for meetings and parties of every size. And there is another expression of local solidarity, of which Chassagne is justly proud. Stored in a garage behind the Mairie are two bright red vans, equipped with powerful pumps and other vital necessities: the village fire engines, which are manned by a volunteer brigade of fifteen young vignerons.

Puligny conveys no such impression of communal pride and cohesion. It has a modest Mairie, a Salle des Fêtes which is just adequate for its purpose and no fire brigade. The very considerable charm of the place consists not in any expression of social homogeneity but quite the reverse; it has all the diversity of a small market town. A grand nineteenth-century château and the modest remains of its fifteenth-century predecessor, several fine houses and numerous cramped ones, an attractive church and an assortment of votive crosses are grouped around various squares (one of which is elegantly shaded by lines of pollarded chestnut trees). There is a distinct shortage of shops and there are no longer any cafés, but Puligny can entertain its visitors at a good hotel, which includes a reputable restaurant. Despite the narrowness of some of its alleys there is a sense of space, lacking in Chassagne and a rare luxury in most other villages of comparable size. And overlaying this stimulating evidence of social diversity there is a feeling of calm prosperity.

'Puligny is more cosmopolitan, Chassagne more viticultural,' claims Loulou Carillon, president of Puligny's mutual aid society of vignerons, the Confrérie of St Bernard. Cosmopolitan is not the adjective that would occur to most people in such rural surroundings, but Puligny certainly seems more open to the world. In its quiet provincial way it evokes the extravagant possibilities of Flaubert, while Chassagne can seem huddled in the claustrophobic melancholia of Balzac. Puligny is characterized by Vincent Leflaive, most engaging of gentlemen-vignerons; Chassagne peers out through the guarded eyes of Pierre

Ramonet, epitome of the peasant grower, and millionaire.

During the years which I spent asking inquisitive questions of Puligny's inhabitants I was only once rudely repulsed, by an old vigneron who mistook me for the tax inspector. In Chassagne, by contrast, I often encountered an instinctive suspicion of strangers, most fiercely expressed by Abbé Colin, the famous priest-vigneron who had succeeded his father as manager of the estate of the Marquis de Laguiche. I went to see him in his retirement, going as directed through the garden of his little house and into the cold kitchen, and there saw an ancient diminutive figure huddled in a stained soutane, a scarf and a beret, whose long, broad but pointed fingers, very red at the ends, were scrabbling at the pages of his breviary. My stumbling explanations were countered with sharp ill temper. 'I don't have any time, I'm waiting for someone. Go away. Leave the gate open.'

It may be unfair to imply that this confused reaction was typical, either of the man or of the village, but some growers in Puligny believe that it was Abbé Colin who did most to fan the flames of rivalry between the two communes, from excessive devotion to the cause of Chassagne. A pity, because he was widely respected as the embodiment of Burgundian tradition, responsible for one of the finest wines of Montrachet.

Nowadays they say that this rivalry is a thing of the past. Monsieur Carillon observes that 'they make good wine everywhere now, even in America, so we must work together', and he emphasizes that he has several friends in Chassagne. 'When we go to the Foire aux Vins at Beaune we all go together and dine together at a restaurant there, a different restaurant each year.' But such formalized contacts are not replicated on a regular, casual basis. On the contrary, there is still a good deal of amour propre which makes each community somewhat dismissive of the other.

Sharing the same surname, the villages remain divided in innumerable other ways, evident even to outsiders. Perhaps it is the name, and the vineyard, which are the real basis of their animosity. Each has been proud to claim Montrachet as its own and reluctant to acknowledge its neighbour's share. Puligny was the first to decide, by a resolution of the town council on 10 February 1878, that it wished to link its name with that of its most famous Cru, but the inhabitants of Chassagne le Haut (as it was then called) were quick to realize their danger and within six months they too applied to the authorities for a change of name. Both requests were granted, on the same day in November 1879, to the bitter chagrin of Puligny, which had conceived the idea in the first place and felt there was greater natural justice in its cause.

The evident geographic boundary between the two villages is not the official line of administrative demarcation but the old road which flows like a stream through a natural break in the hills, down a small valley which descends east from the village of Gamay. South of this road lies Chassagne, perched on the lee of La Grande Montagne. North lies Puligny, sheltered beneath its own hill of Montrachet. But the southernmost tip of this hill (which otherwise lies entirely within the administrative boundaries of Puligny) is claimed by the commune of Chassagne. It has always been thus, contrary to the quite obvious structure of the landscape, and Puligny still feels, half-consciously and with its resentment dulled by centuries of resignation, that its birthright was stolen by its neighbour.

The Place

3 | Vineyards

'My wellbeloved hath a vineyard in a very fruitful hill.'

ISAIAH, 5:1

The Naming of Names

Mists hang so low over the Côte d'Or that you can't see the tops of the hills and smoke rises in streams from every vineyard to meet the clouds. February is the time for pruning and they are burning the cuttings in portable braziers, made from oil-drums chopped in half and mounted on the frames of wheelbarrows.

Steam is also rising from the travelling still which is parked on a corner of the road outside Chassagne, stopping for a fortnight on a tour of the nearby villages which will include Mercurey and Givry in the Côte Chalonnaise. It is operated by Monsieur Champion from Jambes, a cheerful burly man who is the third generation of his family to follow this occupation. He spends the winter months tending his still, a pleasantly warming occupation on a chill February day, and he raises chickens industrially for the rest of the year.

Growers bring trailer loads of marc – the spent skins and pips of the grapes which they have saved since the vintage. Monsieur Champion boils steam through the marc to extract the residue of coarse wine from this unpromising material and distils the results into a fierce colourless liquid which surprisingly enough tastes less fiery at full strength, warm from the still, than it does after a few months' maturation in an old cask. This is the last process of tidying up after the previous autumn's harvest, the point at which distinctions of vineyard and reputation cease to matter, as the waste product of wine is turned into alcohol which will never be labelled or sold but will be quietly consumed by the vigneron, his family and friends.

The peripatetic still is a good place from which to start a tour of the vineyards. Invigorated by a glass of marc and warmed by a few minutes alongside the old copper cylinder of Monsieur Champion's boiler, the wine lover can gaze towards Montrachet and appreciate that despite the penetrating cold of the Burgundian winter this is in many ways the best season for a brisk walk through the vineyards. After their winter pruning the cropped and leafless rows of vines are seen as parallel monochrome lines across the hillside, identifying the contours and boundaries of every *climat*. The walls of an ancient *clos* may long ago have tumbled into ruin and disappeared but an interruption in the vine rows or a slight change in their direction provides graphic evidence of the historic partitions of the land.

The system of Appellation Contrôlée and its four-tier classification of the vineyards of the Côte d'Or recognizes the most important of these traditional divisions and sanctions their names with the authority of law. But it necessarily simplifies a more complex heritage of nicknames and subdivisions, much of which survives only in the memory of the oldest vignerons and in the patterns of the rows. It is worth pausing for a moment to consider these names and classifications, both ancient and modern.

There is a distinction in Burgundian nomenclature between *lieu-dit* (a vineyard area identified by a traditional name) and *climat* (a vineyard defined by topographical features which give an individual character to its wine; a climat may incorporate several lieux-dits). And then there is the *clos*, meaning a vineyard enclosed by a wall. Inevitably there is a certain amount of ambiguity in these terms, most notably with regard to Montrachet itself. In former times the appellation was much more flexible and was applied with varying degrees of justification to vineyards all along the hillside, particularly to those which are now called Chevalier-Montrachet and Bâtard Montrachet. In other words, it was understood in a rather generalized sense to be a climat. Nowadays the name is very strictly reserved for the lieu-dit which was formerly known as Grand Montrachet, the heart of the vineyard which straddles the communal boundary of Puligny and Chassagne. But here too there is a tiny ambiguity, because the section which falls within Chassagne is marked on the most authoritative maps as Le Montrachet while that which falls within Puligny is Montrachet, plain and simple. Montrachet is also quite evidently a clos, its wall more or less intact and embellished with grand stone gateways. Yet no one refers to it as Clos de Montrachet, although the word is used as a mark of distinction for other vineyards whose walls have all but disappeared. Do not expect consistency in the matter of vineyard names.

Their classification, on the other hand, does follow a logical pattern, easy enough to understand. In general terms you may assume that the more narrowly its origin is defined by law, the finer the wine. The best vineyards of Burgundy, the Grands Crus, are identified on the label by the name of their lieu-dit (e.g. Chevalier-Montrachet) without reference to the village to which they belong. They are so grand that everyone is presumed to know their location. Next down the scale are the Premiers Crus, which must be labelled with the village name and usually the vineyard as well (for example, Puligny-Montrachet Premier Cru, Les Pucelles) unless the wine is blended from more than one vineyard, in which case it is simply designated Puligny-Montrachet Premier Cru. Then there are the modest commune wines, from the low-lying 'lieux dits' which cluster around the village: Puligny-Montrachet, without qualification. And at the bottom of the scale, not even entitled to the identity of a village designation, are those basic wines from the least favoured sites, sold simply as appellation Bourgogne.

A typical cross-section of the Côte d'Or would be layered as follows: basic Bourgogne from the flat, poorly drained vineyards at the foot of the slope; village wines as the land begins to rise; then Premiers Crus, then Grands Crus and sometimes another slice of village wines on top, just below the woods and wasteland which crown the hillsides. The best wines come from about two-thirds the way up this gradient, from vineyards which are perfectly placed to catch the sun, sheltered from the wind and frost and exceedingly well drained.

Puligny in this respect is unusual. You climb directly from Puligny Villages to the Grands Crus and immediately above the uppermost vines of Chevalier-Montrachet is nothing but scrub and barren rock. These boundaries seem absurd and arbitrary on the map; what possible topographical peculiarity can condemn Puligny-Montrachet produced in the vineyard of Les Enseignières to be sold on the market at a price which is less than a third that commanded by its neighbour Bâtard-Montrachet, from which it is divided by the width of a narrow road? Why is there no intermediate stage between grandeur and modesty?

Kitchen gardeners know the answer, understanding that a few rows of spinach or beans will flourish in this bed but wither and die in that, a few yards distant. It's a question of shade, moisture, drainage and soil structure. So too in Burgundy, where a walk through the vineyards should be sufficient to convince the observant that the ruthless distinctions of appellation and international demand are justified in actual fact. The lie of the land is decisive.

Crossing the Road

Walking towards Montrachet from Monsieur Champion's still near Chassagne you would cross the old Paris road, the Route Nationale 6, which winds up the valley to Gamay and St-Aubin and swings in a great loop through the hills before heading north, to the capital. It seems inconceivable that this modest road could once have been the main artery from Paris to the south, along which Napoleon's armies marched towards the invasion of Italy. I vividly remember struggling down the Route Nationale, clogged with traffic and roadworks, as I headed for a meeting in Beaune to which I arrived late after a five-hour journey of exhausting difficulty. Now they have built the motorway, and the drive to Paris can comfortably be completed in under three hours, with the added delight of following a particularly beautiful route through landscapes of drama and variety. And the old road, emptied of heavy traffic, offers a pleasurable alternative for those who want to meander from one market town to the next.

In order to arrive at this agreeable state of affairs they very nearly destroyed one of the most famous vineyards in the world. When the motorway was first planned back in 1955 the engineers decided that it should cross the Côte d'Or on a flyover, close to the old Route Nationale. The foot of one of the vast concrete piers needed to support this construction was to be located slap in the middle of Montrachet. They appeared to believe that vines could flourish in the permanent shadow of an enormous flyover, uncontaminated by traffic fumes, and that the tiny vineyard could survive the massive excavations required for the pier's foundations. Unbelievably, this plan was accepted by successive Ministers of Transport and it was not until 1964 that the decision was finally reversed, following prolonged international outcry, and an alternative plan was approved which brought the motorway through a gap in the hills a few miles further north, along the boundary which separates the vineyards of Beaune from those of Savigny.

Thanks to this narrow escape it is still possible to cross the Route Nationale just below Chassagne, walk a few yards up the old track ahead of you and find yourself quite suddenly among the Grands Crus, with the gateways of Montrachet on your left, Bâtard on your right and the boundary with Puligny at the brow of the hill. Beyond lies the long slope of the Premiers Crus, stretching up to Blagny in the distance.

It is a landscape of vigorous simplicity, entirely given over to the vine. A hundred years ago the impression would have been more varied: peach trees and pears grew apparently at random in the vineyards; the vines themselves were pruned as individual bushes (rather than trained on wires in rows) and below the village were pastures grazed by horses and cows. Even the most valued vineyards were broken up by barren patches of scrubland and rock, long since dynamited and bulldozed into cultivation. Less rigorously ordered by the patterns of modern viticulture, the hillside would have supported a more complex ecology, a richer wildlife.

But the fundamentals would have been much the same: red earth, speckled and streaked with limestone; the gnarled black stumps of vines; low stone walls, enclosing irregular patches; the smoke from small bonfires of the prunings rising to mingle with the low-lying clouds along the hilltops; and down below in the village a huddle of houses clustered around the slate-clad steeple of Puligny's church. It may have been prettier once, but there is a boniness about this land which will always survive, giving structure to the wines which it produces.

The Lay of the Land

> 'Full fathom five thy father lies;
> Of his bones are coral made.'
> (Shakespeare, *The Tempest*)

The skeleton beneath the soil is made, like ours, from calcium. It consists of complex layers of limestone, formed many millions of years ago by the fossilization of innumerable sea creatures: oysters, sea-urchins, molluscs, calcareous seaweeds and the like. Some were transformed into reefs of coral or accumulated as vast deposits of shells. Others disintegrated into minute skeletal fragments; nuclei which attracted the pre-

cipitation of carbonate of lime from the primeval seawater, thus forming a semi-porous rock with a structure like the hard roes of herring
(oolitic limestone, known to the English as Cotswold stone). And these
layers of limestone are occasionally interrupted by a thin deposit of marl,
a crumbly oolitic rock which originated from a bonding of calcium carbonate around particles of clay.

Nobody knows whether limestone has any catalytic or chemical effect on the growth of the vine and the constituents of grape juice; none
has ever been proven. But the finest white wines of the world, almost
without exception, are grown on a foundation of limestone and it is
clear that its structure has exceedingly important characteristics in terms
of drainage and water retention. The relatively porous texture of most
limestone (less true of the Bathonian rock which forms the base of the
hill of Montrachet but generally typical of that which underlies the
Grands Crus and Premiers Crus) ensures that the vineyards are well
drained and that the tap roots of the vines are never flooded. But the
rock also acts like a dense sponge, holding a reservoir of moisture even
in times of severe drought. This nourishes the vine and cools the soil,
counteracting the heat of high summer to prolong the ripening season.
And it is this lengthy maturation which is so essential to build complexity of flavour into the grapes.

Above these bones of limestone is a layer of reddish soil, which consists of fine particles of clay and sand, coarser chunks of gravel and marl,
silicates of magnesia and alumina, streaks of iron oxide (particularly in
Montrachet itself) plus trace elements of various other minerals, including copper, zinc, lead, cobalt, beryllium and sodium. The tendency
of most scientists has been to discount these mineral constituents of the
soil but to emphasize its structure and organic nutrients, simply because
it is so difficult to demonstrate the effects of trace elements on taste and
aroma. But I know from my own professional experience with a brew-
ery that the presence of a quarter of a part per million of zinc can be
critical to a successful fermentation, so I tend to look quite closely at
these minute fractions in the soil. Chromium is believed to promote
fertilization, cobalt to shorten the ripening period of fruit and zinc to
alter the balance of acidity and sugar (which may be why it is so vital
to the yeasts). So I feel that the unusually high level of sodium which
has been noted in Montrachet (and in Meursault's finest vineyard, Les
Perrières) must be relevant, if at present inexplicable.

More obvious to anyone who has walked through the vineyards in wet weather is that this reddish-brown earth is extremely sticky; there is a lot of clay in it. Clay soils produce full-flavoured wines, long-lived and impressively powerful but sometimes lacking the finesse of those grown on leaner ground. So it is not surprising to find that clay particles account for 50 per cent of the soil in Bâtard-Montrachet, about 35 per cent in Montrachet and only 20 per cent in Chevalier: an arithmetic progression which almost exactly expresses the contrast between the power of Bâtard, at the bottom of the hill, and the finesse of Chevalier (at the top), with Montrachet itself the perfect synthesis between the two.

The steepness of the slope increases geometrically: from 5 per cent in Bâtard, to 10 per cent in Montrachet and 20 per cent in Chevalier. The more sharply angled towards the sun, the better the exposure to heat and light, and the better the drainage. But in Chevalier's case the drainage is almost too effective; the erosion of the centuries has washed away most of its soil to the vineyards below. And it is Montrachet, in the middle of the slope, which is more sheltered.

Bâtard has collected the deepest and richest soil, but its location could cause severe problems of drainage, were it not for one important factor. Mixed with the cold clay are plenty of pebbles and small broken stones, constituting some 10 per cent of the whole: exactly double the proportion that is found in the slightly lower-lying vineyards which bear the simple village appellation of Puligny. These stones break up the soil sufficiently to allow it to drain, something that is quite noticeable in wet weather, when Bâtard clearly absorbs rainfall more readily than the village vineyards, where the water tends to collect as long puddles in the furrows. The pebbles also have an effect on the microclimate since they act as miniature storage heaters, soaking up the sunshine by day and warming the soil during the night.

The slope as a whole faces roughly south-east, which means that the vines gain maximum benefit from every hour of sunlight, from dawn to dusk. And the scrubland on top of the hills breaks the force of the cold winds from north or west. Mediterranean plants and southern varieties of lizard and snail can be found in the crannies of the rocks above the vineyards and the buzzing of cicadas fills the summer air. But as with the geology, so with the aspect of the vineyards; minor differences in orientation can have a considerable impact on the wine. The fact that

The steepness of the slope increases geometrically: from 5 per cent in Bâtard, to 10 per cent in Montrachet and 20 per cent in Chevalier.

the Chassagne end of Montrachet faces marginally more to the south can seem to result in a weightier character to its wines, as compared to the greater elegance of those from Puligny's half of the vineyard. At any rate it has given rise to an endless and unresolvable debate among those rich enough to sample the results.

Finally there is the question of altitude. The vineyards closest to the village lie at approximately two hundred and thirty metres above sea level. Climb only thirty metres higher and you are in the middle of Montrachet; continue to the three hundred-metre contour line and you have reached the upper limit of Chevalier. Such relatively minor differences are important in terms of aspect and drainage but not of great significance climatically. But a further hundred metres up the hill, high above Blagny, there is a noticeable chill in the air which is quite evidently reflected in the lean austerity of the wines from these stony vineyards, exposed to the most rigorous extremes of Burgundian weather.

For it is worth remembering that this is not (like Bordeaux, for example) a temperate region of climatic moderation. Graphs of the seasonal averages may suggest some similarity in the weather pattern of these two famous wine regions, but in the case of Burgundy such statistical data are utterly misleading. This can be one of the coldest places in France during the winter, one of the hottest at the height of the summer, and it suffers from violent storms. Hail can strip leaves, buds and even branches from the vines during the spring; thunderclaps can ruin a ripening crop shortly before the vintage. And the differences in climate from one year to the next are quite remarkable.

Such intemperate dramas have their effect on the character of each vintage, but the great wines of Burgundy are as much the product of minute variations (of soil and subsoil, aspect and drainage) which are individually almost imperceptible but collectively critical. It is the accumulation of such subtle particularities which distinguishes so clearly the character of each appellation.

From Wild Vines to Numbered Clones

Puligny is now so strongly identified with white wines that it comes as something of a shock to realize that almost all of this land (except Montrachet and its immediate neighbours) used to be planted with red grapes, a state of affairs which persisted well into the twentieth century. Pinot Noir was grown when times were good, Gamay when quantity seemed more important than quality. And even in Montrachet you could find plenty of Bourgogne Aligoté as recently as the 1930s, mixed with Pinot Blanc and Chardonnay.

The fashion has altered with a vengeance: the great white wines of Burgundy now fetch higher prices than most of the reds and the international obsession with Chardonnay has caused Aligoté to be relegated to the humblest appellations. Only two growers (Maroslavac and Chartron) still produce a red Puligny-Montrachet and a few grow the grape up at Blagny; otherwise the vineyards are given over to monoculture of the most extreme sort, dedicated to a single grape variety.

In many ways this is a pity. Neighbouring Chassagne still makes a fair amount of red wine and while no one now would reckon that a bottle of red Chassagne-Morgeot was worth two bottles of Montrachet (as apparently once was the case) Pinot Noir from these slopes can certainly produce appetizing burgundy, of marked individuality. I also mourn the demise of Aligoté in the Grands Crus, though I am probably the only wine lover to do so. But having tasted what a mature bottle of Aligoté is capable of, from eighty-year-old vines grown at Bouzeron in the Côte Chalonnaise, I relish the thought of this variety's potential in Montrachet. It might also contribute intriguing nuances of flavour in a blend. But fashion scorns such options and the laws of appellation forbid them. For better or worse Puligny-Montrachet means Chardonnay.

The grape variety is extremely ancient. Its probable descent from wild strains of *Vitis vinifera* is via a primitive version of Muscat and, like most of the European wine grapes, it came originally from the east, possibly from Lebanon or Syria. Unlike Pinot (which has been known by the same name in Burgundy since at least as early as 1375), Chardonnay's history on the Côte d'Or is a matter of conjecture, because no one knows what it was called in former times. Can it be identified with 'Saulvoignien', a variety planted by the seigneur of Chassagne in 1383, or with 'Noirien Blanc', which was the white grape of Burgundy in the eighteenth century? Was it named after the village in the Mâconnais, or vice versa?

Whatever the truth, the modern strains of Chardonnay are clearly rather different from what was planted before the advent of phylloxera. The old, ungrafted, long-lived Chardonnay vines burrowed deeper into the soil than their modern cousins (grafted on to American rootstocks) and they had smaller berries, producing lower yields and perhaps greater concentration of flavour. According to Pierre Cogny of Bouzeron: 'There's no more real Chardonnay – it yielded so little, from such small grapes, but it made *esstra* wines. It had tiny bunches which would fit into a small glass.' It may still be possible to find some old strains of Chardonnay in the vineyards which (despite being grafted, as all vines must be to protect them from phylloxera) have the smaller berries which were evidently typical before the advent of clonal selection. But such vines are rare.

Clones (genetically identical children, propagated from a selected parent) became the fashion in Burgundy during the 1960s and are now planted everywhere. Previously it had been customary for the growers to take their own cuttings from healthy-looking vines in their vineyards, or for the nurseryman to do so on a similarly ad hoc basis. The traditional method (still practised by several growers in Chassagne) ensured that new plantings consisted of a rich mix of genetic material (something which is believed to contribute to complexity of flavour) but could easily perpetuate weaknesses as well as strengths. In an environment such as the Côte d'Or, where a single crop is grown year after year on the same land, the exhaustion of the soil and inbreeding of the plants can contribute to degeneracy and this indeed happened, with the appearance of *court-noué* or fan-leaf virus, which was first noticed in Puligny in 1950 by Monsieur Varelle of the INAO (the supervisory organization for Appellation Contrôlée). This viral malady of the vine is transmitted by tiny worms which live on the roots. The wood of the vine becomes shorter ('court') between one eye and the next, the leaves shrink and become streaked with yellow and eventually the vine dies, long before its normal life expectancy is achieved. Other varieties of this virus have since been identified, not all of them fatal, but all effecting a significant reduction in yield.

Ideally the infected vineyards should be replanted after the land has been thoroughly fumigated, but in practice that is often difficult because of the highly fragmented landholdings of Burgundy. Even if you manage to eliminate the virus from your own patch, it will probably creep back from your neighbour's. So there has been a considerable effort by the INAO (and by research establishments such as Domaine de l'Espiguette at Le Grau du Roi, in the sands of the Camargue) to develop virus-resistant strains of all the classic grape varieties and to multiply them by clonal propagation. Inevitably this programme has also involved selection for other criteria such as yield, early ripening, suitability to particular soils or (harder to define) for quality.

The result has been to alter the character of the plants in small but significant ways and thereby to alter the character of the wines. Yields have gone up, partly because typical grape size has increased, partly because the vines are healthier, and some would argue that concentration and complexity of flavour have been sacrificed. It also seems possible that the new clones may lack the longevity of most traditional strains of Chardonnay (which could easily flourish for forty or fifty years before replanting was necessary) and so they cannot develop the intensity of flavour which is typical of really old vines. But such concerns are more typical of wine writers than growers who (like most farmers) prefer to minimize their risks.

Some vignerons still undertake what they call 'sélection massale' propagating a wide variety of plants from the healthiest specimens in their vineyards, but most of the best domaines of Puligny plump for safety and buy their clones from Jean-Luc Pascal, himself a native of the village. Jean-Luc's father was a *métayer* (sharecropper) of Domaine Leflaive. In 1955 his lease came to an end and the domaine took the land under direct management, but Pascal was a good worker and a friend of François Virot, the renowned *régisseur* of the domaine. Virot proposed that Pascal should do all their grafts for them and helped to set him up in business as a nurseryman. It was a good time to get started, because the spread of *court-noué* in the vineyards brought Pascal increasing orders from the other growers, who were forced to replant as the virus took hold. The business flourished and is continued today by Jean-Luc, who also looks after the fifteen hectares of vines (in fifteen different appellations) which now constitute his own domaine.

When I arrived at Pascal's modern house on the outskirts of Puligny I was kept at bay by a small but fierce dog, tethered to a long wire that ran the length of the building. It was not until I persuaded Jean-Luc's mother to telephone his wife from next door that I finally gained admittance. Pascal laughed when he arrived, claimed the dog wouldn't hurt a flea, and hauled me off to his grafting shed at the back to explain the intricacies of his métier.

'A good deal of this talk about declining quality is to do with bad pruning, not over-productive clones. Clones give us tranquillity; it's very difficult to be sure when making cuttings from existing vines that

'Those guys in the Midi – they've got no heart.' Jean-Luc Pascal.

the result will be a success. You must mix as many different types of clones as you can when replanting in order to get the best quality, and of course we certainly need more good clones. But you can choose whatever is appropriate for your needs. Take the rootstocks, for example; I would recommend 161/49 for chalky soils and perhaps 3309C for heavier soils, though I'm less convinced about that these days. 5BB is the best for very poor soils. Riparia Gloire is excellent for quality, is very precocious and produces a good degree of alcohol. As far as Chardonnay is concerned, we use clones 95, 76 and 548 for those whose first concern is quality and 96 or 277 for those who want a bit more quantity. But the differences are not huge. The quality/quantity variations might be in the order of 10 to 20 per cent.'

He picked up a plant, took another drag on his Gauloise Jaune and scowled. 'I buy my rootstocks in the Gard, in Vaucluse and the Ardèche. The price has gone up enormously. Each little rootstock now costs me one franc and thirty-three centimes; a year ago I paid sixty centimes. It's those guys in the Midi – they've got no heart!'

Pascal's team of workers do the grafting in March and April, using a machine to make a notch in the rootstock and to cut a matching knob on the end of the vine stem, an omega graft. The combination of rootstock and stem is planted out in May and then each plant is lifted around 15 November and brought back to Pascal's premises, where they are individually inspected to ensure that the graft has taken and the roots have developed. The young vines are stored in beds of sand over the winter before being planted in the vineyards in February, March or April.

'It's a lot of work, and it takes up a lot of space.' Pascal seems momentarily doubtful as to whether it's all worth while. But he expects to sell about half a million vines this year, to Leflaive, Sauzet, Chartron, Carillon, Gérard Chavy and to others further afield. 'I sell plenty of vines to growers in Volnay and Meursault and I'm just beginning to sell in Chassagne, but in Chassagne lots of vignerons do their own grafts. In any case, I don't go out and sell my grafts, I wait for them to come to me.'

The growers will certainly continue to do so, replanting their vineyards with a small range of clones because they can see little alternative and because, as Pascal says, clones give them 'tranquillity'. Even so thoughtful a man as Robert Drouhin, responsible for making the superlative Montrachet of the Marquis de Laguiche, reluctantly acknowledges that 'there should be clonal selection, but you run the risk of changing the character of the vines'.

It's a risk which may be smaller with Chardonnay (which retains its varietal character through thick and thin) than with the more elusive complexity of Pinot Noir. But experience increasingly suggests that the risk may be unacceptable if it means a drastic reduction in the size of the genetic pool, as old strains of Chardonnay disappear. In the long term there seems greater hope in methods of cultivation which strengthen the natural immunity of the plant and revive the exhausted land. Such methods may well prove useful in the fight against *court-noué* and will almost certainly help to combat the spread of *esca*, a fungal growth which penetrates the roots of the vine and eventually kills it, quite suddenly, in midsummer (hence the malady's colloquial name of 'apoplexy'). Esca flourishes in vineyards where herbicides have replaced ploughing; reversion to more traditional practices should prove more efficacious than the application of yet more chemical treatments. The most significant experiment for the future well-being of Puligny could well be that which Anne-Claude Leflaive has initiated at her family domaine, where the techniques of 'bio-dynamic' cultivation are being .given a chance to prove their worth alongside the more conventional assumptions of modern agriculture. I write before these trials have yielded any useful results, but in the hope that they may prove positive, helping to rebuild an ecology which will enable nature's diversity to triumph over man's interference.

The Cross of Montrachet
The road which divides Montrachet from Bâtard continues north towards Meursault, separating the Premiers Crus of the mid-slope and uplands (producing lean and elegant wines) from those at the bottom of the hill, which make Puligny of more immediate appeal and more generous flavour. The distinction may be a bit rough and ready but it serves as a useful rule of thumb, proving that the old tracks across the hill are boundaries of continuing significance. That road, my favourite north-south axis through the vineyards, is crossed by another which descends from Chevalier to the heart of the village and marks the boundary between Grands Crus and Premiers Crus. The point where these two roads meet is the most decisive intersection on the hillside, dividing Montrachet from Le Cailleret, Le Cailleret from Les Pucelles, Les

Pucelles from Bâtard and Bâtard from Montrachet. The junction is marked by an old stone cross, tall and slender, which rests on a simple base inscribed as follows: 'O Crux Ave. 1806. Anne Carillon Veuve Latour de Puligny.' The widow Latour (née Carillon) was a pious lady who erected another cross near Puligny's church and a little shrine on the edge of the village, but this is her masterpiece: the Cross of Montrachet. It has a feeling of grace and inevitability, like a standing stone on some particularly magic spot of Dartmoor, and I am clearly not alone in finding it so. Almost any time that I pass there I notice, sitting on the cross's plinth, a jam-jar full of flowers. Constantly renewed without pretension or expense (these are often the simplest flowers of the field, or a few chrysanthemums), this modest posy is for me a talisman of remembrance and faith; and of thanks for the bounty of the land.

The junction is marked by an old stone cross, tall and slender. The Cross of Montrachet.

4 | Views of the Village

The Pond

Not long ago the street names of Puligny were unmarked, known only to the inhabitants, and the houses unnumbered, as was generally the case in small rural communities throughout France. Only recently did the blue and white plaques appear which already seem so much part of the visual tradition of the place, naming and numbering the lanes and doorways. Pressure from central government and the post office (rather than any desire to make life easier for confused strangers) brought about this change, giving legal definition to the ambiguities of oral habit.

The numbers are entirely artificial, bearing no relation to the local practice of referring to individual houses by the names of their inhabitants ('Turn left at Monsieur So-and-so'), but the street names are those which have stuck to them over the years, for reasons which are mostly self-evident (big road, small road, road behind the church) but sometimes preserve Puligny's history in cryptic form. Nobody knows why Rue du Pot de Fer (the iron pot) is named thus, nor Rue Tripet (something to do with tripe, perhaps?), but there is a clear watery connection which can be followed into the village if you enter it by the road which leads directly downhill from the Cross of Montrachet. This road starts off as Rue Rousseau (the little stream), becomes Rue de Poiseul (the well) as it enters the village and terminates in the Place Johannisberg, which was formerly known as the Place de l'Abreuvoir: the watering place.

There is no sign now of stream, well or pond, unless you listen at-

tentively as you walk down the Rue de Poiseul and catch the sound of
water running along the covered gully at the edge of the road. But formerly there was a stream (at least in wet weather) that trickled into the
horse pond, which itself overflowed into a muddy runnel that ran down
the hill to the Fontaine de Puligny (a small stone structure built to protect the village well) which in turn fed the communal washing trough.
This was, until quite recently, the centre of village society. The men
brought their plough horses to drink at the pond, the women met for
a gossip as they scrubbed the family laundry on the wide stone ledges
which surrounded the washing trough and everyone came to the well
to draw water for their daily needs. Running water was not installed in
Puligny until 1955. And then the horse pond was drained and filled,
the old cross moved across the street to its present position below the
sundial, the wellhead was levelled and covered and the washing trough
converted into the Salle Jean Chartron, where a club for the more elderly inhabitants of Puligny meets every Wednesday. This last metamorphosis is within my recent memory: the old village washplace survived until the nineteen-eighties and I wish it were still there; it had
probably been in continuous use for at least five hundred years.

The Church

> 'Je ne dors jamais bien à mon aise sinon quand
> je suis au sermon, ou quand je prie Dieu.'
> I never sleep comfortably except when I am at a
> sermon or when I pray to God.
> (Rabelais, *Gargantua,* Bk 1)

Rue de l'Abreuvoir becomes Rue de l'Église, joining in fact and name
the original centres of village life. But the pond is drained and the church
is locked, as it has been these last fifteen years or more, to protect it
from thieves and common vandals. It is open for mass on Saturday
evenings (the priest serves five villages) and for occasional feast days;
otherwise you may sometimes wander in there by chance on a quiet
sunny morning, when three or four cheerful local ladies are cleaning it
in preparation for a wedding or a funeral.

The simple classical façade bears the date 1779 and fronts on to a
tiny square which reminds me of one of those quiet corners that you

find in the back streets of Venice, but this Italianate charm conceals a mixture of styles and periods, more evident when you view the church from the side. Then you notice the small slate-covered belfry which sits astride the roof, its neatly overlapping scales bearing witness to its recent restoration. And below, if you are observant, you might spot the single gothic window which identifies the seigneurial chapel, built on to the north side of the thirteenth-century nave by Charles de Mypont in 1496. His tomb was placed before the altar (it has since been moved to the wall) and the chapel was endowed with sufficient lands to support a priest, praying perpetually for the salvation of de Mypont souls. In the mid-eighteenth century the chapel was extended by an aisle, which was then balanced by another on the south side of the church and the façade was rebuilt in its present form. A hundred years later they finally completed the building by the addition of the choir. You would expect the result of this lengthy agglomeration to be a mess but in fact the church has a strong, simple character, enhanced by the dignified restoration which has removed some accumulated ecclesiastical clutter to reveal the well-proportioned architectural harmony of the whole.

Immediately to the north of the church stands a cross, erected in 1795 by Madeleine and Anne Carillon, pious ancestors of a family which still lives in a house almost immediately opposite. The earliest of several such, in and around the village, this cross testifies to one of those moral missions of extraordinary fervour which erupted into the placid devotions of rural faith during the eighteenth and nineteenth centuries. The expression of a form of fundamental Catholicism that seems weighed with guilt, such missions were the Church's response to the violent bouts of anti-clericalism which racked France from the Revolution onwards. But eventually such passions waned and are now mostly a memory, expressed today in political not religous form. Only a persistent trace of anti-Semitism remains as a disagreeable residue of social and dogmatic ferocity, to stain the present with the past.

Declining religious fervour means that most rural parishes have to make do with the shared services of their priest. L'Abbé Menestrier is the curé of Santenay, where he lives, but also has charge of the churches of Chassagne-Montrachet, St-Aubin, Puligny-Montrachet and Meursault. It's a great deal of work and Père Menestrier is often in a hurry, rushing from one funeral or wedding to another, to the occasional distress of the families involved. But for the most part he is well liked and widely respected, as a decent man who understands village life, preaches simply but well and enjoys a glass of good wine.

But Sunday mass on a Saturday evening can never have the feeling of being other than what it is, a makeshift way of fitting the weekly service into a crowded schedule. Puligny doesn't have the full attention of its priest and the delights of Sunday mornings are diminished. In the old days everyone went to church, en famille, and then lingered for a gossip afterwards before strolling home for lunch, or going out to a local restaurant. Sundays combined the steady moral comfort of repetitive ritual and the unhurried social pleasures of the table. Going to church on Saturday is a statement of belief, on Sunday a habitual act of faith, part of the fabric of daily life.

Society

> 'Petite ville, grand renom.'
> Small town, great renown. Written of Chinon,
> Rabelais's native town.
> (Rabelais, *Pantagruel,* Bk 5)

The church's displacement as one of the most important centres of village society leaves a gap which has not been filled. On the contrary, Puligny's potential for social intercourse has diminished during the past half-century; there are now no cafés, few shops and fewer people. It has the air of a village turned inward.

Walk down the narrow streets and lanes and you will pass shuttered windows, some of which appear to have been closed for decades. Mighty stone sockets (intended for the hinges of massive doors) project from the jambs of old archways, relics of a mentality which has remained defensive by instinct, localized by habit. These arches are now closed by metal gates, guarded by dogs that bark at every passing stranger. The most ferocious of these, an Alsatian of heart-stopping malevolence, used to prowl along the top of a wall near the post office, slavering and growling a foot or two above head height. It always seemed about to hurl itself at your jugular and there must have been several elderly pedestrians who came close to death from the sudden terror of its bark. The dog's owner, Jean-Claude Wallerande (sommelier of Le Montrachet),

A house in Puligny guarded by dogs that bark at every passing stranger.

always laughed when reproached about this beast, claiming it was docile at heart, but he was eventually persuaded to give it away to a distant friend.

Such monsters are rare; the invisible guard-dogs often turn out to be yapping terriers, all noise and no real menace, and the shuttered blankness of the houses may suggest a wariness of strangers but implies no aggression. On the contrary, there is a curious restfulness about Puligny; a sense that everyone is entitled to his privacy, visitors included. If you take the street from Place Johannisberg towards the church you will pass a man sitting on a narrow bench outside his house, head in his hands, scowling and angry with the world. But there is no threat or danger of abuse; his turmoil is turned against himself. At the next corner is the post office, defended against break-in by an agreeable door which incorporates the letters PTT in a wrought-iron security grill of unobtrusive strength and period charm. Inside it has the peaceful atmosphere, that gentle dustiness of stamps and glue, which characterizes village post offices everywhere. The price of a bottle of Montrachet may once have been the equivalent of the monthly salary of a postman, but it is no longer so. Postmen are more prosperous. Social disparities, however marked, no longer generate the violent antipathies which once caused France to be the most bitterly communist country in western Europe.

But prosperity is a solvent, not a social glue; and it has not only dissolved some of the traditional hatreds which fissured society but considerably weakened the sense of communal solidarity. Time and again there is testimony to this at the individual level. Equally striking are the records of vanishing traditions.

In the early years of this century, for example, Easter Monday was an occasion for communal rejoicing on a scale which is now unknown. The hillside below Blagny would have been swarming with the villagers of Puligny, Gamay and St-Aubin, dressed in their holiday best as the children rolled brightly painted Easter eggs (hard-boiled the day before) down the steep meadows and through the vines, squealing with delight and competitive excitement as the eggs bounced over the ground, slipped down rabbit holes or became lodged in crevices and were eventually retrieved, more or less intact, to be devoured with a relish that was quite disproportionate to their battered and grubby state but expressed the exuberance of the moment, delight in the day.

As recently as the 1950s, Puligny could muster thirty or forty musi-

The village post office in Puligny.

cians to play in the village band. Now there are two music societies, both non-practising. The most flourishing social clubs of the village are those for the hunters, chasing what little remains of the local wildlife; the tennis players (sixty-five members out of a total village population of 487); and the Club du Troisième Age, for the old.

But there are also two professional organizations, the Syndicat Viticole and the Confrérie de St Bernard, each of which plays an important part in the social life of the village. The former is effectively the wine growers' trade union, meeting to discuss problems of mutual concern, make representations to the INAO about maximum permitted yields (the official *rendement* per hectare, which varies mysteriously with each vintage) and defend their joint interests against interference by the bureaucrats. The Confrérie, founded in 1826, is a mutual aid society with devotional overtones. Its overt purpose is to act the Good Samaritan, providing aid to any member vigneron who is prevented by sickness from undertaking his work in the vineyards, but it also has a social function (as does the Syndicat) which has to some extent superseded its charitable role. The Confrérie's main raison d'être nowadays is to organize two processions annually, one in January on the Feast of St Vincent, patron of wine growers, the other in August for St Bernard.

These processions begin with a glass of wine in a member's cellar before carrying the wooden statue of St Bernard to the church, for a mass of celebration and thanksgiving. Then it's back to the cellar again for another glass of wine before the beginning of a splendid feast which normally lasts, one way or another, from noon to midnight.

Both Syndicat and Confrérie also perform another valuable service to their members, by enabling the vignerons to take turns as Chairmen. These positions bring neither power nor prosperity to the holders but they do entail a most agreeable 'perk': the pleasure of being greeted at official functions as 'Monsieur le Président,' than which there is no higher title in the Republic of France.

Each of these societies, social and professional, organizes trips abroad for their members, as does the Twinning Association which is responsible for Puligny's links with the village of Johannisberg, Prince Metternich's seat in the Rheingau. Travelling together abroad, whether for a long weekend by coach or for a week or two further afield, the inhabitants of Puligny probably see more of one another and forge closer links of friendship than for month after month in the village itself. Daily proximity does not necessarily mean neighbourliness.

Indeed Puligny's social life has to a significant extent retreated in-doors, to the cellars of individual vignerons who occasionally entertain their friends for a glass of wine. And the women meet at the hairdresser, which fulfils the traditional function of such establishments as the cen-tre of rumour and idle gossip. But the real daily social interchange of the village continues, however muted, and revolves around the tradi-tional poles of its unusual geography: the Place du Monument and the Place des Marronniers. The former is the village square, containing the baker, the tobacconist and the war memorial. The latter is the square of a small but sophisticated town, centre of its administration (the Mairie) and hospitality (the hotel). Shady alleys of pollarded chestnut trees give it an air of urban formality and dreamlike stillness.

These two Places are the windows of Puligny's world. One looks in-ward, on the immediate and intensely local preoccupations of a small rural community. The other looks out. In the foreground of this view are the nearby villages, linked by a common culture and ties of social necessity. Further off are the neighbours of mainland Europe, speeding along the autoroutes towards the vineyards of Burgundy. And in the distance (viewed through a haze of regional preconceptions) is a great and foreign vastness which somehow, mysteriously, contributes to Puligny's renown.

5 | Place du Monument

Between the hours of twelve and two, sacred Burgundian lunchtime, life seems suspended in the streets of the village; even the dogs are silent. To walk along the pavements is like exploring a ghost town – each footfall sounds sharply in the deserted stillness and you have the feeling of complete abandonment – as if everyone had suddenly vanished into thin air rather than gone indoors to eat their midday meal, and to snooze.

Nowhere is this sense of emptiness more evident than in the Place du Monument, formerly the Place du Grand Cimetière (a name which recalls its origins as a medieval graveyard). By the eighteenth century this open space had become a public square, much as it is now, with a cross at the centre which has since been replaced by the war memorial, carved in 1921 from the pink sandstone which is quarried above neighbouring Chassagne; an ugly but poignant monument to the thirty-seven men of Puligny who lost their lives in the Great War. After the Second World War a shorter but equally moving list was added to the stumpy obelisk: six names under the heading 'A Nos Morts' and three more under the sad and sombre words 'A Nos Deportés'. On 14 July the memorial is decorated with wreaths and flags, but most days it stands bulky but unnoticed, even by the relatives of those who died.

Near the south-east corner of the square is a slender cross, built in 1856, restored in 1903, and inscribed with a series of mottoes: 'Lord forgive us our sins. It is by the Cross that we come to Glory. To the Immaculate Conception. O Crux Ave.' There is also one of those enigmas which puzzle theologians and historians, since a further inscription reads 'Mission de 1856. Indulgence de 100 Jours.' The sale of indulgences, promising a remission of the sinner's time of penitence in Purgatory, was one of the scandals which provoked the Reformation. And the whole business of indulgences is confusing. What does a hundred days mean after death? How do you measure eternity? Is this indulgence granted to those who pray at this cross or read the inscription or ponder its ambiguities? Heaven knows.

Only in the silent emptiness of the midday break is anyone likely to study such things or to notice the other half-obliterated traces of a time when the Place du Monument was the bustling centre of a populous village. You can still just decipher faded lettering on old stone walls, indicating the former premises of two rival tonneliers, Dupard and Rozet. You might be able to recognize the erstwhile Café du Centre, now shuttered to the world, and you could imagine the time when old men would gather here on summer evenings, to play boules in the dust below the chestnut trees.

Little of that remains, but there is one spot in the square, a simple bench beneath the trees, which is to its habitués the centre of village society, a place to meet, chat and watch the world go by. From this quiet corner you can observe Michel Mourlin repairing a window of his house or Madame Robaire going home after a long day's work at the hotel or an English wine merchant crossing the square on his way to see Olivier Leflaive. A cluster of cronies congregates on the bench in the afternoon, but it's a good vantage point at any time from which to enjoy the restful patterns and small surprises of the passing day.

One morning in early spring my daydreaming was disturbed by the clatter of a cement-mixer – three men were mending the roof of the house behind me. Then it stopped and in the sudden stillness I heard one of the workmen calling down to his mate on the pavement, a dog barking and an unexpected cuckoo, the first of the year, repeating itself among the trees in the park of the Château de Puligny. A fat woman emerged from the house next door, purse in hand and dog at heel, still barking. I had a bet with myself that she was heading for the bakery. A few minutes later she returned, smiling, with three baguettes. Then out popped the baker, leaving his wife to mind the shop while he went to have a word with the butcher, whose van was parked at the entrance to the Rue de la Mairie.

Two old fellows stopped for a chat in the middle of the road, one leaning on a bicycle, the other on a stick. Ten minutes later the stick waved goodbye, just as a younger man and his child came walking down from the post office and paused to greet the cyclist. With foot to pedal the old boy remained gossiping in the road for a while longer before heaving himself on to the saddle and wobbling off towards the Mairie. At which moment an elderly woman who was trotting up the pavement with her bag of groceries stopped for a word with the father and his son. And so it continued, like a slow dance choreographed with perfect timing to weave together the erratic pathways of disparate lives.

The intersection of these meanderings shifts during the course of the day. In the mornings you could pinpoint a spot in the middle of the road, just outside the bakery, but in the afternoon all the paths lead to the bench under the trees, which catches the warmth of the westerly sun.

At three o'clock, if the day is fine, the first of the regulars arrive. André Goudrand and his wife Marguerite have retired to Puligny from Chalon, where he kept a pharmacy and she worked as chambermaid at the hotel. He walks with some difficulty, leaning on a crutch, and she is beginning to show signs of arthritis in the wrists, but they take cheerful pleasure in each other's company and are amiable gossips. 'Of course it's expensive living here, everything in the shops costs so much and with his leg he can't drive so we don't go out to the supermarkets in the big towns like everyone else does. We're dependent on the épicerie here, and the baker, and the butcher who comes here on Tuesdays and Fridays. But we have friends.' There's a contented sigh from both of them. André slaps his hands on his knees and leans forward as he gazes across the square. 'Ah yes,' he says, eventually, and leans back again on the bench.

Although they are both in their sixties they don't go much to weekly meetings of the Club du Troisième Age, when the old people get together to play cards or plan a coach trip abroad or, this year, to make flowers for the decorations which will cover the village at the Fête St Vincent. 'No, I prefer to make my flowers at home. . . and we meet our friends here.'

Next to arrive is Michel Boissard, a vigneron who worked for Domaine Chartron before his retirement and who now, in his seventies, seems as fit as a fiddle; a walking advertisement for wine. Finally, at four

The regulars. Michel Boissard, Marguerite and André Goudrand, Pierrot Lombard.

o'clock precisely, along comes the doyen of the group, Pierrot Lombard. His is an unmistakably French figure: large beret, prominent nose and walrus moustache, blue workman's trousers which flap around the ankles of his sturdy boots. Pierrot walks slightly stooped, slowly and with the aid of a stick, but his voice is firm and he chews his words with pleasure, looking back on a long and dignified life.

'I'm ninety-two, the oldest vigneron in the village. I've lived here always, except for the war. But I'm not the oldest inhabitant. No, that's Monsieur Beck, who used to be a railwayman at Paris. He's ninety-four. But he doesn't get about much now.' This is said with a degree of satisfaction at his own vigorous longevity as he plumps himself down on the bench beside the others and rests his hands on his stick, enjoying the autumn sunshine while the first yellowing leaves fall gently, almost silently to the ground.

An hour later they are still there, chatting peaceably together between interludes of companionable silence, as they do every day while the fine weather lasts.

The Butcher

> 'Heaven sends us good meat,
> but the Devil sends us cooks.'
> (David Garrick, *On Doctor Goldsmith's Characteristical Cookery*)

There used to be two butchers in Puligny but the last one closed in the mid-seventies. Since then the villagers have had to rely on the travelling butcher, Monsieur Bruchard. He takes his van to Volnay on Wednesday and Saturday mornings, St-Romain on Saturday afternoons and Puligny on Tuesday and Friday mornings. The rest of the week he spends behind the counter of his shop at Meursault.

Parked in a side street just off the Place du Monument, Monsieur Bruchard serves customers from a neatly organized cold shelf which is revealed when he swings up the side of the van. 'Our little shops are all disappearing, it's happening all over the world. There used to be half a dozen butchers on the square in Meursault, now there are three. With us it's a family clientele – you have to wait your turn, they talk, you know them. The old people and the middle-aged are still faithful but the young couldn't care less about you. They buy their beefsteak at the supermarkets. The mentality has changed. It's quality that keeps me going. I can't compete with the big shops on price but I can on quality.'

I watch in queasy fascination as he slices some ham, noticing that three fingers of his left hand have been chopped off at the first joint. 'I make all my own pâtés, my saucisson sec, my jambon cru. My speciality is jambon persillée.'

A middle-aged lady comes up to buy a kilo of beef. The purchase is wrapped and paid for. As the woman turns to go she asks Monsieur Bruchard, 'For Boeuf Bourgignon, you use water?' It seems astounding that she doesn't know. 'Wine,' says the butcher firmly, then seeing her glance of dismay he adds, 'And water. Wine and water.'

It is midday, the flap on the side of the van is lowered, the rear door shut and the travelling butcher heads home to Meursault, for his lunch.

The Baker

> 'Qu'ils mangent de la brioche.' Let them eat cake.
> (Marie Antoinette)

Marital relations are a mystery to outsiders – who knows the hidden strengths or stresses of any partnership? But the business of being a baker's wife seems a dull métier, especially in Puligny, especially during the vintage. For most of the year Madame Fontaine works alongside her husband throughout the day (Patrick bakes, Sandrine sells the results of his labour). In the afternoon, while the shop is quiet and he is preparing the elaborate range of pâtisserie in which they both take considerable pride, there is the chance of a few minutes' gossip. But in the evening he goes to bed early, soon after supper, because he has to get up at 3 a.m. in order to fire the stove and knead the first batch of dough for the breakfast baguettes. And for two or three weeks during the harvest they hardly see one another at all. Hundreds of pickers need feeding, dozens more loaves need baking. Monsieur Fontaine abandons the pâtisserie for the duration, starts work at ten in the evening, bakes all night and sleeps as best he can through the clear autumn days. His wife continues to serve in the shop and comforts herself by counting the takings. They have a monopoly in the village and they are appreciated by their neighbours. 'Ça marche bien ici' (i.e. they are doing well financially).

In other ways they are less content. The Fontaines came to Puligny from the Morvan in 1986. They had been used to living in a small friendly village near Saulieu where everyone talked to each other and all the children played together in the street, running in and out of each other's houses. 'Here it's different, our boy has no companions when he plays. It's not as if there aren't any other children – it's just that everyone stays shut up, separate. The thing that disturbs me most about Puligny is that when you cross paths with someone in the street you never know whether they're going to say hello or not.' Challenged as to whether she says hello in such circumstances, Madame has to admit that she's often too shy to do so. This business of greeting one another has enormous implications at every level of society in France: 'Elle me dit bonjour' is resonant with meaning, far beyond the basic recognition of neighbours.

But the business is good and the Fontaines take considerable pride in what they bake. 'We make up to ten different types of bread, from simple baguettes to pain a l'oignon. All the bread is made *sans fèves*, without any bean flour [unlike much commercial bread in France]. It's yellower in colour, like old-time bread, and it's entitled to the appellation Banette, which means that it's made from pure cereal flour, without any additives. We buy the flour from a mill at Chagny. It goes well here. We also make croûtons and gougères. And pâtisserie – every day we make something different. Boules de neige [snowballs] are my husband's speciality. They're made with strawberries, cream, mousseline mixed with chantilly and they're covered in white chocolate. It's our own recipe and we only make it at weekends or on special occasions but the people here like it very much.'

All of which is produced in a startlingly small kitchen at the side of the shop and baked in a gas oven from Germany of which the Fontaines are exceedingly proud. It's a compact family operation.

I was standing in front of the counter one morning in mid-October, chatting to Madame about local education (her son is at the Puligny infants' school), when the door opened suddenly and in came a woman in a hurry. 'Only twenty-five today,' she said breathlessly and began loading a couple of dozen baguettes into the two large bags she carried with her. I recognized Madame Boudot, from Domaine Sauzet, who explained that the vintage was nearly over, some of the pickers had already gone and the rest would be leaving tomorrow. She was looking forward to the end of it, and not having to cook for the masses. But today they were still picking, it was close to noon and she must rush back with the bread for the midday meal.

I realized then that only two commodities continue to be made and sold in Puligny, the biblical staples of bread and wine. The more the business of wine becomes all-pervasive, to the point of obsession, the more the village needs that small bakery on the Place du Monument to leaven the loaf of daily life. The bakery has always been there (the street is marked 'Rue du Four' on the eighteenth-century map of Puligny) and I hope it always will be. As long as the warm smell of the morning's bread continues to waft down the street and mingle with the scent of fermenting wine, so long is it possible to have faith in the promise of Ecclesiastes: 'Go thy way, eat thy bread with joy and drink thy wine with a merry heart; for God now accepteth thy works.'

The Épicerie

> J'ai du bon tabac dans ma tabatière
> J'ai du bon tabac, tu n'en auras pas!

Bebel Bachelet, La Bebel, sells bags of corks and balls of string, and cheese, newspapers, postcards, cigarettes, ice-cream, cabbages, needles and thread, soap and heaven knows what else from her shop on the Place du Monument, open seven days a week, from seven-thirty in the morning to seven at night, but firmly closed for two hours every lunchtime and all afternoon on Tuesday and Sunday. 'No it's not tiring.' she says. 'It's a matter of habit.'

Her father, Abel Meny, christened her Marie-Rose, but every baby in France gets called Bebel (bébé-bel: beautiful babe) and with her it stuck. The alphabetical sequence of Abel and Bebel proved irresistible, as did the conjunction of Bebel and Bachelet after she got married. 'So now the shop has four names. Some people in the village still refer to it as "Chez Meny", others call it Bachelet's or Bebel's or Marie-Rose's place.'

It was Abel who bought the shop, in 1921. He had been wounded in the Great War and thought that the épicerie would provide him with a decent and not too strenuous living. It was a shrewd move because the shop was the only one in Puligny to be licensed as a tobacconist.

Perhaps for that reason more than any other it has survived when the others have closed. 'There used to be four épiceries in the village, each with its speciality. One sold chickens, another repaired bicycles, the third stocked children's toys and dolls. We've always had the tobacco licence.' Bebel is in no doubt of the importance of this village monopoly and her view is widely shared. 'Everyone's got a car so they all go shopping at the supermarkets in Chagny,' says Madame Robaire. 'But Madame Bachelet survives because it's a bureau de tabac. People smoke, so of course they go there, and buy other things as well."

Indeed they do. 'I sell everything here, you have to in the country.' And since her only rival, a shop by the post office, closed in 1990, Madame Bachelet has also taken in the village laundry and dry-cleaning, so that her back room is even more cluttered than before.

A solemn little girl was next to be served and asked for a Camembert. 'How do you want it?' said Bebel. 'As usual,' the girl shrugged. 'Ready to eat?' asked another customer, helpfully. 'Oui,' replied the monosyllabic girl, but as she left she bade goodbye to each of us with polite exactitude. 'Au revoir M'sieur [to me]. Au revoir Mesdames.'

The next customer also bought some cheese and then asked for white thread. 'For hand or machine?' demanded Bebel. 'For machine.' The woman explained to everyone in the shop that she had bought a blouse which was too big for her and that she wanted to alter it, demonstrating exactly where it needed taking in and flapping her elbows like a chicken as she did so. 'But you should take it back,' exclaimed her neighbour. 'Oh, I'm the worst customer I know. Everything I buy is wrong.' She, too, bade a meticulous farewell as she left.

It was my turn next. I paid for some postcards and a book. 'Is that your soap?' asked Madame B, noticing a bar sitting on the counter – but we all realized at the same time that it had been left behind by the woman who was entertaining us a moment earlier. 'Oh, it's Madame Gaugeon,' exclaimed Bebel and rushed out of the shop with the soap, calling across the square: 'Madame Gaugeon, Madame Gaugeon!' A small figure turned in the distance and bustled back towards us. They met by the War Memorial.

Bebel's husband was a Bachelet, one of an intricate clan from Chassagne, so she's related by marriage to half the inhabitants of Puligny's traditional rival. But he was in the French colonial army and they spent many years away from Burgundy in North Africa: Algeria, Morocco,

'I sell everything here, you have to in the country.' La Bebel.

Sénégal. 'I was in Sénégal forty years ago and I enjoyed it. But I went back recently and it was lamentable. Only the railway station and the Mairie were in a decent state.' Monsieur Bachelet retired in 1971 and they returned to Puligny where Marie-Rose took charge of her father's shop.

'Many people from Bresse used to come here in search of work. If they found a vigneron to employ them they would have the right to a case of wine each month. They saved what they earned and bought a few pigs, or a row of vines. Old man Sauzet started by selling biscuits, he had a shop in the village. That's how he made the money to buy his domaine. We were all used to hard work. I still get up at six every morning and might go to the chicken market before opening the shop. But now there's television and cars. . .'

Cackling away between puffs on her habitual cigarette as she paused for a rest in the back room behind the counter, one eye on the glass door into the shop, one beadily fixed on me, La Bebel looked for a moment like a character from the lithographs of Toulouse-Lautrec or the photographs of Brassai, quintessentially French; a shrewd old girl with a heart of gold. But she always wears a tracksuit and there's not much sentiment wasted on times past.

The bell rang as a customer came in from the Place, and Madame Bachelet popped through to the counter. 'Bonjour Paulette. . .' The small transaction completed she returned to the back room, picked up her smouldering cigarette and resumed her reminiscences. 'Of course there were good times and a different feeling then. Take Monsieur Jo, for example. Jo Leflaive who died in 1982. I loved him, he was a real aristocrat.'

There was a brief pause, prompting silent speculation, but then she was off again, cheerfully resilient. 'People say there's not the sense of community that there was, but we still do things together. We go on holiday together. Last time we went to Ceylon, a party of sixteen from the village: two families of Chavy, Leclerc, Michel Thussaud, Deveze. . . this year I'm going to Yugoslavia with the Crédit Agricole. My daughter looks after the shop while I'm away. She's married to Jean-Claude Bidault who works for Domaine Leflaive, driving a tractor. The other daughter lives at Villefranche.'

Not much sunlight penetrates through the shop to Bebel's den; it's like being at the back of a very small café, watching the world go by, chatting to the patronne between customers. For many of its habitués her épicerie fulfils just such a function, a place for gossip and sympathy. And Madame Bachelet takes professional pride in her métier.

'You've got to work in commerce. In the shop you must speak to everyone differently. If it's Olivier or if it's a young mother, one of whose children is ill – you talk differently to each. You must reflect their interests. And the business has helped me, too, in many ways. When my husband died in 1982 it helped me get over my grief – I couldn't weep in front of my customers! It's my life. I'm sixty-three now, my mother went on working until she was eighty-two. As long as I can lift my feet, I'll continue!'

6 | Place des Marronniers

At noon during the vintage in the chestnut tree square all is peaceful. A large pheasant runs across the grass and jumps on to the wide stone windowsill of the kitchen at Domaine Leflaive, whence the faint clatter of pots and pans and the smells of another harvest lunch announce the imminent arrival of a hungry team of pickers. A couple of waitresses at Le Montrachet can be seen through the windows of the restaurant, preparing a table for a much smaller party of foreign visitors. An owl hoots unexpectedly in the distance. The bright green and gold leaves of the trees hardly move in the still air of the crisp autumn day but there is an occasional thud as a chestnut hits the ground, the fresh spiky husk splits open and a nut bounces on to the path, already littered with a thick scattering of them, many still covered in that polished bloom which lasts only a few hours before they darken and dull. As I pause beneath the trees another husk falls beside me and breaks open with such force that the chestnut bounces upward to head height, within an inch of my eye. I am reminded of a traditional vignerons' recipe: roast a few of the new season's chestnuts, crush them in a glass, mix with partially fermented young wine and drink as a nourishing restorative at the end of a hard-working afternoon.

The shadows cast by the formal alleys of pollarded chestnut trees give the Place des Marronniers an impression of cool stillness and modest grandeur, like a miniature park. Even when young men are playing boules here, or schoolchildren chasing a football, there is a dignity to

The shadows cast by the formal alleys of pollarded chestnut trees.

the square which is quite different to the constant social intercourse of the Place du Monument. When, rarely, the chestnut tree square fills up with people and noise (the Quatorze Juillet or other village feasts), you have the same sense as when you glance from one of Seurat's preparatory studies of the empty landscape of La Grande Jatte to the finished work, peopled with numerous figures dressed in their Sunday best; the scene is unchanged and the characters are temporary extras, whose comings and goings barely disturb the dreamlike archetype which is the place.

Partly this is to do with the buildings which surround the square. None of them is especially remarkable in itself but they share a general architectural congruity, decency, clarity and calm. Built in the same stone rubble as the rest of the village, some of these houses have touches of fantasy (the delightful first-floor balcony and verandah of a former café, and the rather grandiose façade of Bernard Clerc's cellars) but the overall impression is of well-maintained gentility.

This is clearly the smart end of the village. The west side comprises a line of rather fine private houses, the most agreeable of which belongs to Vincent Leflaive. His family domaine occupies a range of buildings which stretches along the whole of the south edge of the Place, while the east has a couple of houses set back behind tall walls (including one grand but derelict mansion, shuttered and empty as I write) and the hotel, Le Montrachet. Low box hedges define a small space on the pavement, protecting a few outside tables from the street, and there are always some cars with foreign number plates parked opposite, under the trees. The north side of the square is filled by the old Café Titard (later Fontenille's studio, now an annexe to the hotel), the Mairie and a modern reception room. Of all these buildings the most unassuming, unexpectedly, is the Mairie. There is no evidence here of the municipal self-importance which produced the extraordinary pink sandstone pomposity of the Mairie in neighbouring Chassagne.

The Place des Marronniers was a late addition to Puligny, built in the early nineteenth century at a time when the village had some pretensions to social grandeur, but it now has the well-worn charm of an English country house, and the gentle mystery of Magritte.

The Mairie

'Politicians are the same everywhere. They promise to
build bridges even where there are no rivers.'
(Nikita Khrushchev, October 1960)
'In France we make revolutions but not reforms.'
(Louis Napoleon, 1849)

In the spring of 1989 there was a revolution in Puligny. Jean Chartron, longtime mayor of the village, regarded the office as his almost by divine right. His father had been mayor before him and his great-grandfather before that – but he lost the elections to a relative newcomer, Louis Lafond, who owned not a single vine in Puligny and whose work (for the Chalonnaise wine producer André Delorme) was entirely to do with book-keeping and office management.

The system of rural elections is quite complex. Communities large and small throughout France go to the polls every six years to elect a list of fifteen people for the municipal council, one of whom will be mayor. Local politicians of all complexions spend many hours haggling with their cronies, putting together slates of candidates for the municipal council, trading favours for promises of allegiance. If the population of the place is over 3,000, the electors must choose one list or another, fifteen people who are more or less of a like political mind. In smaller communities there is the luxury of real choice. The voters may select any fifteen individuals from the lists presented to them or may even add other names of their own preference; popular local characters who have not formally stood for office. In Puligny, for example, there is always a small write-in vote for Monsieur Robaire, husband of the femme de ménage at the Hôtel Le Montrachet. But the election takes place in two stages, a few weeks apart, in order to eliminate such minor participants from the second round, leaving the voters with a straight choice in the final ballot.

Such a system can lead to entertaining mayhem. In 1989, three lists were presented to the electors of Puligny, a total of forty-five people standing for municipal office, not counting those who were hoping for their friends to write their names on the ballot form; candidacy seemed a test of social distinction. Puligny's population at the time was 469 (including children and minors), which meant that approximately one in eight of all adults was on the lists. This was grass-roots democracy at its most immediate, and feelings ran high. There were accusations of vote-splitting, families divided in their loyalties, fisticuffs in public places.

The first ballot on 26 March eliminated the no-hopers, leaving the then mayor Jean Chartron (a member of the RPR, the Gaullists) to slug it out with his challenger Louis Lafond, a socialist. Chartron's team consisted of a dozen vignerons, plus one or two others like Thierry Gazagnes, manager of the Montrachet hotel, who denied any political allegiance but whose sympathies certainly lay with the right. Such an alliance could normally have been expected to win (Puligny is traditionally right-wing and firmly viticole) but the times were unusual. In the first place, the socialists had been doing well nationally following Mitterrand's re-election as President a year or two earlier. In the second place it was time for a change. Chartron and his cronies had been in charge for too long and plenty of people had accumulated grudges of one sort or another against the ancien régime. But there was no solidly established alliance of villagers with a common purpose. As Thierry Gazagnes commented shortly after the election, 'It's a funny village. There are a few clans and everyone else is for themselves. There is no community, no feeling of belonging to a community, to the village. Each individual does everything differently; it's the answer and the cause of our problems. And it's something that's particular to Puligny; you go to Chassagne and there's a group.'

So Monsieur Lafond saw his chance and persuaded an assortment of like-minded villagers to join him. He claims that, 'My intention was not to be mayor but to have a number of people on the council who were different. But I found it very difficult to make another list, to find people capable and willing to care for the affairs of the commune. They lacked experience, and of course the old clans formed alliances against us. There was quite a lot of animosity. There were some viticulteurs who would have liked to be on my list but didn't want to oppose their friends who were grouped with Chartron. But plenty of people here used to work on the railways and they tend to vote for the left.' And the new team at least had the attraction of diversity and evident commitment; several of them took two weeks from their annual holidays in the run-up to the elections in order to canvass votes, talking to everyone about the need for change.

In the event, it was a close-run thing; the anarchic character of vil-

'My intention was not to be mayor.' Louis Lafond.

lage society was expressed by the fact that the voters chose seven candidates from Chartron's list, and eight from Lafond's. Chartron himself lost his seat, leaving Loulou Carillon to carry the banner for the conservatives (his father is said to have been convinced when Mitterrand was elected that the socialists would take away all his vineyards); and Lafond became mayor, with a disparate assortment of allies. These included a dentist from Meursault who had moved to Puligny shortly before the elections; Stanislas Bzicot, 'petit viticulteur' (a cheerful busy fellow, much liked in the village); Madame Pascale Matrot, a young mother from Blagny, whose husband runs a highly-regarded domaine in Meursault; Monsieur Lavaud, retired, who represented Puligny's considerable population of the Troisième Age; Bernard Verjus, a great talker who works in Lorraine for the telephone company and is little seen in the village; Madame Gilbert, whose husband runs Puligny's post office.

After their first year in office, it was the general opinion of Puligny that the new team talked a lot but achieved rather less. The agreeable Monsieur Lafond, by contrast, had won considerable respect and affection from villagers of all persuasions. He is indeed quite evidently a decent man, capable, honest, hard-working and intelligent. Originally from the Beaujolais region, he worked in the Rhône before joining Delorme at Rully. In 1977 he brought his family to live in Puligny, in a modest house near the church, and six years later he was one of only two candidates not on Chartron's list to be elected to the council. Now he is mayor.

In a big city that office would give him enormous power, both directly and through patronage, but Puligny is much too small for that. The mayor does have responsibilities for law and order and the commune is empowered to raise certain local taxes, both for general purposes and for specific projects (such as the constant battle against hillside erosion), but Monsieur Lafond sees his job more in terms of coordination and persuasion. He must cooperate with neighbouring communes to provide joint technical services, to deal with the disposal of industrial waste and to organize local schooling (schools are always based at the Mairies); and he must persuade the villagers of Puligny to recognize their own problems and to deal with them. The minutes of a typical meeting of the council record decisions about anti-erosion works in the vineyards, the sale of some poplars belonging to the commune and a fine which was imposed on a vigneron for leaving mud all over the road, but Lafond's major concern is much more basic; the steady and apparently unstoppable decline in Puligny's population.

'This year the shop opposite the post office was closed, and we had to close the school at the Mairie and send the children to Chassagne. When I came here the population was 529, now it is 469. Partly it's a problem of housing. Often when a house comes up for sale it is bought by a viticulteur, either for additional cellars or to lodge his pickers at harvest time, and there are very few new houses being built.'

Thierry Gazagnes had made the same point to me as we chatted at the hotel. 'There used to be lots of small properties with a few ouvrées, two pigs and five rows of vines. Now they have to go where the work is, but it's very hard to buy houses here. You'd be amazed at what Leflaive, Clerc and Carillon own in the village. It's the peasant mentality – they don't need to sell these houses and so they keep them just in case – and use them once a year at harvest time to lodge the vendangeurs.' Monsieur Lafond shrugged good-humouredly at this apparently intractable problem. 'The commune owns some land on the other side of the Route Nationale but it's not part of the local plan to build there. But a lot of people from Beaune might like to live here if houses were available, and if the social life was more active. We have started a Comité des Fêtes (something many other villages already have) to try organize bigger events on the Quatorze Juillet and other feast days. We try to make much more effort but it's difficult to alter a mentality. That's why I think the St Vincent Tournante [see Chapter 14] is so important for the village – because people have had to work together for a year or eighteen months before the event, and that creates more real ties than organizing the occasional fête.'

Monsieur Lafond sighs with good-humoured resignation, reflecting on the difficulty of translating his revolution into lasting reform. 'Further south the people are much closer to one another, much more open than here. It was difficult when we arrived here, very difficult – and I think it's something to do with money. When they've got less they appreciate each other more.'

The Village School

> 'Soap and education are not as sudden as a massacre,
> but they are more deadly in the long run.'
> (Mark Twain, *The Facts Concerning the Recent Resignation*)

In most villages of France, school is at the Mairie and until recently this was true of Puligny. Another building on the outskirts houses the 'maternelle' and 'intermediate' classes (and a few children go to the private school in Chagny), but between the ages of eight and ten most boys and girls of Puligny have elbowed each other through a doorway next to the public noticeboard and crammed into a single room, to be taught everything prescribed by the curriculum. Thus it was for generations, until finally in 1990 the class at the Mairie was closed because of diminishing numbers, and the children transferred to Chassagne. The school there is also situated at the Mairie, but in a much grander building which has plenty of space for the additional pupils. Regret is tempered with optimism: tussling together in the classroom may lead to a rapprochement which will finally dissolve the sectarian suspicions that have for so long divided the 'cochons' of Puligny from the 'machurés' of Chassagne. Social engineering begins at the blackboard.

What follows is the record of one afternoon in the now defunct school at Puligny, shortly before it was closed, a snapshot for the scrapbooks of local historians.

'Finish your exercises,' said Madame Matignan. On the board was written out

      je connais
      tu connais
      il connait etc.

A plump and mischievous girl went up to the board and began to write, left-handed: banane, cochon. Then she crossed out what she had done and started again: cheval, cochon, rabot, banane. Sitting at the back of the class of fifteen children, I spent several fruitless minutes trying to establish a connection between horse, pig, woodplane and banana. Another group read aloud in turn to the teacher, the girls more fluently than the boys.

'Each image depicts a story but it is the sequence of images which gives us the full story. What is the word for that?' asked Madame Matignan. 'Iradgiquement,' ventured one boy, bolder than the rest. Chronologiquement,' corrected the teacher with a sigh. She was relaxed but firm, never raising her voice and speaking very clearly to the children – but it was hard to avoid confusion with three classes proceeding simultaneously in the same room.

Suddenly the lights went out and the computer screen in the corner flipped to blank. 'Oh, l'ordinateur, Madame,' cried a pupil. The teacher shrugged – evidently this was commonplace – and handed out a photocopied series of questions to another section of the class. When the lights came on again there was a different image on the screen. Madame patiently entered the correct sequence of commands to return to the original place in the program.

The test was concerned with calories. 'If Madame Dubois spends an hour in bed she will expend sixty-five calories. . . now you've got to calculate how many calories are expended on each activity by Madame Dubois and by Monsieur Dubois (who spends so much time sleeping, so much time in his office, etc.) then say which of them has expended more energy. And the Dubois have two children who do various things as well. . .'

'Oh, Madame, c'est trop difficile,' cried a ponytailed blonde, but the class settled resignedly to its task. On this day and at this time, in every primary school in France, pupils were learning about the Dubois family and their diet, about calories and energy; rehearsing thereby the constant preoccupations of later life – with the stomach and the liver, eating and digestion. Thus are cultural imperatives transmitted, from one generation to the next.

They used their calculators to multiply calories and the teacher went from desk to desk, helping the more confused to get started. One girl demanded the answers from her friend, the ponytail, who danced up to the teacher for an explanation and then sat down again, despondent. All of this was mimed rather exaggeratedly, to her audience of boys.

The golfers on the computer finally manoeuvred the ball on to the green but their putting was hopeless – it took a great deal of random selection before they managed to sink it in the hole. Eventually they succeeded and the screen flashed BRAVO. They jumped up and down excitedly, 'Madame, c'est marqué Bravo.'

A thickset girl was blowing bubble-gum, two boys at the back were quarrelling about the answers to the test and another went to ask a question of the teacher but was distracted by the game of computer golf and stood giving advice to the new player who managed to nudge his ball on to the green, narrowly escaping getting stuck in a bunker. 'Madame, I'm really gifted at this,' he exclaimed proudly, but three missed putts later his ball was in the rough and he called for help. 'I can't get the ball to move.' The teacher entered a new trajectory and the picture changed. 'Ah, it shifts for you,' exclaimed the boy admiringly. Almost immediately he and his friend managed to reduce the screen to a tangle of red blotches and everyone gathered round to watch. Madame Matignan unscrambled things once more and then went through the answers to the test with the other class.

These revealed that Monsieur Dubois expended the most energy, Madame Dubois would grow fat and their child Florence was in danger of malnutrition. The total number of calories expended by the family was 9,537, correctly calculated by the oldest girl at the back but clearly a complete puzzle to most of the class, including the tub of a girl in the front row who might have benefited most from a proper understanding of diet.

While Madame sat down to mark the papers there was general pandemonium, with everyone running around, talking to each other and fighting in the corners. I looked around me, observing the educational debris of several generations, the litter of changing priorities.

The room itself was light and cheerful, overlooking the Place des Marronniers. The desks were modern, but extremely solid and evidently designed to take punishment. Curiously enough they incorporated old-fashioned inkwells which clearly had not been used since they were made – mine was stuffed with the shavings from a pencil sharpener. Shelves of books and papers surrounded the room to desk level. Twentieth-century technology was represented by a slide projector, a tape recorder, a couple of speakers and a small hand duplicator as well as the inordinately slow micro-computer in the corner. Behind the teacher's desk hung some very large instruments of geometry. A map of the administrative region of Burgundy faced a black sheet, marked with musical staves.

Stained wooden frames, battered at the corners, surrounded the visual aids of an earlier generation, stacked at the back of the classroom. One was a lurid dental chart, designed to frighten children into brushing their teeth. It showed a mouthful of ivory choppers, a ceramic denture fixed by steel pivot to a dead root and a fearsome collection of primitive apparatus. Another attractively illustrated the main species of edible mushroom and the third was a map of Europe at the time of Louis XI of France and Charles the Bold, Duke of Burgundy. This apparently banal exercise in historical cartography was charged with social and political significance.

Gazing at this map, Burgundian children must have marvelled at the extent of Charles's vast domaine, stretching north from his dukedom of Burgundy to incorporate the Franche-Comté, Alsace, Lorraine and Luxembourg, Picardy and Artois, Flanders, Brabant and Holland – this was the richest state of fifteenth-century Europe, effectively independent of feudal overlords. But Louis XI, cunning and cold, secretly financed the Swiss to attack his rebellious subject and Charles was killed at the battle of Nancy in 1477. His frozen corpse, half naked and gnawed by wolves, was discovered in an icy stream two days after the defeat of his armies. Scavengers had stripped him of his magnificent armour and plundered the jewels which studded his flamboyant clothes. And all his French fiefs were confiscated by the crown.

So the map represented victory for the centralized state over local autonomy, the beginning of a process which reached its fullest expression at the court of Versailles and was only briefly interrupted by the chaotic events of 1789. The French Revolution destroyed the privileges of aristocrats, not the power of the monarchy – which was revived under Napoleon and has been reincarnated ever since by way of a series of elected kings. Mitterrand as President of the Republic exerts greater personal power than most of his royal predecessors.

Charles the Bold's death at Nancy signalled not only his own failure to achieve secession from the Crown but the failure of the Dukes of Anjou, Brittany and Bourbon, most of whose vast domaines were annexed to the state over the following fifty years. Burgundy is now associated with the glories of past history or with wine, not with aspirations of independence, and the children of France prefer to idle or flirt or hit each other over the head, rather than set fire to the Mairie in the name of Liberty, Equality or Fraternity. It may have been unreasonable to yearn for a spark of the Revolution in the classroom at Puligny, but as I listened to the pupils singing anodyne songs from the solfege syllabus, I longed for the Marseillaise.

Instead we had their teacher plonking out a tune on the small syn-thesizer in the corner. Some of the children started to sing and others called for silence, loudly hissing 'Sch. . .' When order was restored they were led by Madame Matignan in a chorus which involved a lot of ac-tion and clapping, imitating the actions of the story, and everyone joined in vigorously except a small girl in green who still sat at her desk, reso-lutely picking her nose as she tried to puzzle out the answers to the test. One voice carried on boldly for half a bar after the rest had finished, then tailed off into self-conscious silence. Two or three more songs fol-lowed, including one about an owl (much flapping of wings) and then they began a round, one half of the class singing against the other. They all liked this – even the mournful girl in green left her desk to join the round, and her surprisingly clear voice sounded with touching accuracy above the ragged enthusiasm of the rest.

Madame returned to the board and began writing out the homework for the evening. Behind her back the fat girl cheerfully assaulted one of the boys (the not-so-gifted golf player) and gave him such a fierce kick in the knee that he went up to teacher to complain. She continued writ-ing out the questions. One section of the class had work from their read-ing book, another lot had maths. The ponytailed blonde expressed loud incredulity that they should be asked to do so much.

Suddenly everyone started packing up their satchels. Class was over and they went out into the square for 'gym'. As the children played foot-ball and chased noisily round the chestnut trees, Madame Matignan slumped on the bench, pale with the demands of the day. Cropped hair, narrow face and body, black bomber jacket, jeans and sneakers; her ner-vous energy was consumed in exhaustion. Half huddled, half stretched, she rested with the air of someone for whom this brief interlude was a vital respite but with no sense of repose, seeming already preoccupied with the cares of the evening and her home in Noallay. The children laughed and tussled with one another, but their teacher was utterly drained, her eyes turned inward.

The Hotel

> 'Cela est bien dit,' repondit Candide, 'mais il faut
> cultiver notre jardin.' 'That is well said,' replied
> Candide, 'but we must cultivate our garden.'
> (Voltaire, *Candide*, 1759)

Marcelle Robaire has a small triangular face, like a cat. She reminds me of those old photographs of Colette and there is something similarly evocative about the vivid simplicity of her language, and her tenacity. Meeting her at the head of the stairs, folding the hotel sheets, or hurrying home after work, I have always been struck by the way she holds herself, like a diminutive street urchin ready to do battle against the world, and by her immediacy. Madame Robaire's greeting is usually accompanied by a morsel of gossip or an expressive sigh, as if you were continuing a conversation which had only momentarily been interrupted. But behind the quick grin and the sidelong glance of complicity there is always the feeling that she has borne a great deal of hardship, with the resignation of a generous heart.

Marcelle has been married for over forty years to Louis, who used to work for the village but is now retired. 'We were both orphans, brought up by the state. We married when I was twenty. I used to work with my husband on a little farm. I looked after the cows.' That was in the isolated village of Bessey-en-Chaume, up in the hills to the north. They had four children (one of whom died in a car accident and another from illness) and it was to give them better schooling that the Robaires moved to Puligny, in 1960.

'It shocked me when we came here, my husband and I. In my village the men met in the evening to play cards and the women roasted chestnuts on the fire. But here, the viticulteurs do their accounts in the evening. They don't care much for each other, perhaps because the wine makes them rich. We were on the committee for the village fêtes and everyone else on the committee was greasing each other's palms. Recently I was ill and no one came to see me except Suzanne [Gazagnes], who came to make me a tisane. It's not like a little village here where they'd say, Oh, Marcelle is ill, let's see what we can do to help.'

Soon after her arrival in Puligny, Madame Robaire went to work as femme de ménage for Roland Thevenin, who was then living with his family at the château. Marcelle quickly became indispensable to them. She did everything, cleaning the big house, cooking for the family, helping to prepare feasts and festivities for visiting celebrities. It was tremendously hard work but there was a sense of space and splendour. Then in 1981 Roland Thevenin separated from his wife; the château was abandoned and sold. After eighteen years' service, Marcelle was out of a job.

So she went to work at the hotel, Le Montrachet, which had just been sold to Dr Roland Collet and his wife Christine. 'When she bought it, it was nothing. There were eight bedrooms, very simple, and then they converted nine more on top. I looked after all those rooms. The big room downstairs which is now the dining-room had been a ballroom for the village fêtes.'

Presumably it was built as a café hotel in the mid-nineteenth century and its main purpose then, as now, was to welcome visitors with an interest in wine. Whatever its early history, it had by the second half of this century settled into a state of respectable mediocrity. It survived as a huge bar, after all the others in the village had closed, but its bedrooms were typical of provincial French hotels at that period – faded flowery wallpaper, sagging beds (sometimes three to a room) and a cabinet de toilette in the corner with distinctly dubious plumbing. Such was its state when the Collets bought it from its previous owner, Michel Rossignol of Volnay.

Roland Collet was a doctor specializing in radiology who lived in Paris but worked for most of the week at a clinic near Lille. Christine was the daughter of hoteliers from Chamonix. She had a flair for design and wanted her own professional challenge, compatible with bringing up their young children. A love of good wine brought Dr Collet to Puligny. The hotel was for sale. They bought it.

Christine set about the renovations with enthusiasm. The kitchen was extended, the old ballroom/bar converted into a restaurant and Michel Bezout recruited as chef. His cooking was modern but not wilfully bizarre, and of sufficient quality to attract serious attention. And initially, at any rate, the range of menus was not overpriced.

In 1982 nine bedrooms (each with its own bathroom) were converted from the attics of the second floor. The décor was modern and restfully simple, the beds firm and the bathrooms small but well equipped. Everything showed evidence of a discriminating sense of style. Le Montrachet became a favourite resting place both for the wine trade and for

The Hôtel Le Montrachet has the elusive magic of all good hotels.

wine-loving tourists. It filled a need, because at that time there was almost nowhere else of any character if you wanted to spend a few days in
Burgundy outside the tourist-cluttered streets of Beaune and it had the
elusive magic of all good hotels. Christine Collet, beautiful and intelligent, welcomed the guests as they arrived and supervised her small staff.
Michel Bezout cooked food of appetizing elegance. The indispensable
Madame Robaire looked after the linen as if it were her own and became
a much-loved talisman for the regulars; in some indefinable way her presence seemed to guarantee the personality of the place.

And so for a while all went well. The team was completed by the arrival of Jean-Claude Wallerand, an experienced sommelier whom Roland
had recruited from La Belle Epoque, one of his favourite restaurants in
Lille. The guide-books took favourable notice and business flourished.
But there were tensions, increasingly evident to frequent visitors if perhaps imperceptible to the more transient clientele. The Collets' children
were growing up; Roland's career made it difficult to spend every weekend in Burgundy; when he did come it seemed more for the sake of eating and drinking noisily with his cronies than to be with the family. In
order to regain their privacy the Collets bought a lovely house on the
other side of the square, but the very fact of this necessary self-contain-
ment meant that Christine's presence was missed from the daily toing
and froing of the hotel.

So one day I returned to Le Montrachet for lunch and found the Collets sitting at a corner table in the restaurant, entertaining another couple to whom they were selling the business. Roland was talking contin-
uously, about money, the success of the place, how much the bar took,
the renown of the restaurant, the psychology of the customers. Christine, who had created it all, sat silent.

They sold Le Montrachet, sold their house across the square, moved
back to Paris and stayed together. Dr Collet's career in radiography has
continued to flourish, Christine has opened a shop selling fabrics and
braids. 'It's better now. She telephones me often.' Madame Robaire
leaves almost everything unsaid, but cannot conceal how much she
misses Christine, and all the fun of the early years at the hotel.

The purchaser was another Parisian, Jean-Pierre Faraut, who bought
the place with a group of associates at the beginning of 1987. At
Christine's suggestion he recruited her brother Thierry Gazagnes as man-

ager, with a share of the business. Thierry had trained at a hotel school in France (just across Lake Leman from Lausanne) and had spent seven years in Canada, working at big hotels in Montreal and Toronto. There he had met and married Suzanne (herself experienced in hotel management). Their first child was born two weeks before they flew back from Canada to Puligny, in February 1987.

'Immediately we had to undertake a great deal of investment. After the first few years under the Collets nothing much had been done and the hotel desperately needed renovation. We redecorated the bedrooms on the first floor and installed more bathrooms, and then did the dining-room, front desk and bar.' In 1989 they acquired Fontenille's old house and studio, just across the street, and took a year to convert it into ten bedrooms and a caveau, where they sell a representative selection of wines from all the best producers of the village. Undoubtedly all of this is seen by most visitors as a series of improvements, but Thierry and Suzanne's taste is less adventurous than that of Christine Collet and the style is 'repro Bourguignon'; safe but dull. It is certainly an advantage not to come down to breakfast and be confronted by a metallic bas-relief of dismembered segments of heads and limbs, apparently bursting through the wall (one of Fontenille's more bizarre sculptures, bought by the Collets). It is also true that the rooms in the new annexe are spacious and the dining-room is now distinctly more comfortable than it used to be. They still serve the delicious jams made by Christine and Thierry's parents from blueberries and other wild fruits which they harvest in Chamonix, but the place has lost some of its charm.

Madame Robaire regrets the changes ('It's not the same as it was under Christine'), and Thierry himself acknowledges the difficulties of the succession. 'It was very hard for the first two years, especially for Suzanne. We had no friends here and I had been used to working with a large team in a 600-bedroom hotel. Now I have to be on duty all the time and it has been a big adjustment for the people working here; from working with my sister to working with me. And it's been hard financially.' Suzanne is well liked in the village, particularly by the other young mothers, and she organizes cooking classes for the children which have proved very popular; but Thierry is a more prickly character and still encounters resistance.

'We get no help from the village. It's a very peasant mentality. If people see twenty-five Mercedes in front of the hotel they think we're millionaires. Maybe they're too lucky, they don't have to do any effort of promotion. They would love to have a place like this in Chassagne.'

Maybe, but there are signs of middle-aged spread. Michel Bezout's food may have gained a star in the Michelin but his menu scarcely changes from year to year. Jean-Claude Wallerand guards a wine list which is eminently respectable, but fossilized. Madame Robaire has recently retired so there is a decided dearth of local gossip. A discreet professionalism, rising prices and unadventurous quality threaten the character which made Le Montrachet so well loved. That may be what the international clientele now requires, but for my part I preferred the vivid personality of a more haphazard past.

In pursuit of which I found myself sitting at Marcelle Robaire's kitchen table, talking about vegetables and politics. It was shortly after the village election, when Thierry Gazagnes had failed to gain a seat on the council, as one of the right-wing candidates on the slate of Jean-Louis Chartron, but Louis Robaire (who was not a candidate) had gathered an unexpected handful of write-in votes. I asked Marcelle for her opinion of the outcome.

'Now we have a good mayor. I voted for him, but the council is no good. They talk a lot and do nothing. Before we had a useless mayor and a good council. I was always for de Gaulle and Giscard. I never changed. My husband voted for Giscard and then he voted for Mitterrand, but I've never changed. I voted for de Gaulle, then Pompidou, then Giscard, then Barre.' But this stalwart of the right also voted for Monsieur Lafond, the socialist mayor. Nothing is simple.

Now in their retirement Marcelle and Louis follow Voltaire's advice, and cultivate their garden. 'We have more than a hectare at the back of the house and we grow a bit of everything; potatoes, beans, tomatoes, carrots, salads. We eat it all, with the children and our friends, and we sell some potatoes.'

Quatorze Juillet

Once there would have been bands playing in the streets and choirs singing in the squares. Now there is a disco in the evening and a barbecue with Merguez sausages; the spicy sort which the 'pieds noirs' brought back from North Africa. In the morning they have children's games (sack races, egg and spoon) and during the long stretch in the middle of the day young men play boules under the chestnut trees, watched by a few visitors, wilting in the summer heat as they drink kir on the terrace of the hotel. There is the usual interplay of characters. One (bearded, loud, with a cigarette stub attached to his lip) makes a great deal of fuss, to no evident purpose. Another, tall and gangling, tosses his first two boules high in the air but they drop well short of the mark and he hurls the third furiously, way past it. A quiet player, with none of the bobbing and weaving of his rivals, pauses, looks long and carefully at the lay of the match and then tosses his boule to lie perfectly, alongside the cochonnet. It seems a classic case of the silent genius beating his showy competitors, but one of them, fat and talkative, comes to the mark with hardly a glance down the shady alley. Crack: his opponent's boule is knocked out of the way and his own curls back to nudge the cochonnet and win the game.

The drowsy afternoon stretches almost motionless towards the evening, when a small crowd begins to gather for the barbecue. The air seems heavier by the moment and then, just as the disco has begun to blaze there is another crash as the most tremendous thunderstorm explodes overhead and sudden torrents of rain send the dancers scattering for shelter. Within seconds the streets are awash and the gutters gurgling. All the dust and debris of a dry summer is carried away like a cloudy film on the surface of the drainwater. The festivities are over.

In neighbouring Meursault, by contrast, they have a firework display every year (weather permitting) and the crowd in the village square is swollen by thousands of visitors from nearby villages, until they stand shoulder to shoulder in the dusk. Small boys hurl noisy firecrackers at each other, on the edge of the throng, and at half-past ten the mayor makes a brief speech of welcome. Then the lights of the square go out and the fireworks begin, with mortars bursting high overhead and Roman candles pouring waterfalls of gold and silver down the front of the town hall. It is a slow and rather ragged affair but the crowd is not impatient and the fireworks are good, with entertaining effects like a sky full of wriggling, squealing, explosive worms. There is applause for each set piece, each new star. And when it is over the families and small children set off home, while the boys and girls stay to drink at the bars and dance to the disco. Late at night, early in the morning, their motocyclettes can still be heard, buzzing noisily as they struggle with the extra weight of a pillion passenger, zooming like bees around the village before heading into the dark.

Long before that, the houses of Puligny are shuttered; the village asleep.

7 | Arts & Crafts

"The sculpture that we see in the monuments and exhibitions of Europe affords us so lamentable a spectacle of barbarism and lumpishness that my Futurist eye withdraws from it in horror and disgust."

UMBERTO BOCCIONI
Technical Manifesto of Futurist Sculpture, 11 April 1912

The Sculptor

Michel Fontenille, sculptor, used until quite recently to occupy a house on the corner of the Place des Marronniers – immediately across the street from the hotel, of which it now forms an annexe. Before the change of ownership it was possible to discern the faint remains of the words CAFÉ TITARD, painted on the stone wall above a narrow front door – which was shaded by an old metal canopy adorned with an enchanting frieze of pears and grapes. 'It's because the vineyards were formerly full of fruit trees under which the workers took their ease, eating a juicy pear in the shade. Now all those trees are uprooted because they were so inconvenient for the tractors.' Fontenille's good-humoured voice betrays a strong feeling of times having changed for the worse, somewhat surprising in so cheerful a fellow. 'This house was built in 1824. It was originally a relais, a hotel-restaurant, and my studio used to be the village ballroom. The population of Puligny is now six hundred, but before the war there were nine hundred people living here – there were two brass bands and eleven cafés. When I arrived in 1974 the hotel across the road was a café. Now they're going to buy this house to enlarge the hotel.'

Indeed they did, and much is altered. There is still the splendid verandah on the first floor but the front door has been moved, its beautiful canopy has disappeared and the faded letters which recorded the building's former incarnation as a café have vanished from the immaculately re-pointed façade. It is no longer possible to open the door under

An old metal canopy, adorned with a frieze of pears and grapes.

the frieze of pears and grapes and tumble into Fontenille's dusty studio (now converted into a small caveau selling expensive wine to the tourists), nor to climb up narrow stairs to the unexpectedly sleek room on the first floor which served as a gallery to display the sculptures and as a sitting-room, opening on to the verandah. A much grander stair-case now leads to a corridor and a line of hotel bedrooms, the walls of which have been plastered with that textured finish so beloved of French architects. It is perhaps appropriate that Fontenille's house has reverted to approximately its original use, but I regret the change.

Conservation destroys the past. The varnished joinery, neatly pointed stone walls and well-insulated roofs of so many of the houses which have recently been restored in Puligny suggest the too-perfectly pre-served glamour of a millionairess of uncertain age, fresh from the ex-pensive care of a plastic surgeon. An accumulation of small decrepitudes and casual accretions is for me the agreeable evidence of character and history, infinitely preferable to a facelift which cleans away every trace of life's vicissitudes. Scrubbing and sandblasting can too easily obliter-ate all sense of identity, of visual continuity with the modest vignerons who built these houses in the first place. The impression is of money, not of rural life.

Fontenille himself combines an enthusiasm for the history and tra-ditions of his region with the instincts of a boulevardier. Looking like a cross between a bon vivant and a King Charles spaniel, he enjoys good wine and company, music and conversation – but his daily preoccupa-tion is sculpture. He makes reliefs (often from dental plaster, occasion-ally from resin, bronze or other materials) and his images evoke a clas-sical tradition, fragmented and replicated like reflections in broken water. These days he uses colour more than he used to, which adds an entertaining dimension to works which can otherwise seem elegantly chilly. Occasionally his sculptures are fully three-dimensional and en-tirely abstract – which I find more satisfying than the slightly mannered decorative images of his neo-classical assemblies.

Fontenille's clients are mostly private patrons in France, but he has exported works to Germany, Belgium, Australia, Hong Kong and Canada. His commissions include a relief for the entrance to the Bobar tractor factory in Beaune and (some years ago) for the bar at the Hôtel Le Montrachet. The latter is no longer on view. One of his most inter-esting exhibitions was held in conjunction with an association for the blind, at Chalon. Visitors were encouraged to explore his reliefs by touch, and the catalogue was printed in braille.

Although he worked in Puligny for nearly fifteen years, Fontenille never felt himself fully integrated into the village and most of his friends came from Beaune or Dijon. 'Here in Puligny people don't talk much about anything except wine, and that's very constricting. It's different in Beaune [where he now lives] – there's some music, it's a different culture. Here it's like the Morvan,* a very closed society. They have a great fear of vagabonds. Ten years ago there were no big dogs here but then my brother-in-law, who's very fond of animals, gave a Bouvier de Flandres to Bernard Clerc. Two or three other vignerons got big dogs as well, so everyone had to have a big dog. Now the place is full of dangerous animals, like that monster which prowls on the wall by the post office and terrifies all the passers-by. They have the habit of peasants here, always wanting what others have.'

Fontenille pauses briefly but resumes with the air of a man infuriated by the place he loves. 'They're not open to the world, because the world comes to them – they don't have to make any effort to go out and sell their wines – unlike some other regions – and they know very little of the wines from elsewhere. They are sure that Burgundy makes the best wines in the world, so they learn nothing from others.'

The next time we meet is at Olivier Leflaive's enormous party to celebrate the fifth anniversary of his business. Michel Fontenille is in tremendous form, revived by his move to Beaune, by the party atmosphere, the company of good friends and the stimulation of international gossip, transcending the narrow boundaries of regional chauvinism. It is hard to see how such a character could possibly fit happily into Puligny today, but equally difficult to contemplate the future of a village which, more than ever before, is obsessed with the business of wine, to the exclusion of the interior life.

---

*A mountainous region north-west of Beaune and south of Avallon.

The Bookbinder

'To enter into discussions on all these questions with
comrades who have long ago ceased to read and who
live exclusively on the muddled recollections of their
youth is not a very easy thing to do; besides it is useless.'
(Leon Trotsky, *The New Course*, 1923)

In country parishes there is often a villager who stands apart from his
neighbours but knows the place better than anyone, a sceptic who has
learnt all its secrets, its relationships, its intrigues; has gathered all the
scraps of oral history to which his contemporaries are indifferent and
which strangers ignore; who watches the erosion of apparently un-
changing customs, loves his corner of the world and criticizes its inhabitants with the pungent ferocity that only a native could express.
Such a one is Monsieur Alexandre, bookbinder of Puligny.

In a small alley near the church, the Rue Tripet, hangs a faded blue
sign inscribed in letters of gold: RELIEVR. A glazed door opens on to
precipitous stone steps which descend to a semi-subterranean world,
the dark workshop of Jean-Louis Alexandre. Pale, bespectacled mole,
shrewd and entertaining, he stands at his bench below the window
(which is at pavement level) and gazes at the knees of passers-by, longing for the sun, dreaming of Morocco. In the gloom at the back are a
couple of binding presses and piles of books, racks of paper and rolls of
leather. On the bench, the clutter of his trade: a jar of flour paste, bottles of dye, some tins of English saddle soap from Brecknell, Turner &
Sons of Great Dunmow, rolls of gold leaf on transparent tape; a line of
embossing tools and the bronze letter punches which are heated on a
little rack above a gas flame; a damp sponge in a soup plate; scraps of
calf-skin and a cluster of scalpels.

Monsieur Alexandre restores old bindings and makes new ones. He
learnt his trade at twenty, from a bookbinder in Dijon. 'I loved books,
perhaps that was one of the reasons.' To bind a book in linen he charges
around 150 francs. In leather, with fine marbled paper, it will cost you
twice as much.

His father was the village baker and the family has local roots – they
came from Pommard. Monsieur Alexandre's brother lives in Paris and
he, alone, in the village. 'I was born here, it's sufficient reason to stay.

Yes, I've been tempted to leave but the only thing that lures me is the sun.' He bends over the vise where he is lettering the spine of a book and tapes another line of gold leaf over dark green leather. Picking up one of the tools that has been warming on the rack he tests it on the wet sponge. It sizzles, so he presses harder, to cool the hot metal, then carefully aligns it over the gold leaf and leans down, with steady weight. Peeling back the tape, the bookbinder reveals the crisp line of gold which now underlines the 'nerve' or ridge across the spine. He gives me a sharp, birdlike glance, pauses and then looks down again. 'I long for a sunny country. There's not enough sun in Burgundy. The winters are too long – eight months.' Monsieur Alexandre's gaze is now fixed on the grey stone wall, across the narrow street. 'I have very few friends, I am interested in painting, I travel a little. I go often to Spain, to Greece and Morocco. I'll finish my days in Spain, in the south.' Aware that such talk is a little premature (he is still in his thirties) he smiles suddenly, removes the finished book from the vice and inserts another volume of the *Pharmacopée Française.*

Bookbinding is an archaic craft, preserving past habits. The English hark back to the eighteenth century. Plain brown calfskin and Baskerville lettering evoke the sober dress and pleasant conversation of an educated country gentleman, but the marbled boards or endpapers remind us that his waistcoat was a riot of embroidered silks and his Wedgwood drabware cups were lined, unexpectedly, with the clear greenish-blue of a thrush's egg. Swirling combinations of vivid pinks, blues and yellows echo the flamestitch patterns of eighteenth-century upholstery. These are the bright colours which the East India Company brought to Georgian London, enlivening the fashionable coffee-house brown with the gaudy splendours of an oriental bazaar.

French marbling has an altogether different hue. Dark green and maroon are woven into disciplined patterns of rich sobriety, bookbinder's equivalent of the braided plush and heavily carved mahogany which reassured the nineteenth-century bourgeois of his moral and social worth. Encased in a hard carapace of polished and mottled Morocco, these books seem weapons for schoolmasters and logicians, each page another layer in the pile of differentiations with which the intellect rebuilds our cluttered reality into the ordered constructs of Gallic grammar. The lettering on spine and title page is that curiously unattractive typeface which the French evolved in the 1850s and have stuck to ever since. It reminds one of Balzac, bringing back gloomy memories of struggling through the grim history of *Eugénie Grandet*.

A comparable sense of provincial claustrophobia envelops Monsieur Alexandre. He sighs. 'I don't live much in the village – I live outside it. The villagers don't interest me very much. The vignerons are nouveaux riches and we haven't the same interests. They've got rich too quickly. A crisis in the wine business would be wonderful for life here. What I dislike about Puligny is that the wine is everything – it's very oppressive. Even before the changes the people weren't that interesting. Peasants only think of money – you can't show them anything; they're not interested in anything beautiful. The first question they ask is how much it costs.' He glances up with a rueful smile. 'I am hard on my fellow citizens, I know.'

In the silence which follows, the bookbinder undoes the vise, stacks the last volume of the *Pharmacopée* with its fellows and brings to the bench an old work of local history which needs some repairs to its spine. He cuts a piece of leather and begins to scrape and smooth it with an ivory spatula. It is quiet except for the hissing of the gas flame.

I ask why there is no café in Puligny. Monsieur Alexandre bends down to blow away the scrapings and sighs again as he straightens.

'People don't want to meet each other. A café is a place to meet and they don't have time, it costs too much money. If they are not in their cellars or out in the vineyards it costs too much. I think peasants have always been individualists, not thinking of others. Perhaps when times were hard there was a greater community spirit.'

There is another pause but I keep quiet, aware that I have tapped into a well of resentment which will come bubbling up again. Sure enough, Monsieur Alexandre begins to speak with the quiet fury of an old cat, spitting at the village dogs.

'Peasants don't respect nature. Once I thought they did – and perhaps indeed they did when they had nothing else – but now they don't. I've watched them. They destroy the houses and they destroy the land. Despite the problems that storms and rain can cause by eroding the hills, they have removed the walls between the vineyards and there are ravines as a result. They have cut down all the trees and they use weed-killers. This year they've destroyed even more. There's nothing left but concrete, lawns and vines. They have no thought for the long term. People talk about the countryman's common sense. They have no sense at all. When I go walking on the hillsides here I'm always in a rage, because a wall is gone or the flowers are gone. It's difficult now to find any peaceful corners, to find violets flowering beside a wall. I've even got to the stage where I hardly drink the wine any more. It may be an excessive reaction but I don't think it's as good as it was.'

He shakes his head and laughs, embarrassed at his vehemence, and dips a brush into the glue pot. Carefully, neatly, he spreads the flour and water paste over the leather patch and fits it into place on the spine, pressing it down with his spatula. The join is scarcely visible.

Guessing that it will cheer him up, I mention the recent presidential election at which the wily socialist Mitterrand trounced his right-wing opponents: ambitious Chirac, ponderous Barre and racist Le Pen. Alexandre is reassured by the result, but 68 per cent of the population of Puligny voted for Chirac. 'Loulou Carillon's father is afraid Mitterrand will take away all his vineyards – he fears him more than the Russians. In the first round, eighty-three people in Puligny voted for Le Pen. It's very difficult to try to imagine who they were. Most of them have never seen an immigrant in their lives.'

For a moment I see the gleam of Robespierre in his eyes, smoking out enemies of the Revolution, but the bookbinder's good-humoured pessimism finds sufficient expression in the modest contemplation of his neighbour's follies. There is no bitterness; rather the gleeful relish of the bright schoolboy, bespectacled swot, who delights in shocking his fellows with dreadful tales of his family, lurid hints of domestic repression and unspeakable secrets. Glancing up from his work he tells me that he has plenty of private customers in the region but none in the village itself. 'A book in five years, perhaps. The vignerons aren't very interested in books. Books don't make money for them, so they're useless.' He shakes his head with another heavy sigh, mourning the resolute philistinism of his neighbours.

At this very moment the classic Burgundian silhouette of a villager darkens the doorway.

His rotundity clothed in a shapeless jersey, full of holes, and a pair of baggy blue trousers, faded and patched, an old peasant with a belly like a barrel of wine hobbles down the steps, arthritic feet in carpet slippers, a stick in one hand and a book in the other. Monsieur Vollard, a retired vineyard worker, wheezes with the effort of manoeuvring this old lame body into the shop and blinks as he adjusts his rheumy eyes to the sub-

His rotundity clothed in a shapeless jersey. Monsieur Vollard in the workshop of Jean-Louis Alexandre.

terranean gloom.

'Good'ay M'sseurs. Can you rebind this M'sieur Alexandre? I found it in the house I've just bought. It must have belonged to the previous owner, who was a nurse during the war.'

His patois is so broad as to be almost unintelligible, but the book-binder takes the battered medical textbook with the tender care that such a historic commission deserves, quotes a modest price and says that it will be ready in a fortnight. As the old peasant climbs laboriously up to the street, Jean-Louis Alexandre turns to me, spreads wide his arms and shrugs in silent, rueful amazement. Chuckling quietly to himself, he resumes work with the air of a man disarmed. There is nothing to be said. Pigs have wings.

Such moments are rare and the daily reality for a man like Alexandre is more disheartening, stifled by a monoculture which begins in the fields and ends by shuttering the mind. On my next visit I discovered that his disillusionment with village life had reached crisis point.

'I've bought a house with a friend, an old house with a lovely garden, at Nolay. It's about fifteen or twenty kilometres from here, up in the hills towards Autun. We're signing the contract this afternoon but it's a secret, I don't want you to tell anyone in Puligny yet. The house needs a lot of work on it so it will be a year or two before I move but I'll have my studio there and it's in the real countryside, not like here. It's a re-gion of cows. I'm leaving the vines for the cows, and for the garden. There are very few houses in Puligny with gardens; they're too densely built together.'

I asked about his history of Puligny, long awaited. 'I'm submerged by work, so there's no time for my history. . . and with this house to work on as well. . .' He shrugged and resumed the patient piecing to-gether of a book which he was rebinding for a library at Chambéry. He repaired the corner of a page by worrying away at a scrap of old paper, thinning one edge of it, before dabbing the torn corner of the original page with a paste of flour and water and matching the new with the old. He sandwiched the join between sheets of tissue and paper and then rubbed over the line of repair with his ivory spatula. When fin-ished, the join was almost invisible.

'If I can't find a scrap of paper that matches the original I may have to tint it, in which case I use a weak brew of cold tea.'

At the back of his workroom the commissions pile up, year by year. The bookbinder's customers must be patient. 'Almost all my work now is restoration, for libraries. So it doesn't matter where I work; my professional clients will contact me as easily in Nolay as they do here in Puligny.' Monsieur Alexandre opened the Livre d'Or of the Hôtel Dieu at Beaune, choosing to show me the entries for 19 November 1658. Vast, self-confident signatures sprawled across the page: Louis Quatorze roy de France; Anne de Mantoue, princesse palatine; Anne d'Austriche; Philippe de France duc danjou. And then he brought out the treasure which he had been commissioned to repair for the village itself, with funds provided by the Mairie, by Domaine Leflaive and by Domaine Chartron: Le Terrier de la Seigneurie de Puligny et Mypont. As we gazed at page after lovely page of this eighteenth-century land register, Jean-Louis Alexandre pointed out its peculiarities and fascinations, pieced together the complexities of local history which were revealed in such detail by these extraordinary maps and spoke with affectionate passion of Puligny and its past. But the present had lost its allure. 'I shall be gone by Easter.' And firmly he closed the book.

The Growers

8 | The Châteaux of Puligny

'You see it's like a portmanteau – there are two meanings packed up into one word.'

LEWIS CARROLL
Through the Looking Glass

'Château' has two quite distinct connotations – fortified castle and grand country house. In many places the second meaning gradually evolved from the first, as the strongholds of local barons (built to safeguard their families and retainers, their villagers and as many cows and sheep as could be crammed within the walls) were enlarged and altered in more peaceful times, rebuilt with a view to luxury rather than protection or domination, surrounded by parks and formal gardens, embellished with ornament. The high walls which surrounded these mansions now had social rather than military significance: they guarded the grand bourgeois from unwelcome intrusion by the peasants at his gate.

In Puligny there was no such continuity in the evolution of castle to country house. Le Vieux Château was built at the top of the village in the fifteenth century, commanding the approaches from Meursault and Chassagne and with a wide view over the plain: a fortified manor house for the local Seigneur, Jean Perron de Mypont. Grouped around a series of courtyards, its mangled and disjointed remains reveal quite clearly their medieval origins despite numerous alterations which have taken place over the centuries, as the château has been split up between different owners and its outer walls used as a quarry to supply building stone for other houses in the village. A former *dependance* which still exists further up the hill was already shown as a separate property (owned by Monsieur Dugon) on the eighteenth-century map which the Seigneur of Puligny commissioned to show the extent of his domaine around the village, but the main structure of the old buildings (clearly identified as the Château de Puligny) still remained in the possession of the seigneur. That was in about 1740.

More recently a courtyard in front of the château became separated from the rest and is now shared by various owners, principally the Carillon family and a retired stonemason, Monsieur Llorca. This section of the château was badly defaced in 1904 when medieval stone windows and doorways were removed for sale to American antique dealers, and its recent 'restoration' has done little to improve matters. Only the core of the château, the old house which was rebuilt for the Seigneurs de Puligny in the seventeenth century, retains a dignified and tranquil air, a sense of history – reflecting thereby the character of its present owner, Stephan Maroslavac.

By the middle of the eighteenth century three of the most substantial houses in Puligny were owned by the Edouhard family. Two faced each other across the Place du Grand Cimetière and the third was nearby, on a corner formed by the junction of the Rue de But and the Rue de Bois. During the course of the following century this house was enlarged, remodelled and finally rebuilt, as a grand residence for a family on the make. The exact architectural sequence is hard to determine. Its former owner, Roland Thevenin, claims that the château dates back to Napoleonic times and that it welcomed from the outset a series of distinguished visitors: Carnot, organizer of the first modern army in France in the years following the Revolution; Ney, Napoleon's bravest marshal, whose heroism in Russia prevented defeat from becoming annihilation; Napoleon's mother, who is said to have broken her flight from Fontainebleau here on the night of 23 July, 1815, as her son was beginning his final journey to St Helena; Lamartine, romantic poet and republican politician, brief hero of the Revolution of '48. Others repudiate such stories as the inventions of successive generations of Edouhards (eager social climbers who ennobled themselves to d'Esdhouard) and argue that the present building cannot be earlier than about 1850. Whatever the truth, it is clear that it was designed to impress.

Naturally enough there were extensive outbuildings (stables and carriage houses, storerooms and cellars), a fifteen-acre park and a general air of bourgeois grandeur. Unlike the Vieux Château, which merges with democratic confusion into the huddle of neighbouring houses and gardens, the 'new' château and its park are surrounded by a high stone wall and it faces firmly away from the village. At some point it has also abrogated the title of its predecessor and is now described, with upstart indifference, as the Château de Puligny.

Curiously enough, it was this château which first caught the eye of Stephan Maroslavac, but when he tried to buy it, in 1941, the occupying Germans vetoed its sale to this Croatian immigrant in favour of a bid by the prosperous local négociant and estate owner Roland Thevenin. That decision (repeated in somewhat different circumstances by the French Ministry of Agriculture when the château again came on the market in 1988 and was sold to a bank) ensured that the architectural character of the two châteaux continues to be mirrored in the personality of their owners. It also reflects a tendency in France, no matter who's in charge, for a combination of snobbery and chauvinism to preserve the social and economic order. The prejudices of a deposed aristocracy have become the familiar habits of the heirs to the Revolution.

Le Vieux Château

I found him in his cellar, a true underground cellar, perhaps the only such in Puligny. With great courtesy he beckoned me to go before him up the stone steps to the yard in front of the house, but it was not until we emerged into the mild autumn sunlight that I properly took in the handsome old face, unstooped stature and energetic dignity of this remarkable octogenarian. With an old cap on his head, a fine moustache, well-worn tweed jacket buttoned over his pullover, baggy trousers and sturdy shoes, Stephan Maroslavac looks what he is, a cross between an intelligent peasant and a gentleman farmer. There is an air of aristocracy.

Maroslavac was twenty-eight years old when, with his wife Katerina Kovacevic and their two infant children (one a newborn baby), he decided to leave the village of Miholhjca in Croatia, where his agricultural family had lived for two generations. Why did they go? He smiled at the simplicity of my question. 'I left to find something better, to get something for myself and my family, and to be happy.' It is clear that he achieved those ends.

Inside the house he sat at table in the comfortable front room, an old-fashioned place which is a mixture of office and dining-room, sitting-room and hall. As Katerina (now Katherine) closed the door to her

Stephan Maroslavac looks what he is, a cross between an intelligent peasant and a gentleman farmer.

kitchen at the back, the old man riffled through a pile of files until he found what he was looking for, a cutting from a Yugoslav newspaper, a long article by a reporter from his homeland who met the Maroslavacs at St Juan-les-Pins on the Côte d'Azur, where they spend four months every winter. Sight of the article prodded his own memory. 'We lived close to the border with Hungary, in what is now Yugoslavia but was then part of the Austrian empire. I was twelve years old when the Great War started. I remember the commotion when news reached the village of the assassination of Archduke Franz Ferdinand, at Sarajevo. That started it. There were so many upheavals. We left in July 1930.'

After a long journey through central Europe, Stephan and Katerina found their way to Ivry-en-Montagne, in Burgundy, where he had heard of a job going in the plaster works. A year or two later Maroslavac moved across the hills and down to Puligny, as an agricultural labourer working for the domaine of Reynold de Seresin. Then, after five years of careful saving, he managed to take over thirty hectares on his own account, working the land *en métayage* – sharing the crop with the owner. In 1939, just before the outbreak of war, he concluded an agreement to farm fifty hectares of land which belonged to the Château de Puligny (then the property of old Madame Hardorf, descendant of its eighteenth-century owners) and he moved his family into a corner of the farm buildings near the château.

Nowadays the richest vignerons of the village count themselves lucky to cultivate twenty hectares of vineyards but at that time land was worth a good deal less and in any case much of it was pasture, not vineyards. Maroslavac, like his neighbours, grazed cows and pigs and fed his horses on meadows which are now given over to the production of Bourgogne Blanc.

In 1941 it seemed that his chance had come to establish himself as a man of property. The Château de Puligny, with its fine park and extensive domaine, was put up for sale and as *métayer* of the land Maroslavac should have had a prior claim to purchase the place, as he wanted to do. But the Germans insisted that it be sold to a Frenchman, so the château was bought by Roland Thevenin. Maroslavac stayed on as sharecropper until 1947 and then moved into the house in La Grande Rue, next to Chartron's place, where his son lives now.

He became *métayer* of the Comtesse de Montlivaut's estate, which was based on her home at Blagny, and he is still remembered by the family with affection and admiration. Jean-Louis de Montlivaut was impressed by his extraordinary strength. 'He would roll full barrels of wine up the ramp from the cellar single-handed. Normally it needed two men and a rope.'

By that time Stephan was beginning to piece together a sizeable domaine. 'I was helped a great deal by my friends when I was younger. They gave me a hand when I needed anything and they lent me money.' There must have been something about Maroslavac then, as there is now, which commands immediate confidence and respect. His fellow vignerons were themselves hard pressed in those days, before the prosperity of recent times, but they seem to have trusted their savings to him with hardly a second thought.

Finally, in 1954, Maroslavac bought the other château, Le Vieux Château, at the top of the village. Or rather he bought the remnants: a house in considerable disrepair (originally medieval but apparently re-modelled in the seventeenth century); the remains of a fortified wall and gateway; a small barn and what had for centuries been a walled vineyard, nearly a hectare in extent, L'Enclos du Château. And under the house was a cellar, almost the only true cellar in Puligny – since the water table in these parts is so high that to dig a hole is to dig a pond, everywhere except here, on the slope at the top of the village.

Stephan re-roofed the house, cleared and replanted the abandoned vineyard and filled the cellar with barrels of maturing wine. Comfortably established in what has remained his home ever since, he continued to augment his domaine. Together with his son Stephan and eventually his grandson Roland, Maroslavac bought a few rows of vines here, a few *ares* there. Their most important purchase was twenty years ago when Stephan père et fils acquired three hectares of stony land, high above the Premier Cru vineyard of Les Folatières. Overgrown with scrub oak and brambles, with most of its meagre soil eroded by rainfall on to the vineyards below, this apparently unpromising patch had lain uncultivated since the devastation of phylloxera at the turn of the century. The Maroslavacs brought a heavy *concusseur* to pulverize the rock into submission, enabling them to plough the virgin land and then to plant it with cuttings of Chardonnay taken from the best plants in their vineyards. They obtained official entitlement to the appellation Champ Gain, Puligny Premier Cru, and the wines have proved to be some of the best from their domaine.

It's a marvellous site from which you look down on the village far below and across the plain to a distant spot on the horizon where, very early in the morning, the rising sun reflects off the snows of Mont Blanc. Stephan Maroslavac, the son, points across the vineyard to the east, 'When you can see the mountain clearly for a moment like that, at dawn, it's a sign of changing weather. It means that rain is coming.'

Champ Gain is situated at an altitude of around 340 metres – only the vineyards of Blagny are higher – so the vintage is often a day or two later than for the other Premiers Crus, but there's seldom any risk of hail. 'I was astonished that we got such good harvests from this land but I think it's because it was virgin soil which had not been exhausted by a succession of replantings.' Even now, in mid-October 1990, the vines still look remarkably healthy. Despite an exceptionally dry summer, the bright green leaves are only just beginning to show a few streaks of yellow, while further down the slope you can easily spot changes of colour and thinning foliage, signs which identify those patches of vines which are less well nourished or nurtured.

The family domaine now includes six hectares belonging to old Stephan, about twenty-two hectares farmed by his son (a mixture of ownership, métayage and fermage), and eight hectares owned by the grandson Roland. Most of the work in the vineyards and at the harvest is organized by Stephan the younger (now sixty years old) from his house and cellars in Grande Rue, at the bottom of the village. In addition to the Champ Gain, he produces Puligny Premier Cru from Les Referts, Les Folatières and Les Pucelles; some Meursault-Blagny; a fair amount of Puligny Village, Bourgogne Blanc and Aligoté; a rare red Puligny; St-Aubin and Santenay, Bourgogne Rouge and Passe-Tout-Grains. And he makes a sparkling Crémant from Bourgogne Grand Ordinaire (one of the most absurd appellations ever conceived, combining adjectives which are diametrically opposed).

Maroslavac is one of only three vignerons in Puligny to use a harvesting machine (the others are Pascal and Henri Clerc). He bought his first harvester, a Loiseau prototype, in 1982 and found that it worked well but wasn't sturdy enough, so traded it in the following year for another Loiseau. That machine was replaced in its turn by a Braud, his current favourite. The machine saves time and money – it can harvest one and a half hectares in a ten-hour day, a task that would otherwise require a team of at least twenty pickers (who have to be fed and housed, as well as paid). But the machine loses time in the smaller vineyards so Maroslavac employs human pickers to supplement the work of his mechanical harvester and is in a good position to compare the results. He claims that in most years there's no great difference, though others have found problems with rapid oxidation of the broken grapes and insufficient selectivity between ripe and rotten, producing a lack of finesse in the finished wine. A great deal seems to depend on the skill of the driver and the setting of the machine. In 1990, curiously enough, Maroslavac felt that the machine-harvested wines were noticeably better. He attributes this to the belief that when the rods of the harvester beat the bushes to knock off the grapes they tended to bruise the stems and unripe berries causing the release of *verjus* (literally 'green juice') which was sufficient to produce a good level of natural acidity in wines which otherwise (because of the hot dry summer) tended to be a bit flabby – needing the controlled addition of tartaric acid in order to have the necessary balance between ripe fruit and structural definition. 'It was a wonderful harvest this year, but quite bizarre. The natural degrees of sugar were really exceptional but we lost half a degree, even three-quarters of a degree in a single day, following the rain. Aligoté grown on the plain, where it didn't suffer from the drought, came in at 12.7°. There's a lot of talk about high yields and indeed we reached 72 hectolitres per hectare in one vineyard but it was much lower in most others – and the overall average for the domaine was no more than sixty hectolitres per hectare.'

That still seems high by comparison with a number of other quality-conscious growers, but Maroslavac's attitude is relaxed. His cellars are neat and extremely clean, his vineyards well cared for and his wines decently made – but he has always sold most of his production to the négociants, keeping only modest quantities for sale to private customers, restaurants and a few importers overseas. 'When we can get such a good price for our Crus in bulk there doesn't seem much point in taking the trouble to bottle them.' It's the attitude of a farmer, seeking a decent return on his annual labours, rather than a vigneron whose passion is for the quality of the final product. This judgement is endorsed by his pragmatic decisions in the cellar. Wine destined for the négoces is vinified in tank, that for his own bottling is fermented in cask.

We went down to the cellar to taste the results, a cross-section of the 1989 vintage, bottled in September 1990. This in itself is indicative;

most of the finest domaines would expect to mature at least their best wines for eighteen months in cask – earlier bottling is appropriate for the modest appellations but simply an administrative convenience for the rest.

Puligny Le Château was surprisingly rich in colour, had aromas of toasted grapefruit and was soft, rather rustic on the palate – I suspected a machine-harvested wine. The Premier Cru Referts, by contrast, was markedly more concentrated, rich and fine, with an attractively spicy length of flavour. Pucelles was disappointing – charming and open in style but lacking the grandeur of the best wines of this appellation. Champ Gain had not yet developed much character on the nose but had an attractive sweet/sour palate, reminiscent of greengages, and lingering persistence. The red Puligny, a real rarity these days, also seemed closed-up in terms of aroma but was appetizingly astringent to taste, like sucking cherry-stones. It's the sort of wine which I tend to enjoy very much myself but find impossible to sell to my customers.

As he wrapped up a bottle for me to take away and we talked about the universal problem of getting payment from restaurateurs, I was struck by the similarities between father and son but also by their differences. When I left the old man he told me, laughing, that I wouldn't get his son to chat very much (as he himself had done) 'because he's always so busy. You'll have to talk to him as he works.' In fact the younger Stephan had been quite unexpectedly generous with his time, had taken me to see his harvesting machine, driven me up the hillside to Champ Gain, talked quite openly in answer to my numerous questions. But there isn't the same impression of conversation rooted in long-sought achievement, wisdom tempered by hardship. Stephan the son was brought up in France, married a Frenchwoman (Jeannine Tremeau, who brought vineyards as her dowry) and has lived through times of increasing prosperity. A capable and agreeable man, he drives a Mercedes (like all the prosperous vignerons of Burgundy), works hard and is sceptical of government. His preoccupations are those of the present.

Stephan senior, eighty-eight years old, is the living embodiment of Europe's troubled history in this century. But he has a wonderful and somewhat unexpected serenity. When I asked about the changes in village life during his time here I expected the nostalgia of an old man for the good things that are past – for the close and supportive community, the more deliberate pace, the moral certainties of an earlier age. On the contrary. 'I had to keep five or six horses to work my land before the war, now we have tractors. There's been a great deal of progress. And we lack for nothing in our old age.'

It's the testament of a quite remarkable old man who has lived through a past which others less closely connected to it view without a full comprehension of the privations and difficulties. The question is not whether his grandchildren are better off, in myriad different ways, but whether they have managed to guard the appetite for life which Stephan Maroslavac still savours with such relish and digests with such apparent ease.

Château de Puligny

Roland Thevenin, fanatical Bonapartist, former mayor of St-Romain, erstwhile owner of the Château de Puligny, friend of the famous, man of affaires and poet, lives alone now, up at Santenay, in an ugly but substantial nineteenth-century house with an immaculate tennis court and well-maintained gardens (of the depressing sort, infested with monkey-puzzle trees). There is plenty of evidence of wealth but little sign that the old man, now in his mid-eighties, has achieved much tranquillity in the autumn of his life. Sitting at his kitchen table, clasping a large bowl of coffee in his powerful knobbly fingers, Thevenin looks like a shrewd but grumpy toad as he reflects on the changes that he has seen and the present state of politics in France. 'The government always tries to block those who make progress, who want to construct things. Little functionaries spend their lives seeing how to fuck us up.'

Before the war Thevenin was based up in the hills behind Meursault, at St-Romain, a forgotten appellation which he made locally famous as 'Mon Village'. Administering a cluster of family domaines and a successful négociant business, he had fingers in many pies.

'St-Romain was the place where the Marseillaise was sung for the first time. Rouget de Lisle, its author, was born not far from here, at Lons-le-Saulnier.'

The first part of this statement is surprising from so passionate a historian and certainly owes more to local bias than recorded fact. According to most reputable authorities, Rouget de Lisle wrote words and music for what became the anthem of the Revolution (and of France) during the course of a single night, in April 1792, at the suggestion of the Mayor of Strasbourg – before whom it was first performed three

Roland Thevenin, fanatical Bonapartist and former mayor of St-Romain.

days later. Thevenin is more reliable on the events of his own lifetime, itself the subject of much local gossip and any amount of inaccurate scandal.

'I bought the Château de Puligny in 1941, from old Madame Hardorf, whose family had been there a long time.'

Thevenin omits to mention the German veto on the sale of the estate to its tenant, the Croatian immigrant Stephan Maroslavac, and there is understandable obscurity about why he himself should have been the preferred purchaser.

'In those days I kept twenty-five cows on the meadows below Puligny and I had a park of 300-year-old trees in front of the house. I used to lend the park to the musicians, the village band, who would play there on all the great feast days. That was where Puligny used to celebrate the Fourteenth of July.'

It is not only Thevenin who recalls those times with nostalgia. Madame Robaire, chambermaid at the hotel and one of the great gossips of the village, is equally certain that this was a golden age. 'The first St Vincent Tournante was celebrated there in '61, just after I arrived in the village, with all the children dressed up. It was wonderful. I went to work for Domaine Roland Thevenin in 1963, as *femme de ménage*. I did the cooking, the cleaning. He lived there then, with his wife and three children. His son worked in the vineyards with two employees – they did it all – and there were two women in the cellars. There were thirty rooms in the house – and I did everything, with no help. It was very agreeable – we worked hard but it was good. Lots of foreigners came to taste the wines and there were parties with ambassadors from everywhere, from Japan even, and Tino Rossi, Maurice Chevalier. All the Grandes Fêtes were celebrated there. We would make a Buffet Campagnard – pâtés and sausages and good home-made bread – *la grosse miche* [big cob loaves] – country bread. There were white railings all around the park. Horses and trees. It was magnificent, it was the Belle Époque. But in 1981 he separated from his wife and left – she was fed up with all his girlfriends – so I had to leave too, and I'd worked eighteen years for them. He sold the Folatières vineyard to Chartron, Le Montrachet to the Duc de Magenta* and the château was sold for

---

*In fact Thevenin's treasured morsel of Montrachet was bought for a record sum by the Domaine de la Romanée-Conti. Philippe de Magenta acquired Puligny Clos de la Garenne.

500,000 francs. It's all finished now – now it's a factory. He lives by himself, all alone at Santenay, and his wife lives at the Moulin aux Moines, at St-Aubin. She's OK.'

The château was bought (in 1985) by Michel Laroche, a well-known grower and négociant from Chablis, as the focus of a domaine which he planned to create on the Côte d'Or, based on vineyards acquired from the Ropiteau family of Meursault and Monthélie. Laroche is also said to have had in mind the tremendous success of nearby Château de Meursault, a truly grand classical house which faces towards the main road across a well-tended vineyard, luring tourists to tour, taste and buy. Much of the production of its domaine is humble Bourgogne Blanc, but graced by the château label such wine mysteriously sells at almost the same price as a famous Meursault. Laroche evidently hoped to achieve similar results at the Château de Puligny. As a first step to this end he uprooted its lovely park – thus allowing the house to be visible from the Route Nationale – and cleared the ground in order to plant a five-hectare vineyard which he designated Clos du Château. Unlike Maroslavac's L'Enclos du Château, which is entitled to the appellation Puligny, this new Clos du Château can only produce wine with the modest designation Bourgogne. Few locally have forgiven Laroche for this act of vandalism, least of all Roland Thevenin.

'They've cut down all my trees to plant vines – as if there weren't already enough vines in Burgundy. They don't see that Burgundy is not just about the vines but the viticulteurs who live here, who work here; the life of the countryside. But Puligny doesn't have the spirit of a village now because most of the vineyards belong to people who want to destroy rather than to build. For them the land simply represents a certain value.'

Retreating from contemplation of the present and all its woes, Roland Thevenin takes me to admire his collection of Napoleonic memorabilia and tokens of France's military history. There are portraits and letters, flags and medals and helmets, swords, sashes and the tricolour. It is a sad display, assertive of past glories, tinged with the macabre. It occurs to me that Thevenin is not someone with whom to discuss the Dreyfus affair.

But he seems happy enough with the latest turn of events at the château, which has changed hands once again, in intriguing circumstances.

After owning the place for three years and doing little with it other than replacing trees with vines, Laroche decided to sell and managed to pull off a considerable financial coup in so doing. The dilapidated Château de Puligny, its ravaged park and recently acquired domaine (twenty hectares dispersed between the appellations of Meursault and Monthélie, St-Aubin and St-Romain, plus a smallholding in Puligny itself) was suddenly presented as a French national treasure, a jewel beyond price. As soon as the Japanese giant Suntory joined the bidding it became clear that there would be considerable political pressure to find 'a French solution', as was the case a decade earlier with the sale of Château Margaux, in Bordeaux. Just in time, a white knight plodded to the rescue – in the somewhat ponderous guise of Crédit Foncier de France, a banking and property conglomerate which, among other things, is the long-standing owner of a couple of unremarkable châteaux in Bordeaux and (far more significantly) the freeholder in Paris of both the Place de la Madeleine and the Place Vendôme, probably the most valuable real estate in France. One of the main board directors was lunching at the Ritz (Crédit Foncier's tenants in Place Vendôme) when he drank a decent bottle of Burgundy instead of his usual claret. In an expansive mood, he decided that it was time the company owned a domaine on the Côte d'Or.

So they paid 33 million francs for the privilege and claim that this was a bargain – Suntory was apparently prepared to pay ten million more but their purchase was vetoed by the Ministry of Agriculture. Crédit Foncier became proprietor at Puligny and Claude Schneider, their local director based at Dijon, was put in charge of an expensive programme of further investment. Additional vineyards have been purchased in the Côte de Nuits, the château has been re-roofed, restoration work has begun on its interior and a brand new complex of offices, vinification plant and cellars has been constructed at a discreet distance from the house, half hidden by the few remaining trees at the edge of the former park. Described by Madame Robaire as 'a factory', this is the architecture of airports and industrial estates, not 'vieux Bourgogne', but it is enviably well equipped for its task, with all the latest winemaking technology.

Such investment is clearly for the long term, with an eye to prestige. Crédit Foncier is seen as the saviour of part of France's patrimony, Château de Puligny is a glamorous brand name to enhance the value of the more modest appellations in its domaine, the directors can drink their own burgundy when lunching at the Ritz and the place will eventually be a luxurious country retreat at which to entertain the bank's most valued business associates. The purchase made some sort of sense to them and was exceedingly welcome to Michel Laroche.

Sole survivor from Laroche's brief ownership of the château is the young winemaker and oenologist Jacques Montagnon, who arrived here from Chablis in 1988. A cheerful fellow who seems to relish the challenge of making red wines as well as white, Montagnon is clearly delighted at all the new toys he has been given to play with. Grapes arrive from the vineyards for sorting on the latest *triage* tables, pressing in the latest Bucher pneumatic presses and fermenting in the temperature-controlled, computer-linked stainless steel vats of the cuverie (which is named in honour of Roland Thevenin). Red wines have the benefit of an ingenious pneumatic system for punching down the *châpeau* in order to ensure maximum extract of colour from the cap of skins and pulp and both red and white wines are matured in oak casks (to the accompaniment of piped musak) before bottling in the domaine's own heavy, embossed bottles, corked with the finest Spanish corks from Sagrera, suppliers to the Domaine de la Romanée-Conti. Finally, the bottles are stored before sale in an air-conditioned warehouse, with the humidity controlled to a constant 15 per cent.

1989 was the first vintage under the new régime and the results look promising. Of the whites, I tasted an attractive Côtes de Nuits Villages (rare exception to the general redness of this appellation), a pleasant Meursault and a Puligny-Montrachet of real concentration. The château owns only a single hectare of vines in this appellation – and naturally enough they want more, but there are seldom any vineyards for sale. Of the domaine's red wines the undoubted star was not the Pommard or the Côte de Nuits but the much less fashionable appellation of nearby Monthélie. The vineyards were originally planted by the wild man of that village, André Ropiteau, who went bankrupt before he could harvest the fruits of his labours – but he chose a particularly good site and Jacques Montagnon frankly acknowledges the pleasure that he has taken in vinifying this wine, and his pride in the end result. Because it exhibited from the start such an attractive character of wild fruit (woodland strawberries, in particular) he decided to give it only a couple of months' maturation in cask, preferring to guard its youthful vivacity rather than add the complexity of new oak. It's odd that this should be the wine which I found the most delicious and individual in the tasting but it also provides encouraging grounds for supposing that the enthusiasms of the winemaker can survive the technological sophistication of his winery.

The day after my visit to the château I met Monsieur and Madame Schneider emerging from the Hôtel Le Montrachet with their lunch guest, Roland Thevenin. He was looking red-faced, cheerful and well fed – just like a schoolboy given a treat by his parents on Speech Day – and the impression was reinforced by the fact of being buttoned into a suit and shirt and tie which seemed uncomfortably tight on his short frame. The Schneiders, by contrast, had the cosmopolitan, self-confident air of busy and successful executives, sparing an hour or two in their smoothly planned schedules to fulfil their parental obligations. I felt a slight sense of foreboding at this unexpected reversal of generations. But the moment passed. Thevenin grinned with a flicker of ancient malevolence, the Schneiders waved a cheerfully insouciant goodbye and my unease evaporated in the autumn sunshine. Occasionally it returns.

9 | Petits Producteurs

The landscape of Burgundy is fragmented between innumerable owners; it takes a great effort of will to overcome this tendency to partition, first to augment a domaine, then to hold it intact over several generations. The laws of inheritance are divisive and the cyclic fortunes of agricultural life return sooner or later to ruin. Smallholdings are sold when too small to cultivate economically and are consolidated into bigger domaines, which are then riven by some catastrophe and divided as the spoils among their rivals. But the unprecedented period of steadily increasing prosperity which has been Burgundy's fortune over the past few decades has strengthened the capacity of the big domaines to weather temporary adversity and provided a considerable incentive for their owners to find ways of maintaining them from one generation to the next. Methods have been devised which bypass the laws of inheritance, most notably by turning these estates into limited companies, with individual members of the families as shareholders. The result has been to tip the balance between consolidation and fragmentation, in favour of the former. The number of individual domaines is decreasing and their size becoming larger. At the 1990 vintage over sixty proprietors were registered in Puligny but less than a third of them had vineyard holdings of any significance. In a decade's time that number could well be halved.

Between the handful of big domaines and the rest, the small producers, there is a gulf at least as great as that which separates any other social classes, bound together in economic interdependence. The petits

The cyclic fortunes of agricultural life return sooner or later to ruin.

producteurs are differentiated from their richer neighbours by three vital characteristics: they sell their wine in bulk to the négoces, as a cash crop in which they have no further interest; they are intensely local in their preoccupations because they have no contact with customers from outside Burgundy, or from abroad; their prosperity is less secure than that of the big proprietors, less likely to survive the upheavals of inheritance.

I shall introduce you to all the grandes domaines of Puligny at some point in this book but the petits producteurs are too numerous for me to include more than a short selection. My choice may seem arbitrary but is not entirely unrepresentative. Two are workers who have earned their livelihood from other employment and cultivated their vines at weekends, another is a traditionalist whose future is decidedly uncertain and one is an immigrant to the village who has made good. Finally there is Gérard Chavy, who is no longer a petit producteur but runs what is effectively a grande domaine in miniature. He is included here as an example of a small producer who has successfully made the transition to grander things.

As a cross-section of a class this is sufficient to give a flavour of its diversity but only prolonged and close acquaintance could do justice to the dense strata of Burgundian habit and expression which lie buried beneath such individual differences. The petits producteurs may be more vulnerable than their prosperous cousins but collectively they embody the continuity of local culture, undiluted by the aspirations of gentility.

Jean Ponelle
I glimpsed an ancient wine press through a gateway, went into the tiny courtyard for a closer look and found myself confronted by the suspicious glare of an old and angry man. But a couple of expressions of interest were sufficient to unleash a torrent of resentment.

'I'm seventy-two years old and a vigneron. I was a soldier during the war and then I married and then I went to work for Domaine Leflaive as a vineyard worker. Twenty-six years I worked for them and then I was chucked out; by Joe (you know, the brother that died?), for *nothing!* I took him to the tribunal and he lost, he had to pay and so then I went to work for Chartron until I retired.'

All this was spat out in broad patois and with bitter glee – but it was impossible to fathom why he had been dismissed by Leflaive.

Jean Ponelle and his wife still cultivate a couple of hectares of vines, producing basic Bourgogne – red, white and Aligoté. They do all the work themselves throughout the year but at the vintage their family comes to help; six children and twelve grandchildren. The simple arithmetic progression from one generation to the next is dramatic evidence of the declining birthrate which now afflicts France, after centuries of state exhortation to be fecund and fill the land.

Suddenly he turned on me, his suspicious gaze on my notebook and pen. 'Are you the taxman?' It took a lot of mollification to convince him otherwise. Then he resumed his litany of complaint. 'There used to be three cafés, two bakers, a butcher and four grocers. It was better before than now.' More muttering, as he went about his work, cleaning down the yard. 'I used that old press until three years ago but they don't like it, the négoces. And they don't pay as they should all at once, after the harvest. Now they spread out the payments in four slices, throughout the year. And the price of Bourgogne is so *low*.'

I got the impression that he still felt I was a spy from the tax office, taking evidence to defraud him. But his grumpiness was evidently habitual and also in some way representative – of all the small growers who can see fortunes being made by the fashionable domaines, and (as ever) by the négoces; and who find themselves excluded from the increasing prosperity of their neighbours. Those with tiny vineyards, of basic appellations, have always had to find employment in order to make a decent living – and have generally found themselves working as labourers for the big domaines. It is a situation which breeds envy, and the labourer sometimes avenges himself on his employer by petty theft, of the materials he needs to cultivate his smallholding or a few kilos of sugar to fortify his wines. The honourable employee can regard such perks as his by right, and the generous employer may wink at this practice, sanctioned by habit. But the slightest altercation between the two can lead each to make an issue of the fact and expose social differences which both had hitherto ignored.

In practice these differences are increasing. When Jean Ponelle dies and his tiny landholding is divided between six children the likelihood is that each will agree to sell – and the vineyards will be bought by one of the more prosperous proprietors of Puligny. There will, in future, be very few petits viticulteurs working for the grandes domaines during the week and cultivating their own patch at the weekends. Instead of this community of understanding and interest (however riven with jealousy) there will be a more straightforward and ruthless division of the spoils – between the owners and the workers.

François Llorca

There used to be plenty of labourers who could build and repair the drystone walls which protected the hillside vineyards against erosion and animals. It was a necessary part of the vineyard worker's repertoire of skills, since the land had in any case to be cleared of the larger stones to make cultivation possible. Now there is hardly anyone able to pile this rubble into a solid boundary. Hence the fact that François Llorca, though reputedly expensive to employ, has been able to earn a decent living as a stonemason, extracting the raw material of his trade from the ancient quarries on the hill below Blagny and using it to rebuild long stretches of those vineyard walls.

I much prefer the modest, anonymous character of that work to the grotesque stonemasonry of Bernard Clerc's chalet, which Llorca helped to construct near the entrance to one of the hillside quarries, or the mimicry of traditional idioms which he has employed in the village. His work in the church is decent enough but Llorca's most notable (and most controversial) restoration has been to the range of old buildings which houses his cellars, part of the Cour du Vieux Château. Ten years ago this courtyard still showed the scars of a visit by American antique dealers, in 1904. They vandalized the place, carrying off all the old mullioned windows and arched doorways, leaving blank holes in the ancient façade. Now there is no trace of their depredations, but Llorca's reconstruction owes little to historical authenticity. True, he rescued a twelfth-century window from another old château which had fallen into ruins and installed it on the first floor, carving two or three more to match; they look well enough, though rather too early in style for the rest of the building. But there are other details of folkloric fantasy which mar the decent simplicity of the original. More serious, to my mind, is the fact that Llorca's ground-floor cellars occupy what was once a fine vaulted room which he believes may originally have been the château's chapel and then became a reception room. The remains of a seventeenth-century fireplace are now brutalized by a modern boiler and its associated pipework, installed without any regard for the damage that has been done to its surroundings.

Here lie a dozen casks which contain the entire harvest of Llorca's modest domaine. Perhaps one or two of these barrels hold Puligny-Montrachet, from a small vineyard which he bought quite recently, but most are filled with simple Bourgogne and Aligoté, the produce of a hectare and a half of vines which his wife brought as her dowry when they were married in 1952. She is a native of Puligny and one of the great characters of the village, an excitable gossip who provides much entertainment for her neighbours. Born Mlle Jobard, she is related to a large family of local vineyard owners, name of Lartus. Llorca himself is Spanish by ancestry, though born and brought up in France. His parents arrived from Alicante in 1929 and François was born in Burgundy the following year. He was apprenticed to a stonemason in Dijon, where he worked for several years before moving to Beaune and then, on his marriage, to Puligny. 'There used to be cows and horses grazing the meadows below the village then. Now they're all planted with vines. Things have changed a lot, but it's the same with everything.' And he shrugs, evidently unperturbed.

Llorca and his wife have three children but each has left the village: 'There's not enough to live on here.' They return for a weekend at the vintage to join family and friends in gathering the harvest. But neither they nor Llorca himself have time or inclination to look after the wine in the cellars. Most is sold to the négoces soon after the picking, to Chanson of Beaune or Ropiteau of Meursault. It's a cash crop. But I visited Llorca once before his wine had disappeared into the négociant's blend, and tasted each appellation from the cask. The best was the Aligoté, agreeably unpretentious. The Bourgogne Blanc and Puligny-Montrachet had been picked too soon and chaptalized to bring the alcoholic level up from 11.5° to 13°; typical of a small producer for whom the price of a few sacks of sugar is well worth the trouble that they save, by allowing him to gather his harvest at a weekend when he is conveniently free rather than waiting for the grapes to be fully ripe. Such low levels of natural alcohol are also an indication of high yields, bane of modern viticulture.

If this were simple vin de pays, sold at a few francs a litre, Llorca's attitude might be less regrettable. But for Puligny-Montrachet, supposedly one of the finest white wines in the world, it's a very great pity that he should be content with such mediocrity. Worse still is the cynical attitude of the négociant, who buys such stuff knowing that its certificate of appellation will make it saleable, regardless of quality. Pity the poor consumer, lured by a famous name, who finds nothing but disappointment in every glass.

Daniel Joly

Just above the Vieux Château, at the bottom of a vineyard called La Rue aux Vaches, stands a cluster of buildings which originally formed a 'dependance' of the château and must once have been a classic Burgundian farm. You can still spot one fine ancient window on the first floor of the house, and the broken remnants of a stone fireplace are stacked against a wall in the unbelievably scruffy yard, below a rickety shelf heaped with various plastic containers, pipe connectors, a brush and a few dirty rags. Inappropriate and haphazard alterations have ruined the original dignity of these buildings and the muddy yard is stacked with a miscellaneous collection of old wooden casks. It is a place which seems to have forgotten its history, or to despise it.

Daniel Joly, too, appears disinterested in the past. I mention that his family must be one of the oldest in the village; the name is mentioned in the eighteenth-century land register of the seigneurs of Puligny and is inscribed on the base of the stone cross which marks the site of the horse pond, together with a date, 1805. Monsieur Joly merely shrugs, apparently ignorant of both facts, and claims that his grandfather came here at the beginning of this century. As for the house, he rebuilt it in 1986. So I had suspected, for the inside could be that of any bourgeois house in France, revealing nothing of its origins. Nicole, Daniel Joly's wife, is slightly more forthcoming. She came here from the Morvan to work as a picker at vintage time, met her husband and stayed.

I guess they must be in their late thirties; they have three children still at school and despite Daniel's red face and incipient paunch he still has the gangling gait of an overgrown teenager. And behind the awkwardness there is an evident desire to be friendly, struggling through the inarticulate habits of a man unused to the society of other than his immediate neighbours.

Daniel Joly cultivates nine hectares of vines, some of which he owns, some of which are rented and the rest being held *en métayage*: as a sharecropper. The white wines range from Bourgogne Aligoté to a little Puligny Champ Gain Premier Cru, and he also has a couple of red vineyards in Santenay. Joly's management of this domaine is extremely traditional. He does all his own grafts, using a range of clones as well as making cuttings from the vines in his own vineyards (including some treasured specimens of Pinot Noir at Santenay which are more than sixty years old). Various local ladies are employed to do the pruning and at vintage time they help with the picking. The harvest is entirely by hand, using a team of twenty-five pickers, for fifteen of whom they provide lodging. And they all have to be fed. Nicole Joly does the cooking, together with her mother.

Most of the wine is sold soon after the harvest to the négociants. Joly rattles off a list of names which includes Bouchard, Drouhin, Olivier Leflaive, Chartron and Trebuchet, Mommesin and Thorin; a respectable roll call which suggests that his wine must be good. That which he keeps for himself is matured in oak casks which are at least four years old, and is bottled in the August before the next vintage. The style is decidedly old-fashioned, with a lot of colour, a lot of character and a rustic, oxidized flavour which can be agreeable but which seldom exhibits much finesse. The négociants are probably wise to remove the raw material from Joly's care as soon as they can get their hands on it.

Daniel Joly is a happy-go-lucky fellow who goes fishing and hunting and enjoys the occasional game of tennis. But not with the serious competitors from Chassagne: 'You mustn't make any noise when those players move!' Sometimes he takes himself off on holiday, leaving his family behind. And sometimes not. There is no sense of ambition or even any awareness of what ambition means. Fifty years ago he would have fitted comfortably into the texture of village life, surrounded by the continuing certainties of rural society. But those certainties have ended and Joly seems adrift, without any evident misgivings but with a simple determination to shut his eyes to the future, as he has done to the past.

Camille David

I wandered up a sidestreet of Puligny, a dead-end which had attracted me because it was sunny, and there were geraniums in pots on every ledge and windowsill. At the end of this alley they were pumping wine across the lane, from one cellar to another, so I stopped to watch. Camille David stood beside me, smiling encouragingly as his grandson and a cellarman wrestled with pipes and pumps. He is in his mid-seventies and theoretically retired, but in fact is still very much involved in running his small domaine while his grandson works alongside him, providing the muscle, and prepares to take over his inheritance. They look remarkably alike, despite nearly half a century's gap in age, and they share the same engaging smile. Camille himself preserves a quizzical interest in the world around him and an unusual openness to strangers, which may be a relic of the fact that he, too, was once an outsider here.

'I came here by chance from Paris in 1934. I came to work and I met a very good young girl.' The girl was Mlle Jante, who became his wife. She brought with her a dowry of vines, basis of a domaine which now extends to five hectares and includes parcels in the Premier Cru vineyards of Les Truffières, Les Referts, Champ Gain and Les Folatières, as well as some Puligny 'village' and a patch which produces simple Bourgogne. Camille had not been brought up to the viticultural life but he accepted the challenge with enthusiasm. How did he learn? 'Largely by working on my own, with a little spirit of observation, a willingness to experiment and a few useful books.' Lean and weatherbeaten, he tilts his face when talking to you in a manner that has been caught by his grandson and which reminds me of an alert dog, ready to scamper into the sea after a thrown stick.

The boy, of course, had the proper training. 'He went to the viticulture school at Beaune. He learnt a lot about business but zero, nothing, in practical terms.' This is said with considerable affection, but with all the contempt of a self-taught man for textbook learning and formal schooling.

'I planted all my own vines, from my own grafts. You have to be careful. If it's limestone soil you should choose your rootstock well, some varieties won't do well at all. Often the vignerons here plant Riparia everywhere – but it doesn't do well on limestone. I've even tried to keep some Pinot Blanc in the vineyards but I have to admit it's not been very successful.'

Monsieur David is very conscious of the division that exists within the village between the handful of big domaines and the rest, the petits producteurs. 'It's a division which splits the Syndicat des Vignerons. The big domaines never lend anything to the small ones but we try to give each other a hand. Monsieur Joly has helped me a lot by lending me equipment and my grandson is a mate of Monsieur Bzicot's son. That's how we get along.'

Camille leads me into the cellar and I admire the traditional sim-

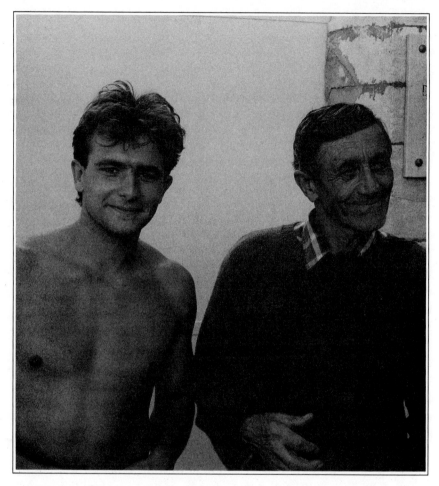

His grandson works alongside him, providing the muscle. Camille David and his heir.

plicity of its layout. 'Fortunately my grandson shares my outlook. We both want to keep that old press, it's part of the heritage of Burgundy, but other things will change. Perhaps we may eventually keep more of our wine in the cellars and have it bottled by a mobile bottling line. Or we may even buy our own line. But at present we sell 95 per cent of our production to Maison Latour – we've been dealing with them for twenty-five years and it would be difficult for us to sell very much more of our wine direct to the consumer. Monsieur Latour is in touch with his clientele but we could not so easily contact the customers. We are in a dead-end down this alley and no one can see we are here. And anyway it would mean that someone would have to be here all the time, to receive visitors and so on. And then there's the space that we'd need to store the wine and the investment in bottles and equipment. It's hard to tell what the future will hold. When I came here before the war 85 per cent of the inhabitants were viticulteurs – now there are only twenty who cultivate their own vines. You have to work very hard and there's very little security in your retirement.'

But I have the impression that this domaine will survive and prosper. They have some valuable vineyards and the succession seems assured. Camille and his grandson are an agreeable and capable pair; they may never make the finest wine of Puligny but it could well be good enough to win a modest following and justify the investment necessary if they are going to sell their production after the lengthy process of maturation and bottling at the domaine. If they lived in Chassagne they would have already taken steps to this end. But there is something about Puligny which appears to keep many small proprietors subservient to the négoces. Perhaps the inhibition which stifles their initiative can be found in that social and economic gulf to which Camille David referred, between the big domaines and the rest. It is a gulf which seems to be growing wider.

Gérard Chavy

There are said to be seven families of Chavy in Puligny, related to each other in the most complex ways, and they have certainly been long established in the village. But the Chavys of Puligny disclaim any connection with those of the same name from Chassagne.

Gérard Chavy is a small, alert, quietly spoken man in his mid-fifties. There is something neat and well ordered about him which is reflected in his house and cellars, in the Rue du Vieux Château. Clearly a cut above the typical small proprietor, he nonetheless lacks the evident self-confidence (self-satisfaction almost) of the bigger producers of Puligny. In part this is modesty and a habit of reserve but in part it expresses the fact that Monsieur Chavy is indeed making that difficult transition from petit producteur to grande domaine.

His father was one of five children, so inherited a very small part of the family vineyards. By careful husbandry he built on his inheritance, buying land when he could, and Gérard has continued to add piece by piece to the domaine. He now owns eleven hectares outright (nothing tenanted, no sharecropping) and most of it is very well situated. They produce a little Bourgogne and some straight Puligny but also have parcels in the Premier Cru vineyards of Les Pucelles, Les Folatières, Les Perrières and Clavaillon. This last is an appellation which he shares with only one other proprietor, Domaine Leflaive.

The oldest vines are around thirty to forty years old and the average age is about twenty-five years, which gives real concentration of flavour. Replanting is done with clones purchased from Monsieur Pascal, but Chavy is insistent on buying a good mixture of different types in order to ensure complexity in the wine. At vintage time there is a large team of up to thirty pickers. Unusually, most of them are local; they only had to provide lodging for seven in 1990, one of whom was Chavy's Japanese importer.

All this trouble would be unrewarding if Monsieur Chavy continued to sell his entire harvest to the négoces, but since 1976 he has been building up the reputation of the domaine-bottled label, so that only a third of the wine is now disposed of in bulk. The rest is vinified in a mixture of stainless steel cuves and oak barrels, one-third of which are renewed each year. Chavy's preferred tonnelier is Damy and the casks are extremely expensive – 2,300 francs each in 1990. The cellars are constantly being enlarged and are scrupulously neat and clean, evident sign of the impeccable care which is taken at each stage of the wine's maturation. As a result, the reputation of this domaine is such that half the wine is now exported (mostly to the USA, plus a bit to Britain, Belgium and Japan) and the rest is sold in France, mainly to private customers.

And each year the quality improves. Chavy's wines are not yet among the very best of the village but they can be very good indeed, slightly nutty in character and with real substance. Perhaps they lack a vivid identity, but Gérard Chavy is a modest man, not given to asserting himself.

This very discretion continues to stand him in good stead. Well liked and local, Chavy is excellently placed to purchase whatever parcels of vines come on to the market as a result of the continued fragmentation of the small domaines. He will pay a fair price and I suspect he will not need to borrow the money from the bank. As long as his two sons, Jean-Louis and Alain, share their father's steadfastness, the estate will continue to expand and the reputation of its wines to grow. But I could also wish for a touch of flamboyance, to lift the flavour of Domaine Chavy from its present honourable expression of bourgeois virtue to that striking individuality which is the prerequisite of great wine.

10 | Grandes Domaines

The vignerons of Puligny have grown rich because their wines are famous throughout the world. But such renown is utterly dependent on an intense and continuing devotion to winemaking at the highest possible level of quality. The gift of the vineyards themselves is not enough.

Sometimes it seems that the growers are seduced by their own self-esteem into believing that their wines will always and effortlessly outclass all potential rivals. To the outsider it is evident that such complacency is dangerous. Good Chardonnay is now made throughout the world; great Chardonnay seems increasingly likely from several favoured sites and gifted winemakers. Burgundy is capable of producing superlative Chardonnay, of supreme quality, but it is also the source of any number of poorly made wines, sold at extortionate prices. And such mediocre examples of renowned appellations can easily breed public disillusion with what is perceived as a Burgundian myth. The consumer whose first taste of Puligny is an expensive bottle of over-cropped, over-sugared, slightly oxidized white wine, its character masked by the impact of new oak but otherwise quite evidently dull, may well come to the conclusion that such is the intrinsic character of one of the world's most famous wines, and that the whole business is a fraud.

Responding to the challenge of their vineyards is the responsibility of the grandes domaines above all others. The small producer who sees his crop vanish into the négociant's soup may be forgiven for regarding cash in hand after the harvest as the principal reward for the long labour of the agricultural year. But the grower who bottles his wine at the domaine and sells it under his own label has undertaken a responsibility which cannot be reduced to such simple commercial imperatives. It is he who makes the collective reputation of the village and its vineyards, as well as his own individual name.

What constitutes a grande domaine? It is an arbitrary line which divides the big producer from the small, but I have taken as my definition a minimum property of ten hectares, the harvest of which is mostly bottled at the domaine and sold under the domaine label, with a significant proportion being exported. The following producers of Puligny at present meet those criteria: Carillon, Chartron, Château de Puligny, Clerc, Leflaive, Maroslavac, Sauzet (with Gérard Chavy in the process of developing from petit producteur to grande domaine). I have included a brief description of each in this book, either grouped in this chapter or scattered in those that precede or follow it. Inevitably they are a mixed bunch, of widely varying quality, and my comments on them cannot be otherwise than partisan and momentary. These portraits are snapshots, taken in a particular light and at a particular time. My view may not always be clear and it is important to bear in mind that things can change very rapidly, for better or worse. If a cellarman dies or one generation of proprietors succeeds another, quality may alter from one vintage to the next. Frequently this happens and the general tendency, at present, is towards a raising of standards throughout Burgundy. Today's dud may well be tomorrow's star.

Carillon

Standing in their cool cellars, with the autumn sunshine slanting in at the open door, I listen to the family Carillon discussing the 1988 vintage. Young Jacques, who trained at the Lycée Viticole in Beaune, talks about their new rotary cuve for vinifying the red wines. It has a stainless steel spiral inside which can be made to turn this way and that to mimic the action of pigeage, the laborious process of punching down the cap of skins and pulp which floats to the surface in the old-fashioned wooden cuves and needs to be well mixed with the fermenting juice for maximum extraction of colour and tannin. Father Louis (a burly man in his fifties) shows me a cask of white wine which is bubbling merrily away and remarks that the fermentations have been tumultuous this year, and the casks overflowing, despite the seven or eight litres of headspace which they always leave in the top of the barrel. Grandfather Robert (smiling, slightly stooped but full of life) recalls that they had the same problem in 1947, though he's not sure they can really make that comparison between the wines. 'Well, there's certainly much more solid matter in the grapes this year than in 1982,' says Louis. 'From each full trailer load of grapes in '82 we could count on twelve casks of wine; this year we've got ten.' At which point Madame Carillon pops out of the door which leads straight from cellar to kitchen, a lettuce in her hand, to remind them that it is nearly time for lunch. And in the background there is the faint almost imperceptible hiss of fermenting wine, one of the friendliest sounds in the world.

This is an extraordinarily united family, with a shared wealth of experience and an inherited understanding of the traditional lore which used to be part of every vigneron's equipment. They chew the grapes to assess the character of the vintage and inspect the sediment from tank or cask to decide whether the berries were really ripe. They understand the characteristics of their soil and vineyards and have an instinctive sense of place. The Carillons have been established in Puligny for centuries (they can trace back to 1632) and are intertwined by relationships with most other families of the village.

Such rootedness is expressed in habits which hark back to the beginning of civilization. When Louis opens a bottle for me to taste and stoops to pour the first few drops on the beaten earth floor of the cellar, it is of course a prudent habit because the wine at the top of a standing bottle is likely to be ever so slightly more oxidized than the rest – but it is also a reflex which echoes the ritual of classical times, when a splash from every jar of wine was poured on the ground as a libation to the gods.

Above the entrance to one of their cellars is a stone engraved with the date 1611, which they found when renovating some of the old *dependances* of the Vieux Château, behind the section owned by Monsieur Llorca, where the original seigneurs of Puligny had stored wheat and hay from their fields below the village. To reach those premises Jacques took me out into the street from the main cellars, past the corner of the church where a cross still stands, erected in 1795 by his ancestors Magdeleine and Anne Carillon, and into the door of an old house which had belonged to his great-grandfather. Through the cellars of the house we suddenly emerged into the tiny walled kitchen garden which is cul-

Through the cellars of the house we suddenly emerged into a tiny walled kitchen garden.
Jacques Carillon.

tivated by old Robert Carillon. He is partly paralysed and claims the garden is poorly kept, but it looked immaculate to me and had the magic of a quite unexpected space in the midst of a jumble of buildings at the heart of the village.

At the end of the garden path Jacques opened another door and we found ourselves in an old courtyard of the château which gave access to the thoroughly modernized and air-conditioned premises where contractors come to do the bottling for them and where the stocks of bottled wine are stored. 'We don't air-condition the barrel cellars because it dries the wine out too much, just as the oak tends to do. That's also why we rarely use more than ten per cent of new oak casks each year.' Carillon bottles between a third and two-thirds of the harvest in any vintage, dependent on demand and quality, and sells the rest to the négoces, most regularly to Drouhin. 'My grandfather sold a bit in bottle to a few private customers locally but it was not until the sixties that we started to sell a significant amount of our production in bottle and began to export our wines. The négoces used to act like kings in the old days – there was a time when they paid five francs a tonneau. Now commerce is changing in our favour. But we still sell some to the négoces for security, because the market in bottled wines is less predictable.'

The Carillon domaine comprises twelve hectares of vines. Three hectares are in Premiers Crus vineyards (Champ Canet, Les Perrières, Les Referts and the recently replanted Les Combettes, plus a fragment of the Grand Cru Bienvenues-Bâtard-Montrachet); between five and six hectares are Puligny-Montrachet, comprised of about twenty different parcels scattered in most of the vineyards which are entitled to the village appellation; and the rest are red, including a hectare in Chassagne, parcels in St-Aubin and Mercurey, plus a little Bourgogne Rouge and Passe-Tout-Grains.

They still pick entirely by hand (though one day they expect to use machines) and the vintage takes nine or ten days with a team of up to forty, including the additional hands needed in the cellar. They get the usual mixture of nationalities and occupations but most are French and most are young. Eighty per cent are lodged in houses owned by Carillon and the rest are local.

Fermentation for the grander whites is in barrel, for the rest in stainless steel. The reds are fermented in open cuves or in the new stainless steel rotary machine, with a cuvaison which can last as long as a fortnight but is normally rather less. The best whites are left on their lees until September and bottled the following February and the reds, too, spend about a year in cask. But Carillon is sparing in the use of new oak. The Bienvenues will be rotated in casks of varying ages, of which between a quarter and a third are new. For the Premiers Crus the proportion will be around fifteen to twenty per cent of new oak. And not all of these are the standard 'pièces' of two hundred and twenty-five litres – I spotted a couple of new demi-muids in the cellars, huge casks more often seen in the Loire. The large size of barrel is intended to minimize the impact of oak. 'We think the wines dry out when aged too much in oak and that it masks the typicité.'

All of which may seem very traditional and rather dull, but the Carillon cellars are some of the cleanest and best organized of any that I know and the wines are full of character. Tasting there is a delight, moving from cask to cask, discussing each appellation and comparing one barrel with the next. Occasionally the door to the kitchen will open and there will be a glimpse into the house; often the various generations of the family will wander in to join whichever of them is taking me through the latest vintage.

The style of the Carillon wines is confirmed by the first taste of their village Puligny, elegant but straightforward in the most agreeable way. The Champ Canet is considerably grander, as you would expect, but has an immediate charm which is very appealing. Quite different is the Perrières: more austere, more substantial and better structured, with a stony length of flavour which promises a long evolution. They make a little Referts, which is also rather unforthcoming when young but has the acidity which gives it vivid definition as it matures, sometimes rather mineral in character. And the Bienvenues, of which they make only between five hundred and eight hundred bottles a year, is always the most substantial, with a touch of spice, but also with some of the lean elegance of the Perrières.

Carillon's red wines are unusually interesting for a producer of Puligny. The St-Aubin is the most straightforward. The vines ripen the earliest because the vineyard is covered in large stones which store and reflect the heat of the sun, and the wine can be a touch too soft in very ripe years but normally has the appetizing astringency which you might expect from a red Chassagne – and it turns out that the vineyard is on the border of Chassagne Premier Cru. But this excellent wine is usually labelled Côte de Beaune Villages, because the name St-Aubin is less easy to sell. The light, cherry-like Mercurey and the more substantial red Chassagne (raspberries, plus a lean, stony character) are both rather grander than the simple village appellations might suggest; in each case half the vines are in Premier Cru vineyards but they are blended with the village wines to make a single cuvée.

Louis Carillon ('Loulou' to one and all in Puligny) stands foursquare at the centre of village life, a man of substance in every sense of the word. His father is widely loved, his mother was the daughter of François Virot (renowned régisseur of Domaine Leflaive who did so much to establish the reputation of Puligny's finest wines) and through his wife he is connected to the intricate clans of Chassagne. Her father was Monsieur Couson, *ébéniste* of that village (he restored old furniture), and her sister is married to Jean Pillot, viticulteur. 'I'm good friends with several of the growers of Chassagne.' And following Jean Chartron's loss of office, Loulou Carillon is now the bastion of the right on Puligny's village council.

So it seemed natural, when Puligny was host for the St Vincent Tournante in January 1991, and a hundred thousand visitors crowded its narrow streets, that it was Monsieur Carillon's turn to be Président of the Confrérie du St Vincent. Dressed in his best suit, with his badge of office around his neck and an air of bluff self-importance radiating into the cold winter air, Monsieur Carillon expressed with greater force than any more cosmopolitan figure could have done the strong, rural foundations which support the glamorous international reputation of Puligny and its wines.

Chartron

On 27 November, 1879, the day that the authorities gave formal recognition to the new name, Puligny-Montrachet, which linked an obscure village to the glory of its most famous vineyard, Jean-Édouard Dupard was a happy man. As mayor of the village he had campaigned tirelessly for the change of designation and in common with all those who dealt in its wines he knew that the official decree would be to his profit. Puligny-Montrachet looked grand on a label. Thus baptized, even the most modest of village wines sounded like a close cousin of Montrachet itself, and could command a suitably enhanced price as a result. Politics and commerce had blended into an emollient balm. But there was a fly in the ointment; on the same day that Puligny was thus ennobled so too was Chassagne, its detested neighbour and rival.

Dupard, nonetheless, was the hero of the hour with his fellow villagers and his prosperity was increasingly assured. He had established himself in Puligny twenty years earlier, in premises on the Place du Monument. You can still just discern the faded letters of his name above a broad stone archway through which they rolled the barrels, both full and empty, that were the staple of his business as tonnelier and wine merchant. It was evidently a successful concern, sufficient to keep Mayor Dupard in bourgeois comfort and to provide a substantial dowry for his daughter.

She married a local viticulteur, Edmond Chartron, and they established a dynasty which is still a force to be reckoned with in the political and commercial life of Puligny. Edmond invested the profits of his father-in-law's business in vineyards, his most notable purchase being the best part of a hectare of Chevalier-Montrachet which he acquired in 1917. The domaine of this marriage can still be identified by the stone gateways (in Chevalier, Clos du Cailleret, Les Folatières and Clos des Pucelles) which bear the name Chartron Dupard. These vineyards remain the core of the family's holdings today, together with others just below the village producing Bourgogne Rouge and a patch in the plain, near the railway line, which is planted with old vines of Aligoté.

Edmond also followed his father-in-law as mayor of Puligny, in which office he was succeeded by his son Jean-Georges and grandson Jean-René, present head of the family. Jean Georges was responsible for the twinning of Puligny with Johannisberg, the renowned wine village in the Reingau. That was in 1966. His son Jean-René became mayor in 1977. As an act of filial piety and family aggrandizement he had the old village washing pool at the corner of the Place des Marronniers converted into a reception room, named after his father. In March 1990 Jean Junior was voted out of office, an upheaval which he clearly had not expected and still finds disagreeable. He claims that he was in trouble with the church, as well as with the left, but it is not clear whether this was a matter of politics or morality. It is certainly true that politics in France has always been regarded as a route for the advancement of self-interest as much as the public good. How far that was true for the Chartrons in a small community like Puligny is hard to say, but the position of mayor cannot have harmed their business.

Chartron's long campaign to improve the classification of his vineyards undoubtedly needed every ounce of political leverage and bureaucratic understanding to achieve success. Despite considerable local opposition Jean-René eventually managed to obtain official approval for segments of vineyard above Le Cailleret to be re-classified Grand Cru (effectively doubling the value of the land) and he is said to nurture a similar ambition for the whole of Clos du Cailleret, a fine Premier Cru vineyard (three hectares in extent) which he owns in its entirety. Geography might appear to favour his claim but the fact is that Le Cailleret has never made wine of comparable substance to its neighbour Montrachet or of comparable elegance to Chevalier, nor does it do so now under Chartron's ownership. It must have been a bitter blow for Jean-René to lose his political power base in the midst of this long campaign but there seems less likelihood now that he will ever succeed in his grandiose scheme.

The timing of the election was particularly galling since it was in 1990 that Chartron finally regained full control of Clos du Cailleret, at the expiry of a contract which had entitled the négociant Robert Drouhin to the entire white wine harvest from this vineyard. Drouhin vinified the wine in his cellars and sold it under his own label, making Clos du Cailleret of such quality that few think Chartron can equal it. But Jean-René must have hoped that the vineyard's return to his full control would have coincided with its elevation to Grand Cru, and that he could have convinced the critics that his winemaking matched its status.

There are indeed those who speak highly of Chartron's wines, but I remain less convinced. Jean-René himself is quite evidently proud of his abilities as an oenologue, insists that he does all his own analyses in the laboratory and claims that he employs a young oenologist primarily to provide expertise in the making of red wines, of which he himself has less experience. The domaine does produce a couple of agreeable reds, including the only red Premier Cru of the village, from Clos du Cailleret. It has something of the stony, appetizing leanness of a red Chassagne and I like it very much. In fact I prefer it to any of Chartron's whites.

Parallel to his running of the domaine, Jean Chartron controls two businesses as a négociant. One is the old family firm of Dupard Aîné, the other a more recently established company which he founded in 1984 in partnership with Louis Trebuchet. Trebuchet (the name means

Chartron has some of the best vineyards in Puligny.

bird trap) had gained considerable experience with another firm of né-gociants in Beaune and is an ambitious man who, like Chartron, has political connections. He is assistant to the mayor of Beaune. The firm of Chartron & Trebuchet specializes, of course, in the wines of Puligny but also handles others from the Côte d'Or. 'We prefer to buy grapes, sometimes must, rarely wine'; in other words they want to exercise con-trol over their raw material at the earliest possible stage. It is a policy which should yield quality, but so far the results have been lacklustre.

Chartron also operates two wine-importing companies in Germany, where he spent twenty-five years before returning to Puligny. It was there, in the Saar, that he met his wife. Her mother was from Alsace, her father a Basque, so their three children have an unusually interna-tional background. And the eldest son, Jean-Michel, is busy learning Japanese with a view to developing further export markets for their wines. All of which suggests a family which has commerce in the veins. But I wonder whether they fully grasp the necessity for some substance behind the label.

This thought was provoked by the curious non-event of my last meet-ing with Monsieur Chartron. I had been invited to a party in his cel-lars to celebrate his re-acquisition of full control over Clos du Cailleret, an event which was supposed to bring together a number of interna-tional journalists and all his closest friends from the village. I found my-self standing outside his house, twenty minutes after the appointed hour, wondering where the party was. Just as I was about to leave, Jean-René glided to a halt on the pavement, talking into the car telephone of his air-conditioned BMW. It felt like a sequence by Fellini, paradigm of the technology of modern communications which renders human contact redundant. The erstwhile mayor of Puligny seemed surprised to see me and announced that since none of the famous journalists had turned up he had rescinded the invitation to his fellow villagers and cancelled the party. Without the media, there was no message.

Chartron has some of the best vineyards in Puligny and has invested in fine equipment for the cellars, but something is lacking: the spark which distinguishes the great winemakers from the rest. Perhaps a new generation may soon be inspired to realize the full potential of this in-heritance. At present you might say that they are marking time.

Clerc

At nine-thirty at night, in the middle of the vintage, Bernard Clerc's yard looks like the premises of a twenty-four-hour breakdown service. An arc light shines on a dripping mechanical harvester and on a welder who is repairing one of the beaters of the machine. Monsieur Clerc himself is busy in a nearby workshop, mending a small pump, surrounded by spare parts for the harvester and other engineering components, less easily identified. Spanners and wrenches, screwdrivers, hammers, files and the specialized tools of the enthusiast are displayed in their slots above the workbench. Bernard has the pale knobbly knuckles and wrinkled brow of the true mechanic and his stained overalls confirm the impression that here is a man who missed his vocation. He should never have been a vigneron; it is not the slow rhythms of agriculture which interest him, nor even the wine itself. He comes alive whenever a machine is involved, and likes nothing better than explaining or dismantling the innards of his latest acquisition. Pipes snake across the floor, connecting presses and pumps and heat exchangers and tanks. Discarded mechanical objects lie on every ledge. You expect to see pools of grease rather than puddles of wine or water. The cellars have the scruffiness of the motorcycle freak, whose machine is more often spread out on the ground as a mass of chains and cogs and gears and a sump full of thick oil than assembled into the sweetly running entity it was designed to be.

Bernard Clerc was, inevitably, one of the first in the village to acquire a mechanical harvester. He bought a prototype machine in 1982 and replaced it with a Braud four or five years later. He uses the harvester in all the vineyards he can get it into (which means not the Grands Crus) and demands that it work day and night. The machine that I witnessed being repaired in the yard was eventually hosed down and sent out again, shortly after ten o'clock. It was expected to complete a further two and a half hectares by dawn. Clerc now employs fifteen pickers where he previously needed sixty and he completes the vintage in six days instead of ten. He claims that the quality of the machine-harvested juice is as good as with the hand-picked crop, but this is said in such a way as to suggest that quality is not the first priority.

Similarly in the cellars, Bernard Clerc claims to prefer the efficacy of his Dabrigeon *égoutoir* ('in an hour you have made the wine') to the slower, gentler and to my mind more refined action of his Bucher pneumatic press. The Grands and Premiers Crus are vinified in oak barrels (from François Frères) and the rest in stainless steel, enamel-lined tanks or cement cuves. Sacks of sugar are stacked in the corners, but that is regrettably typical of most Burgundian cellars. Maturation, on the other hand, takes place in the rare luxury of cool, underground cellars, in an old stone quarry up on the hill at Blagny.

It is here that Bernard lives, in the ugliest house of the commune (a Swiss-style chalet, like a large cuckoo clock). The nineteenth-century façade of his premises in Puligny appears to be that of a grand and spacious house, but in fact the entire ground floor and part of the first floor are occupied by the business of making wine. Bernard's father, the Henri Clerc whose name is perpetuated in that of the domaine, lived over the shop, as it were, and died there in 1971. But Bernard prefers to be up on the hill, with commanding views in every direction over the vineyards and down to the distant village. Perhaps this reflects a certain shyness in society (at a party in his cellars I have seen him scurrying around checking that the pipes of wine were still flowing from tank to tank rather than chatting to his guests), but his eyrie at Blagny also enables him to survey almost all the twenty-six hectares of his domaine, much of which he has patiently acquired since he took charge in 1965. There are parcels in Chevalier and Bâtard and Bienvenues-Bâtard-Montrachet; in the Premier Cru vineyards of Les Pucelles, Les Folatières, Les Combettes and Champ Gain; in the lesser appellations of Puligny and Bourgogne.

Bernard is the principal architect of this domaine. His family has long been established in Puligny (since the seventeenth century on his father's side and the thirteenth on his mother's) but his great-great-grandfather made the family fortunes as a foudrier (constructing large vats and wine casks) rather than as a vigneron. And this relative disinterest in the wine still seems a family trait. Bernard himself is passionate about archaeology (as well as grease-monkey engineering) and his son Laurent, who was expected to join him in the management of the vineyards, has decided on an alternative career. It's not clear whether this is because of or despite his marriage to Veronique Michelot, sultry blonde daughter of the most extrovert vigneron of Meursault. So Bernard Clerc's hopes for the succession rest with his own daughter, Corinne.

She has a substantial task ahead of her. At present about half the production of the domaine is sold to the négoces but most of the rest is exported, and the reputation of the wines is high. In my view that renown is not matched by top quality and I believe that sooner or later Corinne Clerc will be faced with decisions about the management of the vineyards and cellars which could well bring her into conflict with her father's way of doing things. But he is a gentle man and the domaine has the resources to survive. I shall watch their future with fascination.

Sauzet

The cellars are a cluster of tiny, interconnected, stone-vaulted rooms, some of which hold no more than half a dozen barrels. I have difficulty finding sufficient space to stand up in them but Gérard Boudot, who is rather shorter, moves with practised ease from cask to cask, constantly but quietly explaining the differences; in vineyard, or oak, or age of the vines, or picking date. Tasting with him is a fascinating education in the range of factors that must be taken into account by the winemaker, and his response evolves from vintage to vintage.

It is February following the harvest and we start with a white Chassagne. This was the first vineyard to be picked but the wine is still undergoing the malolactic fermentation, the process which transforms the green-apple sharpness of malic acid into the softer, milkier character of lactic acid. In some years the 'malo' follows immediately on from the first, alcoholic, fermentation and in other years it takes time. It can be induced, by inoculating the wine with the appropriate bacteria, but most Burgundians prefer to let nature take its course, simply heating the cellars a few degrees to prevent the sharp cold of midwinter from inhibiting the completion of this natural stage in the wine's evolution. When tasted in mid 'malo', the wine can be cloudy, with a distinct prickle of acidity and gas on the palate, hard to judge. But it is the professional wine buyer's fate always to arrive at the wrong moment; either the wine is undergoing the malolactic or it has just been racked off its lees (sediment) into a clean cask and thereby shaken up, or it has just been fined with the traditional white of egg to clarify it before bottling, or it has recently been bottled and has not yet recovered from the process of being pumped and filtered and generally bruised. You always have to make allowances and sometimes suspect that the grower is using one of these traditional excuses to disguise the fact that the wine really is unexciting.

At Domaine Sauzet I never feel that worry. Gérard Boudot is so evidently an enthusiast of extraordinary competence that I am content to listen to what he says and quietly try to form my own judgements, despite whatever mist of seasonal upheavals may be obscuring the wine. The Chassagne was followed by three different casks of Puligny. One was from a vineyard adjacent to Chassagne and the next from a plot at the other end of the commune, next to the boundary with Meursault. The second was more immediately engaging but the first had better structure, and greater length of flavour. The third cask was a blend from several patches of vines close to the village, some old vines, some young. It had good weight and good balance but lacked, for me, some of the finesse of the first barrel.

We moved on to the first of the Premier Cru vineyards, Champ Canet, and compared a cask from the harvest of 'young' vines (seventeen years old) with another from the old vines (more than thirty years old) and then a third, from vines between twenty and twenty-seven years old. 'The rootstock of this one ripens slower than the others so it's a bit less full but it has good acidity,' said Gérard approvingly as we tasted. All three casks were of Tronçais oak, from Seguin Moreau, tonneliers in Cognac. 'Virot [Jean Virot, the manager of Domaine Leflaive] doesn't like these cask-makers at all – but I love them!' It was said with the defiance of the young turk, challenging the authority of an old man whom he clearly regarded as something of a pedant.

More Premiers Crus followed in swift succession: Referts, Perrières, Truffière (one of my favourites, which we tasted from new oak and from a one-year-old cask, both delicious) and finally Combettes, a vineyard from which Domaine Sauzet consistently produces outstanding wine. The young Combettes seemed very tightly closed but clearly had wonderful structure. 'This always evolves more slowly than the other Premiers Crus,' said Gérard, and lowered his pipette into another barrel. This one was fine, with beautiful balance, a lovely wine. 'The vineyard touches Meursault-Charmes but the wine is always more subtle.' And indeed, this was lighter and more elegant than all but the very finest Meursault.

We moved on to the Grands Crus, tasting a sample of Bienvenues-Bâtard-Montrachet from a barrel of Vosges oak, made by the Meursault tonnelier, Damy. It was so closed that I found it almost impossible to judge. Then a Bâtard-Montrachet, from Tronçais oak. 'This is a mixture of wine from a patch in the Chassagne end of the vineyard, planted with twelve-year-old vines, and from the Puligny end, from old vines.'

I love such detail, and the wine was superb, with a rich elegance, balance and sufficient acidity to give a sinuous length of flavour. We compared this with the same wine from a Damy cask, of Vosges oak. It was quite different, equally alive but much more angular in character.

I have lingered on the details of this tasting because it conveys something of Gérard Boudot's own fascination with his wines, and willingness to experiment. He insists that he doesn't have a fixed programme for any of the vineyards, but treats each as seems appropriate to its character. Nonetheless some general principles hold true, above all the constant pursuit of quality. Which is perhaps somewhat unexpected when you realize that Gérard was a rugby player from Creusot, who happened to marry the granddaughter of old Etienne Sauzet, and who trained as an oenologist before taking over the management of his wife's family domaine. But the very fact the he was not a native of Puligny may have · helped. Unconstrained by strong family traditions, he learnt his own way and always had the challenge to prove himself and win acceptance in a village which often seems to close ranks against outsiders.

Another visit during the vintage. There was the usual seasonal urgency in the cellars as each load of grapes arrived from the vineyards to be emptied into the Bucher pneumatic press ('It's the Rolls-Royce of presses, we get much clearer juice, and better, than we ever did before'), but everyone knew their task and the work was performed efficiently. As soon as the tractor and trailer departed again for the vineyard the hoses were turned on and the floors sprayed vigorously with water until every trace of mud had vanished down the drains. Cleanliness was rigorously maintained, despite the inherent pandemonium of the harvest.

They have a core of about a dozen people who come every year: 'They are well housed, so they come back.' But the full team sits down forty to lunch each day and twenty-seven of them have to be lodged. 'As with other growers, we have houses which only open their shutters for ten days in the year, at vintage time. The population of the village trebles for a few weeks every autumn.'

'Michel, check the temperature of the cooler,' called Gérard, and then we tasted the juice, straight from the press. Les Referts: sweetness, acidity and length of flavour seemed well balanced to me, but unfermented grape juice always tastes good. Making judgements about the future wine is no task for the peripatetic wine merchant; it needs years of experience of the individual vineyards.

'I want the character of each terroir to be evident. I search for maximum finesse. We let the must settle completely at low temperature before racking the clear juice off the sediment of solid particles which could otherwise coarsen the finished wine. Because of this we lose a lot of the natural yeast so we are obliged to add some to get the fermentation going. This year I am experimenting with five different yeasts and also trying it without any addition except a booster crop cultured from the natural yeasts. I like to ferment at between 18° and 20°C and normally start the fermentation in stainless steel cuves in order to keep the temperature low, and then put the must into barrel while it is still fermenting. This year I am using forty per cent new oak, which is more than I used to do, but I tried an experiment with the Combettes last year and thought it gave a very good balance. I use a mixture of three different oaks for each appellation: Vosges and Alliers from Damy and Tronçais from Seguin Moreau. Leflaive keep their wines longer before bottling than I do. I don't systematically keep my wines any particular time after the vintage before bottling them – I decide each one individually. The majority of growers sell their wine in bulk to the négoces because they don't have adequate cellars and also out of habit. I have air-conditioning in all my cellars, but I still sell a bit of Referts every year to Jadot. But ninety per cent of our production is bottled in the domaine.'

From the window of his office in the family house at the top of the village, Gérard Boudot can survey almost all his vineyards as the hill climbs before his eyes. But the number of those vineyards has diminished since the heirs of Etienne Sauzet decided to divide their inheritance, in 1990.

Old man Sauzet is remembered by Bebel Bachelet as a grower who made good, and by a local 'courtier' (broker) as 'a cute old fox, who always over-sugared his wines. But I remember buying 1966 Puligny from him at eight hundred francs per cask, including the cask itself'. Now a new oak barrel itself might cost three thousand. It was Sauzet who established the domaine but Boudot who really made its reputation. The old man had a daughter, Colette, who married a grower from Volnay, Monsieur Boillot. They had two children, the daughter who married Gérard Boudot and a son, Jean-Marc Boillot, who worked for a while as winemaker for Olivier Leflaive, as well as running his own domaine at Volnay. Now the brother and sister have split the old Sauzet domaine between them. Jean-Marc has taken the whole of La Truffière, and parts of the other vineyards. It will be interesting to see what he makes of them. Gérard is left with a reduced but still important domaine, to which he is intent on adding further vineyards by purchase.

Boudot has also decided to augment his production by acting as a négociant-éléveur, buying grapes and must from other growers which he vinifies and matures alongside the wines of the domaine. So confident is he of consistent quality that the négociant and domaine wines are now blended together, appellation by appellation, and sold under a single label. It is a most unusual arrangement which focusses on the winery, not the vines, à la California. Fully as I understand the imperatives of inheritance, I cannot but regret the partition of the domaine.

Gérard Boudot, the outsider, has built an international reputation which vies only with that of Leflaive, for the finest wines of Puligny. Both use the word 'finesse' to express their ambition as winemakers, yet each produces utterly different wines, which somehow reflect the personality of their makers and the history of the two domaines. Sauzet's wines are spicier, more pungent, with a directness and vigour, slightly peasant despite their quite evident refinement. Leflaive's wines are those of a gentleman farmer, with a subtlety and allusiveness that suggests the many-layered civilization of a cultured family. Both express the extraordinary potential of these vineyards at a level which even the best of their rivals can rarely approach.

11 | Uncle Vincent

He's getting old now, nearly eighty, and has noticeably aged since an attack of cancer of the spine, a few years back; but Vincent Leflaive still conveys the spirit of a much younger man, a charmer with the civilized dash of a gentleman farmer whose past is not entirely respectable. There are those who suggest that his earlier career, 'en metallurgie', was in some way connected to arms dealing, and numerous others will imply, with the amused affection of old friends, that Vincent has a light-hearted past of amorous adventure. As with all gossip there is probably a kernel of truth in the embellishments of fancy. The family certainly owned a great foundry at St-Etienne, which made armaments during the war and was afterwards sold to Schneider; and Vincent's habit of gallantry has given rise to dozens of anecdotes. John Armit, for example, recalls that when he was running the wine merchants Corney & Barrow he tried for five years to do business with Vincent Leflaive and finally obtained his agreement after a meeting in Paris. 'I'm quite sure that it was a mutual interest in beautiful women that persuaded him to give me the lion's share of the wine he had available for England.' John has never been persuaded to reveal more, leaving the impression that their encounter was at an elegant 'maison de passe' or as rivals, in the bedroom of a mistress.

Vincent can certainly charm the hearts of young and old alike, with the amusement in his intelligent eyes and a few mischievous phrases.

He looks a bit like a jaunty tortoise, wearing a silk cravat, but he is far more than the Anglo-Saxon caricature of a Gallic adventurer. The warmth and wit of his personality are sufficient in themselves to attract strangers and locals, customers and employees, but what really sets him apart is his adherence to the great social virtues: generosity to his dependants, hospitality to his visitors, courtesy to everyman and a capacity for heroic and hidden resignation in the face of changing times and the failings of his acquaintances, his family or himself. In the highest sense of the word, Vincent Leflaive is a gentleman.

But he can also be unyielding in the pursuit of what he believes to be right and has an exact shrewdness which never allows him to undervalue the marvellous wines he makes and sells.

The Sons of Joseph

The family Leflaive traces its lineage back to 1580. At that time it was based at a small village near Beaune, but on 3 February 1717 Claude Leflaive married Nicole Vallée, widow of Claude Girardin, in the parish church of Puligny and since that date their descendants have lived in the village, occupying for eight generations the house which is now owned by Olivier Leflaive, on the Place du Monument. Claude Leflaive's son (inevitably another Claude) is shown on the eighteenth-century land register of the Seigneur de Puligny as the proprietor of this house and as owner of vineyards around the village. A century later the family possessed five hectares of vines including a parcel of Bâtard-Montrachet. But it was Joseph Leflaive, Vincent's father, who created the present domaine.

Joseph was a brilliant marine engineer who had a varied career in the Far East at the end of the last century and was a member of the team which built the first French submarine. Following his marriage to Camille Biétrix de Villars he took charge of his father-in-law's foundry of La Chaléassière, at St-Etienne. The business made his fortune and he used part of this wealth to buy vineyards around his ancestral village.

Joseph had inherited only two hectares from his father, but between 1905 and 1925 he took advantage of the depressed state of viticulture to buy a further twenty-five hectares, in most of the great vineyards except Le Montrachet itself. Eventually his domaine included holdings in Chevalier, Bâtard, Bienvenues, Les Pucelles, Clavaillon and Les Combettes, as well as Puligny and Blagny. Joseph acquired twenty-five hectares of meadow land, plus numerous buildings in the village, including the present cuverie and cellars.

In 1920 Leflaive was joined by François Virot, who became manager of the domaine and helped to formulate a ten-year programme of replanting the vineyards with the appropriate vines and rootstocks. Virot was one of the most outstanding vignerons of his generation and is remembered as a legendary figure in Burgundy; a man of integrity and wisdom whose contribution was of vital importance to the development of the domaine.

Finally, in 1926, Joseph Leflaive decided to retire from his business at the age of fifty-five and returned to live at Puligny. He wrote that he was 'filled with the conviction that there was work to be done in this community, involving family continuity and the integration of a human being with a place, with the land'.

Joseph Leflaive and François Virot continued the replanting of the domaine, replacing Aligoté and Gamay with Chardonnay, and they gradually developed the renown of the domaine label. Until 1933 sales were still primarily in bulk to the négociants, but they pioneered the concept of domaine-bottling, gradually building up sales to restaurants in France and eventually beginning to export the Leflaive wines to the United States. But essentially life remained much the same as it always had been. Vincent (born 1912, the youngest of six children) remembers a village which had the stillness of a sepia-tinted photograph.

'Sixty years ago we worked the land with horses. We had twenty-six hectares of vines and twenty-six hectares of meadows. Because of phylloxera the vines yielded nothing to live on at the beginning of the century and all the vignerons grazed cows and pigs. We didn't have running water here in Puligny until 1955. In the hot weather I used to bathe myself at the pump in the yard. I lived at my father's house then, where Olivier lives now, and the other family house was the Maison Fleurot, in Place Johannisberg, which was eventually sold to Chavy. There used to be four tonneliers at Puligny, now there's only one in the entire region, at Meursault. There used to be a blacksmith here who could fix anything, even cars, but he's been gone fifty years. There were three cafés in the village; the last to close was Le Coufy, named after an old vigneron who's dead now. What have we left? Two épiceries [now one], the hairdresser, an electrician, a stonemason, a baker and the hotel, which employs three or four people from the village.'

Few of these changes were apparent in the lifetime of the old patriarch, Joseph Leflaive. He celebrated his golden wedding in 1948 and his family gathered round to pay homage. The photograph shows twenty-two of them, from toddlers to grey-haired couples, all plainly in awe of the top-hatted figure of the old man, standing with his wife Camille slightly apart from the rest, the head of his tribe. Even had Joseph not been so dominant a personality, there was no place for his two sons, Jo and Vincent, in the management of the domaine. François Virot knew his job backwards and needed no instruction from the young Leflaives, and in any case, as Vincent recalls, 'Our family domaine didn't make any money in the early days, so both my brother Jo and I made other careers for ourselves. He went into insurance. I worked for Shell in Indo-China, then in textiles in France, then in metallurgy. I spent three years in America between 1947 and 1950 and after my return to France I worked for twenty-five years in Paris, until 1977.'

But in 1953 Joseph Leflaive died, three days short of his eighty-third birthday and the two brothers jointly took charge of the domaine. Jo was forty-five, Vincent forty-one. Jo inherited the family house on the Place du Monument but his business was in Grenoble, so his visits were irregular. Vincent came down from Paris every weekend and needed somewhere to live. In 1954 he managed to buy one of the loveliest houses of Puligny, with a large walled garden, situated close to the cellars of the domaine at the north-west corner of the Place des Marronniers. 'It used to belong to an old family of the village, called Mathouillet. There were two children (one was a daughter who married Dr Clouzelle) and they sold it to a négociant who went bankrupt. I bought it from him. Part of the house was an old bakery – but everyone in the village used to bake their bread in those days. At the end of the garden there was a pond, fed by the land drains from the surrounding vineyards. It was stocked with fish for the village but now it is empty because the tractors have broken up all the drainage gullies.'

Vincent's reminiscences are spiced with details such as these, filled with the colour and texture of a vanished village life, expressed without undue nostalgia but with unrivalled experience and often with a gentle but biting wit. There is no one else in Puligny who remembers as much as he and none who values those memories with such affection, and with so little tendency to judge the events or personalities of the past.

The early days of the brothers' management of the domaine saw little change. Day-to-day operations were still supervised by François Virot; Jo Leflaive took overall charge of the financial and administrative affairs of the business, while Vincent concentrated on technical matters and on sales. They wanted to invest in improvements to vineyards and cellars, in the best equipment, in quality generally, but the wherewithal was lacking. Then along came a tall, affable American with a passion for burgundy: Colonel Frederick Wildman.

'He was on the board of National Distillers and then left and bought a company called Bellows which had imported Leflaive wines into the States. That must have been some time between 1947 and 1959. Wildman spoke French very badly but he was a wonderful man and a tremendous taster. He used to come twice a year, in May and at the vintage, and he helped us a lot because he would pay for his wine at the moment of the vintage, or shortly after. He asked us for 50 per cent of the harvest and I agreed. I have a debt of gratitude to the Colonel. His son Freddie is not involved in the house of Wildman which now belongs to Hiram Walker, which in turn is owned by Allied Lyons. So you English own our American importers. They no longer take as much of the harvest but it is still very important, about twenty-five per cent.

'One other great figure of those days was another American, Schoonmaker, who did so much to promote a real understanding of Burgundy in the States. Now of course we have Americans like Mondavi producing Chardonnays which win competitions against ours. But I'm very happy with what Mondavi is doing and I'm not at all worried by competitions. The Americans tend to make extreme judgements. I think it's to do with their extreme weather – three feet of snow in New York!'

The Pursuit of Quality

One of the great arguments (among those who have some experience of wines made before the widespread use of agro-chemicals and the development of clonal selection) is whether the best wines of the past were finer than anything made now. It is an argument which has particular relevance to Domaine Leflaive, because they regularly produce wine at the maximum legal yield per hectare, yet mysteriously combine this quantity with undoubted and consistent quality. Vincent is untroubled.

'Everything which is past benefits from time. People forget the bad wines and the difficult vintages. They talk a lot about excessive yields these days, but the 1929 harvest was magnificent and we made double the normal *rendement*. Perhaps the best years don't keep so long now as they did formerly, but the less good years last extremely well. In any case the size of the harvest is not really a question of quality; the big difference now is that we have all these controls against insects and diseases, so of course the yields are higher. With our new tractors we can treat the entire domaine in a day and a half, at exactly the right moment. Some things you must treat against within three days or the crop is lost. In fact here we prune rigorously, leaving eight eyes on each vine, whereas at Chassagne they normally prune longer, leaving twelve eyes.'

It is an apologia of some conviction but I remain sceptical. I cannot believe that the use of pesticides and herbicides is other than dangerous for the long-term health of vine and soil and I feel sure that lower yields produce more intense flavour. Perhaps that is unnecessary with so distinctive a grape variety as Chardonnay, particularly for a domaine which emphasizes elegance above all else. In any case, the best wines often seem to be those made by winemakers with the strongest convictions, however eccentric, and Vincent has his own particular hobby-horse.

'I think time is very important for the winemaker. The vintage should not last more than fifteen days and we must harvest as late as possible. Here we never commence before the equinox on 21/22 September, because it signals a change in the weather. And we don't pick when it's raining. Plenty of people harvest too early because they have a contract with the négoces or they have a team of pickers standing idle. We prefer to wait although we still pick by hand. It costs a bit more than using machines but I think the quality is better and in eight years out of ten the weather is good in October and we don't need the speed of a machine. It's only in wet years that the speed of the machine has its advantages. But of course we don't use those huge old presses any more. They were so slow that you could still be pressing at two or three in the morning, and they oxidized the juice. The modern presses work faster and better. It's the same with the pumps – we used to pump the wine by hand, for hours at a time, which fatigued it as much as it did us. Now we deserve to be scolded if we don't make good wine.'

The argument over fermentation in wood or stainless steel is one that flares up from time to time, on both sides of the Atlantic, but once again Vincent takes a pragmatic view.

'All our wines are vinified in wood, either in barrels or the large *foudres*, but this is more difficult because each cask has to be looked after. And if you don't have really good oak it's better to vinify in stainless steel. We have changed the methods of ageing [after their period in cask the wines of the domaine are stored before bottling in stainless steel] but not the vinification.

'The problems these days are in the vineyards, with diseases like *l'esca*, a sort of fungus that can attack the rootstock, causing the vine to die. When we used to plough the vineyards, alternately taking earth away from the roots and then piling it back up against the vines, this disease was not as common. Now we use herbicides (not for the young vines, those under four years old, but for all the older vines) and perhaps that does not protect the plants as well. And we have a big problem with erosion. The rain washes away the soil and every year we have to carry it up the hill again, especially in Chevalier.'

Such tasks are part of the repetitive annual cycle of work at the domaine, but Leflaive has also had to cope with reclamation on a more dramatic scale. For a good many years they have owned a plot in the Premier Cru Folatières, but it was in a very bad way; almost bare rock, with hardly anywhere for the vines to gain a foothold. Eventually, in the early eighties, they spent a fortune dynamiting the rocks and re-planting the vineyard, in order to yield six or seven casks of wine a year.

In the summer of 1991 Leflaive added to this patch of Folatières by the purchase of another plot in the same appellation. At the same time the family fulfilled the dream of every vigneron in Puligny by acquiring from Domaine Fleurot a morsel of Montrachet itself. It's the merest fragment, a couple of ouvrées lying the other side of the village border, in Chassagne; sufficient to make little more than a single barrel of wine each year. But this 'homoeopathic dose', in Vincent's words, is cause for great rejoicing. This is the first time for more than two hundred and fifty years than anyone in Puligny has been able to lay claim to a portion of that 'stony hill'.

Gentlemen Farmers
One of the great strengths of Domaine Leflaive is that it is big enough to employ specialist teams in vineyards and cellars. Dealing with erosion in Chevalier-Montrachet need not cause any interruption in the cellar work. Nor does bottling the wine have to wait for a convenient gap in the seasonal round of urgent tasks in the vineyards. 'It's very difficult to work as a vigneron in the vineyard all day and then do your

Michel Mourlin came rolling along on his bike and braked breathlessly to a halt.

cellar work properly when you get back at six in the evening.' Vincent's comment is a statement of the obvious but runs contrary to the traditional mentality of the peasant grower, which is to do everything himself. And one of the most attractive things about the way his philosophy has been implemented at the domaine is that it seems in no way to demean the individuality of each employee. These are not mere functionaries, but colourful characters in their own right.

The régisseur (manager) of the domaine until his retirement in 1989 was Jean Virot, son of the famous François, whom he succeeded in 1964. It must have been hard to follow in the footsteps of such a father and there is no denying that opinions of Jean Virot have been less generally laudatory. Virot was in charge of a large team at the domaine, probably larger than it need have been had he exercised effective control over their work, and he seldom gave me the impression that he really understood the fundamentals of great winemaking. Vincent has never in my hearing spoken a single word of criticism of his régisseur but he did once suggest, in the lightest possible way, that their outlook was not entirely as one. 'We at the Domaine look for elegance above all. We are very attached to harmony and finesse. Of course we have our differences. I prefer young wines but Jean Virot likes old wines.' Virot indeed seems to have been born an old fogey and it is my belief that the wines of Domaine Leflaive achieved their remarkable quality by some mysterious process of osmosis between Vincent and Michel Mourlin, the head cellarman (and Michel Thusseau, the chef des vignes) which bypassed Virot entirely. Mourlin, too, is now retired but he is a delightful man who was always on the move, muttering to himself as he went. I doubt whether he or Virot ever listened seriously to a word that the other said, a situation that could be highly entertaining to the outsider.

I was standing outside the hotel one morning, contemplating a grey sky, when Jean Virot swung one long leg over his old-fashioned bicycle and came leisurely to a halt beside me. We chatted in a desultory way about the wine market in general and about prices in particular. Virot would not be drawn into anything which might sound like a specific opinion on the subject, preferring oracular pronouncements of Delphic ambiguity. 'It is easier to deceive yourself than to undeceive yourself,' was his last word on the subject, uttered with an air of unctuous authority. Virot's tall, slow-moving figure, topped by a dark beret, his pedantic, lugubrious voice and his Cheshire cat smile were in comical contrast to the short, bustling figure of Michel Mourlin, who came rolling along on his bike at that moment and braked breathlessly to a halt in order to pass the time of day. Peering through the pebble lenses of his spectacles at the cloud-filled sky, he heaved a tremendous sigh. 'Ah well, at least it's not vintage time. No danger of rot now. If you have grey rot it's a misery. With the red wines particularly – you get none of those little purple pellicules that give colour when alcohol contacts them.' Then he jumped on his bike again and headed off to the cellar.

Virot has now been succeeded by Pierre Morey (an exceedingly-well respected vigneron from Meursault) and Michel Mourlin by Jean Jaffelin. But the third member of the critical triumvirate at the domaine remains in place. Michel Thusseau, head of the vineyard team, is a sturdy man in his fifties, who inherited the position from his father, old Louis, one of the most delightful characters of Puligny. With his beret pulled firmly down on his head and an air of no nonsense with his workers, Michel strikes me as an extremely capable man, though perhaps one who might find it difficult to adjust to any changes in viticultural policy. He has a smallholding of his own, which he works at the weekends. Sometimes he sells the harvest to the négociant firm of Olivier Leflaive; driving a hard bargain, it is said, as he tries to pull a fast one over his boss.

Together with the core of loyal workers, devoted to the domaine, these men make a good team, however fallible individually. And Vincent is very much aware of the advantages of such an organization, able to rely on each section to undertake its specialized tasks. He likes to compare this way of working with the traditional peasant proprietor's determination to do everything himself. The epitome of that mentality is Pierre Ramonet, now in his eighties, patriarch of the finest domaine in Chassagne. 'Ramonet's father started buying vineyards at the beginning of the century and they gradually built up a wonderful domaine, but I have seen old Pierre Ramonet preparing his grafts at seven or eight in the evening, at the kitchen table. His sole pleasure other than work is putting on his suit every Sunday and taking his family out to lunch, to Alain Chapelle or Paul Bocuse.'

That comment echoes my own experience of meeting Pierre Ramonet one day, as I was on my way to see his grandson Noël. The old man was standing at the corner outside his house, tall but stooped, with long white hair curling over a shabby collar, his cap pulled low over his brow, wearing a baggy cardigan (stained and full of holes) and a dusty pair of corduroy trousers. To my intense surprise he grabbed my elbow like a lifelong friend and launched into a story, as if we had been interrupted in conversation a few days earlier.

'You know I was in Paris recently for a prostate operation. Well I was getting fed up with being stuck in hospital, so eight days after the operation I said to my doctor, "I'm not staying here tonight, I'm going out to dinner at a good restaurant, I'm going to Taillevent [possibly the finest restaurant in Paris]. Will you come with me?" He seemed a bit taken aback and said, "But there's a two-month waiting list, you can't get a table there, just like that." "Of course I can," I said. And I picked up the phone and got a good table straight away. They all know me, old Ramonet. When you're as well known as I am you can always get a table at the best restaurants.'

Indeed what French restaurateur, anxious to guard his precious allocation of the greatest white wines of Burgundy, could refuse a table to Pierre Ramonet, producer of the finest Montrachet, and which of them would recognize the old man if they met him on the pavement in Chassagne, dressed like a tramp?

Vincent, on the other hand, could never be mistaken for other than he is. His shabbiness in the vineyards at vintage time is that of the gentleman farmer; the inevitable cravat tucked into the collar of his shirt and a handkerchief into the top pocket of a favourite tweed jacket, well worn but evidently well cut. He greets everyone by name and they all respond with a smile of respect and of affection. And he kisses all the girls as he greets them. 'Not *all* of them,' insists Vincent, when I mention this. 'Only the pretty ones.'

Tasting the Wines

Vincent's personality and his enthusiasms are reflected in his wines. The hallmark of the domaine is elegance, even in a simple Bourgogne Blanc or Puligny, and this is particularly apparent when you taste the Premiers Crus. But there is also a characteristic which I can only describe as a refined sexiness, evident in all their best wines, as Vincent himself is well aware. Le Clavaillon, for example, is consistently fine, subtle and sophisticated, a wine for savouring quietly with a friend; but it never has the sheer excitement of its immediate neighbour, Les Pucelles. That, in Leflaive's hands, has a richer, spicier, more floral character, an enticing

'Only the pretty ones.' Vincent Leflaive and a member of the vintage team, October 1988.

allure. 'This Pucelles is a pretty girl,' says Vincent approvingly as he tastes the latest vintage. And at the level of the Grands Crus similar comparisons apply. The Bâtard-Montrachet is always magnificent in a grand, substantial and slightly self-important way. It is often more marked by oak than the other Leflaive wines and sometimes has a distinct taste of acacia honey. 'It's a wine for men of affairs, directeurs-generals, for men of business. But for a tête-à-tête with your wife you must take Chevalier.' And of course he's right, however irritatingly sexist such comparisons may appear. Chevalier is silky, many-layered, with marvellous richness but remarkable finesse. The warm smell of baking bread is often combined with scents of elderflower, hawthorn and lime-blossom. As Leflaive's Chevalier matures you are reminded of fresh straw, marzipan and greengages, with a lingering touch of spice. Tasting a bottle of the '78, eight years after the vintage, Vincent replied to my own exclamation of delight with a nod and a smile. 'It's at its summit now. If you've got a lovely girl, eighteen years old, there's no point in waiting five years.'

The Succession

Since the death of his brother Jo in 1982, Vincent has held together the disparate shareholders in the family domaine (fourteen grandchildren of François Leflaive) and has run the business with inimitable flair. His zest for life and the huge affection which he commands have helped to postpone any serious question of the succession until quite recently. Olivier Leflaive (son of Jo) was made co-gérant with Vincent in 1986 but he was already much occupied with his parallel business as a négociant and seemed (except at vintage times, when he drove the team with cheerful energy) more a representative of one family faction than a vital force in the running of the domaine. Then Vincent contracted cancer of the spine, 'mon petit cancer' as he referred to it cheerfully to his friends. For a while he was expected to die.

The fact that he survived is owing not only to his own unquenchable spirit but to the efforts of his wife, Liliane. For years she has lived in Paris, running a Medical Information Centre, and come down to Puligny only for occasional weekends, 'where I am the wife of my husband'. When Vincent's cancer was diagnosed she immediately took charge, persuading him to accept a course of treatment which involved a carefully controlled diet and a steady intravenous drip of an alternative medication to that prescribed by his doctors. He made a remarkable recovery, after a desperate period of danger, although he is still prone to pain and exhaustion from time to time. There is cause for optimism.

But Vincent accepted his illness as a signal that it was time to retire. His daughter Anne-Claude was appointed co-gérant of the domaine with Olivier Leflaive. Anne-Claude is trained as an oenologist and has a great deal to contribute on the technical side. Olivier has had the experience of working alongside Vincent for several years and is well placed to handle the commercial affairs of the business. Together they now run the domaine but they are responsible to a council of management which represents the main blocks of the family inheritance, divided between the heirs to four of the children of Joseph Leflaive. The other members of the council are Maria Cruz de Suremain and Ludovic de Noue, who appear during the vintage and at other moments of celebration but have no executive role in the domaine. So the third generation of Joseph's family has managed to preserve the vineyards intact and has succeeded in consigning the direction of this inheritance to its two most qualified members, thus far without any major rows; despite the fact that the Leflaives number their fair share of eccentrics and social misfits, some of whom might have been expected to squawk. The question for the future must be whether Anne-Claude's and Olivier's individual strengths can achieve full expression as Vincent's did, or whether the necessity of finding common ground with each other and with the family representatives will cause the domaine's wines to lose any of that characterful identity which is a sign of greatness.

Le Poireau

The transition from one generation to the next was announced on 23 June 1990, at a party to celebrate Vincent's decoration with the order of Chevalier du Mérite Agricole – 'le poireau' (the leek), as it is referred to locally. It was an informal family occasion of great happiness, on a sunny summer afternoon in Puligny. Gathered in the woodshed and other outbuildings of Vincent's house, leading into the garden, was the family (present in force) plus the employees of the domaine, various renowned growers from Burgundy and the Rhône (Gérard Jaboulet, Jean-Jacques Vincent, Hubert de Montille), several English wine merchants and a number of Domaine Leflaive's other importers from mainland Europe. Everyone arrived with a smile.

Soon after five o'clock Liliane Leflaive climbed on to a makeshift stage to announce the order of events and immediately struck the note of affectionate good humour which was echoed by all who followed her. Patrick Leflaive was next, the cheerful and intelligent eldest son of Vincent's brother Jo, who had followed his father into insurance. 'My dear Uncle Vincent,' he began, and then with the greatest affection expressed something of the family's pleasure in Vincent's life and character. The latter, blinking and beaming, clearly touched and trying to look modest, stood listening as praise was gently heaped upon his head. It was also Patrick who announced the formal result of an earlier family conclave, expected by all present, which confirmed that the direction of the domaine was henceforth to be entrusted to his own brother Olivier and to Vincent's daughter Anne-Claude.

Then it was the turn of Hubert de Montille, renowned grower of Volnay, whose gleaming bald dome has been polished by years of wearing the wig of an advocate and judge. Holding his audience entranced, he spoke with all the elegance and wit of which the French language is capable, elaborating a marvellous idyll of the perfect vigneron, endowed with all the virtues. 'Is this Vincent Leflaive? No, it's a dream.' He punctured his own balloon and then blew up another one, more vivid and more real, as he described the character of his subject in terms which we all found instantly recognizable.

The decoration was presented to Vincent by the local Deputé, whose speech had the well-polished patina of the professional politician but was remarkable in one respect. Speaking without notes and without hesitation, he gave a detailed summary of Vincent's life, all the events and dates marshalled, memorized and correct. It was an impressive performance.

Finally it was Vincent's turn. Wearing his habitual cravat and a double-breasted blazer of old-fashioned cut, he looked like a rather rascally yacht owner of the 1930s, but there was a tear at the corner of his reptilian eye and a smile of heart-warming simplicity on his face. Vincent reminded his audience that this was a family occasion and a gathering of friends, asserted that the reputation of the domaine had not been created single-handed but with a team, talked of old François Virot and others of his generation who had re-created the renown of the Côte d'Or and attributed the decoration that he had just received to all those now working at the domaine. 'Jean Virot was the high priest in this work, Michel Mourlin was the canon. As for me, I don't know.' And he stood there, speechless, as we cheered him to the echo.

The Sub-prefect of the Département presented long-service medals to Jean Virot, Michel Mourlin and Michel Thusseau. Rounds of applause greeted each, most warmly for 'Petit Michel', the head cellarman. Virot replied for all of them in his ecclesiastical style, a sermon of praise for his patron, larded with snatches of history. Michel the caviste jumped up to say a couple of words, blinking through his spectacles as he presented Vincent with a garden seat made of willow, a gift from all the employees. And finally it was Liliane again, who gave her husband the presents from the family: a bunch of flowers, a hat and a kiss.

The party ended with everyone drifting into the garden as the shadows of cones and cubes of topiary lengthened on the grass, in the evening sun. And then we strolled across the village to Olivier's where another party was beginning, larger, louder and longer. Five hundred people gathered to celebrate the fifth anniversary of the establishment of Olivier Leflaive Frères, and the festivities continued until dawn. Another style, another generation.

The shadows of cones and cubes of topiary lengthened on the grass, as the party to celebrate Uncle Vincent's decoration ended.

12 | The Family Leflaive

Olivier

His house seems a repository of temporary enthusiasms, filled with a high-tech clutter of uncomfortable modern furniture, computers, musical instruments, faxes, cartons of cigarettes, tennis rackets and executive toys, strewn in all the disorder of a teenager's bedroom. Sometimes his life seems the same. He looks like a middle-aged rock singer turned countryman, recovering from the disillusion of disappointed love. But Olivier Leflaive is also a man of considerable determination, joint boss of the most important family domaine in Puligny and prime mover of a négociant's business which has set new standards of quality.

'Until 1981 I was in show business, organizing shows, a manager, artistic director.' Somewhere along the way he also married, had two daughters and was separated from his wife, who now lives in Grenoble. He retains a preference for blondes and he still sings with his own band OLF, 'just for fun'. It is a threesome consisting of himself, his nephew and his nephew's best friend. They play at the vintage *paulée* and at Olivier's annual summer party in Puligny, and they have borrowed Pink Floyd's studios in London to record a disc, but the music is a medley of Anglo-French rock, evocative of late-night jams in the seventies, and Olivier knows in his heart that it's not very serious.

The domaine is different. 'It's generally an old vocation. My uncle Vincent started aged sixty, me at the age of forty. Young people don't really want to live in these isolated villages and the older generation of peasants always wants to stay in charge to the end. There are often fights

'Until 1981 I was in show business.' Oliver Leflaive at his annual summer party in Puligny.

as a result. But I get on very well with Vincent. He is wise, older, like a father, and I am able to push ahead with new projects. At the domaine in the past two years we've invested more money than in the previous twenty. And I hope that we can regroup the vineyards so that the domaine has a third of its holdings in the Grands Crus, a third in Premiers Crus and a third in Puligny Village. Most viticulteurs have eighty per cent of their vines in the lesser appellations (Bourgogne and Village) and only tiny holdings in the best vineyards. Lamy at St-Aubin, for example, makes only one cask of Bâtard each year; it's difficult to do it well on that scale.

'Domaine Leflaive is different in that respect and also because it is one of the very few (like Laguiche or the Domaine de la Romanée-Conti) where the proprietors don't work in the vineyards themselves. We are a bit despised by the other growers who are in the vines all day and want to do everything themselves: the vineyards, the wines, the financial administration, the sales; everything, because their property is so small. With Domaine Leflaive we are big enough to have a team in the vines, a team in the cellars, specialists where we need them; whereas the small proprietors cannot even employ a maître du chai.

'In fact Puligny has more big domaines than Chassagne, for example. There must be six or seven properties of more than ten hectares, which has permitted their owners to evolve in different ways, more bourgeois than paysan. And they are not very communicative. But the new generation is much more open. I am good friends with Gérard Boudot, for example.'

The trouble was that Domaine Leflaive offered very little scope for real development as far as Olivier was concerned. Not only was Vincent the dominant figure there but the domaine's renown was such that its wines were always on allocation. 'We have refused orders year after year. In France the private customers are limited to twelve bottles a year and we accept no new restaurant clients. And overseas our agents are also strictly rationed.' Not much challenge for someone as interested in promotion as Olivier. In any case he is the restless sort, and wanted to create something of his own.

So, in April 1985, he formally inaugurated the business of Olivier Leflaive Frères, a négociant with a difference. Like all négociants it was dependent for its raw material (grapes, juice or wine) on other growers rather than its own domaine, but unlike most it *had* to achieve the highest standards of quality. It was clear from the start that Olivier could only win family acceptance of his venture if the name Leflaive was going to be associated with standards that could rival the renown of the domaine itself. It says a lot for Olivier's powers of persuasion that eighty per cent of the existing family shareholders in the domaine agreed to take part in the new company, headed by his brother Patrick and his sisters Carole and Marilys.

There were clear advantages to them. Each of the heirs to the domaine owned little more than a hectare of vines (far too many small-holdings to be viable properties on their own) and because of the complexity of its ownership the domaine was unlikely to grow significantly in size. But the new business offered a way forward. In Olivier's words, 'the first object of Olivier Leflaive Frères is to increase the size of the family operation. If the family sees this operation growing they remain attached. The second thing is that it's no fun to say no to a client – we must find a way to augment the Leflaive production to keep the customers happy. As long as the quality remains at the same level as the domaine, Olivier Leflaive Frères is complementary to its efforts. And the third reason is simply that I wanted to do it and I've worked hard to achieve it. Jean-Marc Boillot [his first winemaker] and all the others at the start worked without pay. The first vintage we handled was 1984, which was very difficult.'

Olivier is fond of enumerating the points of his argument, ticking them off on his fingers as he goes. And he continued his exposition by listing the four critical factors for quality: buying grapes or juice (they very rarely buy wine) from good growers with the best sites; unrestricted investment in casks and equipment; patience, let nature take its course; and cleanliness. 'To make good wine you need lots of water; we try to keep the cellars like a hospital.'

To this list I would add a fifth factor of vital importance, the quality of his employees. They are a mixed bunch but mostly young, highly qualified and often slightly eccentric, and there is a quite evident esprit de corps, born of rivalry with the domaine. The original winemaker was Jean-Marc Boillot, highly talented son of a viticultural family from Volnay. His passion was oak and he ran a programme of research into the effects of different oaks, in conjunction with a local laboratory. Tastings with him would often involve comparisons of the same wine from different casks. Boillot's favourite tonnelier was Damy, but he also bought barrels from François Frères, Billon and Seguin Moreau and his budget for oak was big. Although their policy is to renew only a quarter of the barrels each year, Olivier Leflaive Frères can easily spend £100,000 on new oak, every vintage. Boillot's enthusiasm for oak certainly had an effect on the wines, particularly as he was also an enthusiastic 'lees beater'; which means that he liked to leave the wines on their sediment in the barrels and stir it all up regularly to reactivate the yeasts, a process which tends to result in fuller flavour. The result was a style of winemaking which initially seemed to emphasize strong flavours (oak, lees, ripe fruit) over refinement and there were certainly some who felt Boillot was a better maker of red wines than white.

Jean-Marc left in 1989, returning to Volnay to take charge of the family domaine and, more recently, his share of the Sauzet domaine which he inherited jointly with his sister, wife of Gérard Boudot. His successor as winemaker at Olivier Leflaive is Franck Grux, member of a Meursault family of market gardeners; his aunts and uncles still sell vegetables on the market at Beaune. But his mother was a Roulot, from an old family of vignerons, one of three daughters who were all, to their father, substitutes for the son he longed for. To his daughters' continuing fury they were named Simone, Paulette and Noëlle (feminized versions of boys' names, the last of which was choosen because she was born on Christmas Day).

Quietly spoken (until he gets angry), Franck looks more like a pinball wizard than one of Burgundy's best winemakers, and he has a good line in laid-back repartee, particularly when provoked by Ellen Cartsonis, his girlfriend. She is a Greek-American and first announced herself to me on the phone in May 1988 as Olivier's 'directrice commerciale'. He spoke of her at the time as 'my little flirt, my little business flirt.' Their relationship cooled, to the point where Ellen finally quit her job as sales director midway through 1991. It is to be hoped that Franck will not resign in sympathy with her, since his contribution is now of enormous importance to the quality of Olivier Leflaive's wines.

What was good before is now superb. Franck is more discreet in his use of oak, beats the lees less than Boillot, and is very sparing in his use of sugar (none of the white wines were chaptalized in 1989). In that year, too, they bought only juice and grapes, no fermented wine, so were able to exercise control right from the beginning of the winemaking process. And the négociant business is now building its own domaine, so that it is less reliant on buying its raw material from other growers.

But that raw material can be extremely good, if the team at Olivier's gets it to his cellars as soon as possible after the vintage. I hitched a ride once when the van went out to collect some Bâtard-Montrachet from a grower called Gaillot, who runs an extensive domaine from exceedingly modest cellars in the neighbouring hamlet of Corpeau. Dean Korth, a Californian who describes himself as 'the cellar rat', was helping load three empty new barrels into the van, into which the fresh-pressed juice was to be decanted, and then we set off with a clatter into the fog. The driver was a local, who cracked jokes as we went, all of which were rendered entirely unintelligible by the combination of a thick Burgundian accent and the Gauloise Jaune which was perpetually stuck in the corner of his mouth. So I concentrated instead on listening to Dean's life story. Originally from San Francisco, he worked for a Californian wine company, played music on the side, married a French girl he met in Los Angeles and decided to go to France to study wine. So he enrolled in the school of viticulture at Beaune, then worked at Meursault for Dominique Lafon before joining Olivier as general cellarman. He speaks fluent French with an unmistakable Californian accent. 'I enjoy working with the team here but as soon as I open my mouth everyone stares.' In many ways Dean epitomizes the enthusiasm and internationalism which is having such a radical impact on the traditional practices of Burgundy. He may seem an oddball, but this is the face of modern winemaking.

We arrived at a small barn, equipped with a modern Vaslin press, a few traditonal oval fermentation vats, and not much else. You would never guess that this domaine employs between forty and fifty pickers at vintage time and owns vineyards in Chassagne (both red and white) and Puligny, plus a substantial acreage of Aligoté in the plain. But Jean Gaillot is one of those who prefers to concentrate on what he is good at, cultivating the vines, and to sell his entire crop to the négoces. His vats are emptied almost as soon as they are filled and he has no need to invest in expensive casks or the space to store them.

Olivier's casks were unloaded from the van and we hung around while they were filled, chatting to Monsieur Gaillot's cellar-hands. My eye was caught by a bunch of flowers in a jam-jar on the winepress. 'It's for the boss – he's ill with the flu.' They all laughed heartily at his misfortune – ill or not, Monsieur Gaillot was out in the vines with his pick-

Olivier's casks were unloaded from the van and we hung around while they were filled, chatting to Monsieur Gaillot's cellar-hands.

ers, gathering the last of the harvest.

Back in Olivier's air-conditioned cellars, Jean-Marc Boillot rushed by, rolling an empty cask end on end, with the speed and control of long practice, and then gave me an extensive tasting of the previous vintage, during which he expounded at length on his theories on yeasts, the malolactic, oak ageing and chaptalization, while the recently arrived Bâtard-Montrachet was being analysed in the laboratory. It seemed a world away from Monsieur Gaillot's barn.

There is no question that where there is this degree of dedication, the négociant who buys his raw material at the earliest possible stage after the vintage can make great wine. And this is certainly true now at Olivier Leflaive. They buy from the best growers, including famous domaines like Ramonet, and they have allowed an ambitious winemaker to exercise his talents at a much younger age than would normally be likely within the confines of a family domaine. They also make a far wider range of wines than most domaines, using top-quality expertise on the harvest of such villages as Rully, St-Aubin or Pernand-Vergelesses, where expectations of quality would normally be much more modest. Although the key word is always 'finesse', this is harnessed to the clearly stated aim 'to cultivate the differences', to emphasize the typicity of each appellation. And the results are regularly among the finest white wines of Burgundy.

The very success of Olivier Leflaive Frères poses questions for the future. How long can the négociant business continue on its present course of constructive rivalry with Domaine Leflaive and how can Olivier himself maintain a sense of balance as he tries to run both organizations? In particular this is true as the négociant side builds its own domaine. To such problems the answer is frequently the same: Anne-Claude. As she progressively exerts her influence at the domaine she should provide a counterweight to the mercurial character of her cousin Olivier and constitute a focus for the team there to keep up its side of the competition. And the result, if all goes well, could be another period of remarkable achievement for both sides of the family Leflaive.

Anne-Claude

On 2 June 1990, Anne-Claude Leflaive was appointed co-gérant of the domaine, in succession to her father Vincent. She is by far the most technically qualified member of the family ever to have held that position and her arrival completes a team which has changed radically in the past few years, as the old guard reached retirement. It is the beginning of a quiet revolution.

Now in her mid-thirties, Anne-Claude is already grey-haired but has a decidedly youthful grin and a stylish air of energy and enthusiasm. She is always elegantly if casually dressed, in marked contrast to her cousin Olivier, who often looks as if he has slept in his cowboy boots.

She studied commerce for three years in Paris in the seventies (including six months in London and six months in Germany) and from 1973 onwards she came every year to Puligny at the vintage. 'I loved that. I love the vintage.' In 1979 she started a practical 'stage' in the vineyards with Michel Thusseau ('It snowed in '79, it was very cold, very hard') and began a course in oenology at Dijon. But a short while later she left in the midst of her studies, to be with her future husband who was doing his military service in Morocco. On his return to France they married and settled at Dijon, thirty miles north of Puligny. He worked hard at his career in public engineering (building motorways) and Anne-Claude looked after the children, as well as doing some part-time teaching in Adult Education.

But the domaine was always in the background. Anne-Claude was appointed one of the four family representatives who constituted the Conseil du Gestion (Board of Management), and in 1986 she resumed her studies in oenology, completing the course in a year. Having received her diploma as 'technicien oenologue', in June 1987, she constructed her own laboratory at the Domaine and began to put her theories into practice. Now she is joint-director, and travels down the road from Dijon to Puligny at least three days a week.

It was clear from the start that her interests were more technical than managerial, but few people, herself included, can have had any inkling how radical was to be the overhaul of viticulture and vinification at the domaine. She started quietly by studying the vineyards and the techniques in great detail, a project which is still continuing, in order to analyse all the variables which contribute to the final character of the wine from each individual parcel of land. This involves soil analysis, annotation of the different clones that are planted on each plot, study of the vineyard treatments used during the course of each year, study of the maturity of the grapes before the vintage and then detailed recording of every stage of the vinification until the bottling. All of which is complemented by tastings of every batch, trying to identify the differences between each cask or tank of wine. At Vinexpo in Bordeaux Anne-Claude met Monsieur Delon of Château Léoville Lascases who was doing similar studies of his vineyards, to analyse the characteristics of each parcel, and she was also much encouraged by Professor Raymond Bernard at Dijon.

But the work itself has largely been undertaken with Pierre Morey, the new régisseur of the domaine, with whom Anne-Claude has been studying the vineyards since 1987. 'I have complete confidence in him. You can't say enough good things about him.' They go through the vineyards three weeks before the vintage and again two or three times as the picking approaches, analysing the grapes and the health of the vines. 'And we taste the grapes, that's very important, with the characteristics of each vineyard in mind.' As a result of these studies they have recently decided to pick the vineyards parcel by parcel, as indicated by their analysis of the grape maturity, rather than simply harvesting by rote, one appellation after the other. 'We always pick later than the Ban de Vendange [the official start of the vintage] because we look for maximum maturity. The problem is that because of that policy we often find ourselves picking at the equinox when there is a change of the weather. There can be rain and we may lose both alcoholic degree and acidity.' They look for a minimum of 12° of natural alcohol in the basic Puligny, 12.5° for the Premiers Crus and 13° for the Grands Crus.

None of this is particularly startling, merely a refinement of existing practice at the domaine; but Anne-Claude is causing several ripples in the pond of traditional habits by her insistence on one key matter of policy. 'We want to leave as much as possible to nature, to interfere as little as possible.'

The first impact of that determination was on the use of yeasts. 'Before Pierre Morey came we used the advice of the oenological laboratories who said add this yeast or that yeast, and we did it. But I believe it's very important to use the natural yeasts. We stir up the lees two or three times a day to reactivate the yeasts. Before Pierre came that was never done.'

Much more fundamental is Anne-Claude's conversion to the 'organic' point of view, more particularly to the bio-dynamic system as practised by Nicolas Joly of Coulée de Serrant, in the Loire. It happened thus. 'I always buy organic vegetables for myself and in the place that I buy them I saw a poster advertising a conference on the subject at Beaune. So I went. Monsieur Bourguignon, an agricultural engineer and biologist working on the micro-biology of the soil, near Dijon, spoke with great passion.'

Fired with enthusiasm, Anne-Claude organized a conference for local growers at Olivier Leflaive's, on the subject of bio-dynamic cultivation. She got Claude Bourguignon to speak again and also Monsieur Bouchet, who had worked with Joly and who (like Bourguignon) is now a consultant to the domaine. And she found one local grower, Jean-Claude Ratteau, who could also speak with experience and enthusiasm on the subject.

Whether Anne-Claude convinced anyone else is hard to say, but she has certainly convinced herself. The first experiment of the system at the domaine started in October 1990, covering a total of a hectare of vines; divided between basic Puligny, Premier Cru and Grand Cru. The vines were pruned unusually late, in March, and have been treated with concoctions of cow manure and cow's horn, 'dynamized' by stirring for several hours before use, because advocates of the system believe this makes them more active and effective. The timing of such treatments is extremely complex, combining traditional beliefs and high-tech science. They take account of the state of the cosmos and the astrological signs as well as making very precise soil analyses which measure the micro-biological activity of the soil. Other treatments involve silica and similar natural materials, some of which are applied in tiny doses, as in homoeopathy, to achieve the desired results. Synthetic chemicals are out. The bio-dynamic system is based on the writings of Rudolf Steiner and can easily sound cranky in the extreme to the sceptic. But there are two powerful arguments in its favour. One is that it is back to nature with a vengeance, as organic as you can get, which must be good news for all who are concerned about the use of agro-chemicals. The other is that the system has been employed successfully for many years by some astoundingly good winemakers. Apart from Joly, the high priest of bio-dynamic cultivation, you could also point to his neighbour Noël Pinguet at Domaine Huët (unquestionably the most renowned producer of Vouvray) and others in different regions throughout France.

At Domaine Leflaive the experiment will take time. The wines from vineyards treated in this way will be kept separate until the end of the malolactic fermentation and then blended with the harvest of the same appellations which have been cultivated in more standard fashion. Blind tastings will be conducted up to that *assemblage* and the results carefully analysed, to see whether there is any evident qualitative difference in the wines.

Anne-Claude hopes that the results will prove positive and that she can secure family agreement to extend the system to the whole domaine, over a period of four or five years. 'It will be much more economic because we won't have to use all those expensive chemicals. The bio-dynamic system will probably produce a slightly lower yield, of better balanced wines. We prune short now, and we cut off buds and grapes if we think the yield will be too high.' That too is a change of policy at a domaine which for years has regarded high yields as relatively unimportant. Can they preserve Leflaive's legendary elegance if the taste is more concentrated than before?

The question is prompted in part by my notes on a tasting of the '89 vintage of the domaine, which Anne-Claude provided for me immediately after her exposition of the virtues of the bio-dynamic way. The wines were truly splendid, full of fruit but exceedingly well balanced, still rather closed but with the promise of great things. The Clavaillon had its usual elegance and, in this vintage, unexpected depth. The Pucelles was spicy, alive, fascinating. The Bâtard was concentrated and grand and the Chevalier had great length of flavour but had yet to develop its full character. Inevitably the thought occurred, could such wines be better made? Almost immediately I realized that I was falling into the trap set for us by those who are insistent on establishing a league table of the finest wines, with marks out of a hundred calculated to the last decimal point. In fact it is absurd to try to decide in some absolute way whether the finest vintages of Vincent's reign are more or less splendid than those which will be produced by the team of Anne-Claude and Olivier. On the contrary, we should rejoice in the changing character of each generation, secure in the knowledge that whatever the preferences of winemakers or tasters there is still one essential continuum in the history of Domaine Leflaive, the passion for quality.

Colette Imbert

The story of a great domaine is not just about the wines but about the people. Tasting a bottle of Chevalier-Montrachet will give you a flavour of Leflaive, of great splendour and refinement. Talking to Colette Imbert provides a more pungent taste, but no less memorable.

I suppose she must be about fifty but I think of her as ageless. Sturdy, short cropped hair, beautiful from the smile on her face and the vivid immediacy of her character. She works mostly at the 'cantine' where the regular employees of the domaine can eat lunch every working day. There is a system of tickets and she has a budget of £2 a head, with which she provides the most splendid meals. These scraps of her conversation are jottings, noted while following her around the cantine after the end of the vintage, as she cleaned the floor and then prepared the lunch. Alas that my pen could never keep up with the remarkable flow of her words.

'Ah, it's so dirty after three weeks. It's good the vintage, but it's good when it's over.

'It was a happy team, with the usual regulars who come every year. We need the core of habitués, they're like part of the family. I have the impression that they're my children.

'I don't like cooking so much to tell the truth, and we had a cook to help. On Sunday we had to cook for seventy-five people.

'It's a little bit like my own house here. Nobody ever asked me to clean it, but of course I do. There used to be a young girl who worked here with me, but she left to have a baby. I do the cooking, the shopping, the administration, the housework.

'I work for Olivier for an hour in the morning. He said to me, "Colette, you take the role of mistress of the house, you do the flowers and tidy up – and don't forget to clean my car!"

'And when Vincent got ill I went to his house every morning. He's a gentleman, a real gentleman. He telephoned me and said, "Simplement je me paie un petit cancer." So I went whenever he phoned. He had an intravenous drip, some sort of parallel medicine. His wife organized it. And he made a spectacular recovery. Ah, he's a gentleman, in all the excellence of the term.

'I live in the SNCF [railway] buildings, near Chagny. My husband was in the railways; he's retired now. In 1983/4 I started work again, I was a nurse by training, but the place closed just as my husband retired. But I knew Ghislaine and she said Olivier was looking for someone. So I started work for him.

'Then Monsieur Vincent said come and do a bit of work in the office, then in the house, then the cantine. I'm always very reticent about

'It's a little bit like my own house here.' Colette Imbert.

taking on anything else, so I started out of necessity and I continue out of pleasure, perhaps, and respect for the family. Respect and affection mixed up for Vincent.

'I decide what we're going to eat, and I prepare it. I have this little notebook and I write down who eats and when. I am allowed twenty francs per head for each meal. These are the menus for last week:

Salade Frisée, Petits Lardons
Tomates Farcies, Riz
Fromage, Fruits

Salade Composé, Langue de Boeuf
Spaghetti
Fromage, Dessert

Flan aux Olives
Timbales Fruit de Mer
Salade Verte

Crudités
Boeuf aux Carottes
Fromage, Gâteaux

Raclette, Pommes de Terre
Salade Verte
Fromage, Glacés

Avocats aux Crevettes
Hachis Parmentier
Salade Verte
Fromage, Crème Dessert

'I was born in Paris. During the war we moved to near Vichy, in the centre of France. Then I went to school in Lyons, to learn to look after little children. Then a nursing school in the Allier. Then – *what a desolate hole!* – we moved north of Dijon to Les Laumes Alésia. My father who worked in the railways was sent there. We had to keep following him, we had no roots. I was married there and had three children, then we came to live at Chagny, in the hope of moving back to the Allier, but it never happened.

'My grandfather was a railwayman, my father, my husband, my brother-in-law, his son-in-law, my husband's brother – all railwaymen. My dream was that my son should be in the railways too – but he came home one day and said he'd got a job in the EDF [Electricité de France], and he earns a lot more than his father. But I have been lucky because our children have stayed in the region, and I have grandchildren.

'One thing not so many people understand is that I *adore* rugby. Jean-Michel plays, and my son-in-law (he married my daughter). Once when Jean-Michel scored a tremendous try at school, I found myself running along the touchline, cheering him on and I arrived at the same time as him – and everyone cheered! I was just wearing these shoes, not proper running boots.

'I get here between 7.30 and 8.00 in the morning and I normally go home at 2.00. I don't like resting much, I like to be active.

'Something I appreciated from the very first day was that this is a special domaine because they have respect for everyone who works for them. The paulée this year was held in the outbuildings of Vincent's house – and it was very much appreciated by the workers. Anne-Claude put a huge amount into organizing it. They gave presents to all the new vendangeurs and a tremendous meal and so on. They don't always get properly appreciated for it, and that upsets me. They say, 'Oh well, they've got money, it's paternalism.' If that's paternalism I could wish it for every worker.

'The paulée is for the workers, for everyone. They don't like it when visitors join them for the feast.

'What do I like best? I detest the accounts and the money – I was terrible at mathematics at school – but I love to read and I love to talk. And I love to make the cooking look good. I like the pleasure of putting yellow sweetcorn next to bright red tomatoes.'

Celebrations

13 | Vintage

Harvest Festival

Burgundians approach every vintage with a mixture of joy and trepidation. The sense of imminent relief at a harvest safely gathered is clouded by anxiety. A tempest could still destroy the crop which has been nurtured with such constant care while another storm, inevitable and feared, exhilarating as thunder, whirls its unpredictable way through the quiet habits of rural life: the arrival of the harvesters. Like a sudden wind which sets the leaves swirling in the street, bangs doors and shutters and is followed at once by a lull in which you hear inexplicable laughter from an upper room, or a child crying, the pickers are a social tornado. Their breath is anarchy.

Camaraderie and exuberance are fuelled by hard work and wine. Liaisons which at other times would seem inconceivable flower for a moment of madness. Days of exhaustion roll into nights of reckless oblivion until the final day, when the pickers roar back from vineyard to village in a cacophony of triumph; the final night, celebrated with songs and ribaldry at a harvest feast, the paulée; and the sudden sobriety of the morning, dispersal and parting.

Most of the villagers forget their habitual wariness of strangers and smile with indulgent complicity at the antics of these invaders. A few grudge the vagrants their gaudy licence and batten their doors against threatening disorder. Behind shuttered windows they wait for the harvest to be over and their dogs growl at every passer-by. But there are others for whom the vintage is a seasonal fever, eagerly anticipated. They

Camaraderie and exuberance are fuelled by hard work and wine. Members of Leflaive's team, October 1988.

await the pickers as liberators, and harbingers of excess.

Vintagers arrive singly, in couples and groups from the poorest regions of rural France, from the cities, from abroad: students chasing the harvest from one wine district to another, criss-crossing the continent before heading towards the east; a truck-driver and his girlfriend, taking a break from the road; a cluster of high-spirited nurses from a hospital in Rouen; the unemployed, glad of work and companionship. Some are returning for their third or fourth season working for the same domaine, while others come without engagement and simply proffer their services to anyone in need of extra labour. For most it is a working holiday and all have an air of carnival, unconstrained by familiar circumstance and social obligation. They relish the vintage like Mardi Gras, as a time of celebration and licence. With dormitories in tempting proximity 'nuits blanches' are common, followed by a grey awakening.

For their employers, the growers, it is a matter of hard work. The traditional habit of regarding the harvesters as a necessary bane meant that in the old days they were often provided with the most basic accommodation and furnishings, in ruinous hovels; not simply out of meanness but because it was thought that if you put them in a proper house they would only wreck it. And the food was simple. Most growers would fatten a few rabbits before the vintage, to fill out the pot-au-feu, because meat from the butcher was far too expensive. Old Pierre Ramonet is said to have been confronted by his pickers, years ago, with the demand that he provide them with a hot shower, and meat once a day. 'I don't have a shower and I eat my meat on Sundays,' Ramonet replied, and sacked the lot. Nowadays expectations are higher. Houses which stand empty for the rest of the year must be made habitable, dormitories swept and someone organized to cook the pickers' meals. And their equipment (now provided by the domaines) must be checked and prepared. Innumerable pairs of secateurs have to be cleaned, oiled and sharpened, baskets and buckets washed and counted, squeaky piles of waterproof clothing taken out of store. Mechanical things need servicing: tractors and trailers and presses and cooling apparatus. The cellars are cleaned, tanks sterilized and sacks of sugar stockpiled against anticipated need. Are there enough casks and have they been steamed and sulphured? These and uncountable smaller tasks must be remembered now, because once the vintage begins nobody has time for anything but the job in hand.

There is the panoply of officialdom, the necessary proof that all is regulated. A week before the day which the growers have long ago determined is the beginning (already notified to their pickers) a notice appears on the board of the Mairie, signed by the Prefect of Burgundy. It decrees the earliest permissible dates for harvesting each grape variety and appellation. In 1988, for example, the producers of sparkling burgundy (Crémant de Bourgogne) were allowed to start the vintage on 19 September, while growers in the Hautes Côtes de Nuits (whose grapes ripen last) had to contain their impatience for eleven days further. This decree was displayed alongside the minutes of a meeting of viticulteurs (at which Bernard Clerc had pointed out the text of an Article of 1941 allowing each grower to buy up to five per cent of grapes, must or wine to improve the quality of his harvest, and asked for clarification) and a notice setting out minimum rates of pay for the harvesters. Twenty-nine francs an hour for pickers, thirty for porters; deductions of five francs a day for lodging, forty-four francs for nourishment and nineteen point seventy-eight francs for tax and social security; a detailed sum showed that a picker could expect to earn a net wage of one hundred and sixty-three point twenty-two francs, about £15 per day.

To begin at the beginning, on the earliest permissible date, is not necessarily the wisest choice. Local proverbs proffer ambiguous advice. On the one hand the warning ('Quand le rondeau est près, la pluie n'est pas loin' – the new moon brings rain); on the other the comfort ('Si la lune renouvelle en eau, trois jours après il fait beau' – if the moon renews itself in water three days later it will be fine). I prefer the pungent summary: 'Vendanges tot, vendage tard! Vendanges tard, vendage tot.' When the harvest is early, you can afford to wait for the grapes to be fully ripe, and pick late; when the harvest is late, you should hurry, because bad weather may ruin all. Some growers allow familiar habit to relieve them of the burden of this annual decision and always harvest early, or late, in unquestioning allegiance to ancestral tradition. Others (driven by financial necessity) have no other thought than the requirement to sell their wine as soon as possible to the négoces and pay off the accumulated créditors of their agricultural year. Serious producers commit themselves to an anxious gamble, made between weather forecasts.

Pick too soon and you must rely heavily on artifice to make good the defects of nature, adding sugar (the 'sun in sacks') to vats full of unripe grapes. That, nonetheless, is the safer choice. By waiting you may enjoy the warmth of an Indian summer, bringing the grapes to full maturity, but you also risk the autumn storms. Rain dilutes the hoped-for concentration and may cause that greater calamity, grey rot, to spread like a plague through the vineyards, tainting the resultant wine with the smell of decay. Worse, for the white wines, can be thunder, which causes what Jean Marc Boillot calls a 'déclatement des cellules' in the Chardonnay grape, resulting in berries the colour of chocolate, dying from the inside.

The vignerons of the village are not natural risk-takers and the gambler's nervous energy (exhilaration bordering on panic) may be heavily concealed by rural stoicism, but there is an urgency to the vintage which is shared by all, a sense of controlled frenzy. Having made his choice, the vigneron must stick to it and he keeps his nerve by mocking his neighbours. There is always a chorus of voices declaring, on the one hand, that those who picked early missed the vital days of sunshine which transformed a mediocre harvest into a great vintage and, on the other, that those who picked late gathered rain, over-ripeness and rot. 'Chacun défend son bifsteak.'

Sturm und Drang

Monday, 3 October. As I drove up from the Mâconnais after lunch with a grower in Quintaine, the sky darkened and the heavens opened with an earth-shaking crash of thunder. The deluge was so torrential that the road became a river, the car felt like a submarine and my progress slowed to the pace of a middle-aged swimmer, with visibility reduced to a matter of yards. The downpour lasted well over an hour and when it finally eased the low-lying vineyards were flooded and the hillsides were fissured with torrents which exposed the bare limestone beneath its thin covering of red earth. The sky was clear again but the weight of water which had fallen felt sufficient to have stripped every grape from the vines. Having arranged to spend the second week of the 1988 vintage with Domaine Leflaive, it seemed that I was returning in time to witness a catastrophe.

Another crash greeted me in Puligny. Arriving a few minutes after the impact, I could almost hear its echo ricocheting around the village, but already a small crowd had gathered and the sounds of screeching metal and fractured glass had been replaced by the noise of everyone giving his own opinion of events, oblivious of the others. The evening air was filled with gossip.

Two cars were locked together, one astride a battered roadsign, the other surrounded by remnants of the ugly municipal flowerpot which had adorned a small triangle at the intersection of the Rue de l'Abreuvoir and La Grande Rue, opposite the cellars of the widow Moroni. A tremendously fat vigneron leant on one of the wrecks, holding forth to his cronies, while the drivers swapped addresses and insurance details, peering at their documents by the light of a torch. Young men on bicycles swooped through the dark, calling to one another, and passers-by stopped to discuss the incident.

It seemed it was the girl's fault. A picker with the team at Domaine Leflaive, recklessly well charged with wine, she was driving too fast, heading up a one-way street the wrong way. No one was hurt and no one seemed angry, or even much surprised.

Eventually a truck appeared, laden with *marc* (the skins and pips of spent grapes), and the driver was persuaded to hitch a tow rope to one of the vehicles. The car was pulled free, losing some of its bodywork in the process, and a young boy jumped in, furiously, and turned the ignition. To everyone's amazement the engine started and he clattered into the night. Encouraged by this the girl's boyfriend did likewise, disappearing with the ominous grinding sound of mechanical disintegration. The crowd dispersed, the excitement over. I turned over the uprooted roadsign. It said STOP.

A pale light glowed through the mist in the Place des Marronniers, silhouetting a young picker in the call-box, telephoning home. Behind her in the shadows, three local boys were perched like crows on a broad windowsill of the Salle Jean Chartron while Bernard Clerc's dog barked, unseen, from the floodlit yard where an ungainly clutter of tractors and a mechanical harvester dripped in the clammy night. On the other side of the square you could peer into the uncurtained windows of the Domaine Leflaive, where the tired team of pickers still lingered over their supper. In the bar of the Hôtel Le Montrachet old Monsieur Robaire, on crutches, was chatting to a younger vigneron over a glass of 'fine', while an American couple in the restaurant chose their wine with the aid of a guidebook. Providentially they ignored its advice to drink Le Montrachet (expensive, and rarely well made) in favour of an excellent Puligny-Clavaillon from Leflaive.

Upstairs, an hour later, I wondered for the thousandth time why the French prefer such a complicated system to drain their bathwater. What possessed a nineteenth-century inventor to replace the simple Anglo-Saxon plug with this complex mechanism of ratchets and rods – a dial to raise a valve? Constant adjustment is necessary to ensure that the bath doesn't drain as you fill, or resolutely refuse to empty. I saw myself reflected in the distorting mirror of the shiny dial like a boiled crab, stranded on the fishmonger's marble slab: not the most encouraging start to a good night's sleep or a hard-working vintage. I also felt an uncertain sense of nervous anticipation, like the first day at a new school.

A Day in Chevalier

Tuesday, 4 October. The next morning was grey and misty. When I met Olivier Leflaive in the street, at half-past nine, he had already been working for two hours as a 'porter' in the vineyards and had just returned to collect provisions for the rest of the team. Had there been much damage from yesterday's downpour? Olivier seemed unperturbed. 'We had to stop picking for the afternoon but the grapes are extremely healthy and there's no rot. If we get a few days of decent weather all will be well.' I followed him into the tiny kitchen at the domaine, assailed by delicious smells of cooking, as he called 'Casse-croûte, casse-croûte', clapping his hands in his urgency to load up with supplies and be gone.

Three people were at work, preparing the pickers' lunch, and the secretary, Ghislaine, was sitting at the window, writing out a shopping list as Bruno the cook called out his requirement. 'Lemons, carrots, more onions, charcuterie for the casse-croûte – what are we going to have this time? How many days' casse-croûte? Olivier, when are you going to finish – Sunday?' 'Oh no, we must finish Saturday,' said Olivier firmly, as he concentrated on pouring coffee through a funnel into the assortment of empty wine bottles which were stacked ready for him, clustered in plastic bottle baskets. Then we grabbed the coffee, wine and filled baguettes, piled everything into the back of the car and headed out of the village, up the hills towards the vineyards.

'If we're going to make comparisons, it's like '82,' said Olivier, lighting another cigarette. 'There's big quantity and good quality, plenty of tartaric acid but not much malic – after the 'malo' it should be correct.' His furrowed brow suggested that this was a statement of optimism rather than certainty – much more rain and the quality could plummet.

The car stopped in a slither of red mud. Olivier looked sceptically at my brogues and offered me a pair of boots. As I pushed my right foot into the Wellington, something squelched and I drew it out again in alarm. One of the pickers had booby-trapped the boot with a bunch of grapes. 'Oh, the pigs,' laughed Olivier, realizing it was meant for him.

It was nearly ten in the morning but still misty in the vineyards and the red mud stuck to everything, making it heavy going for the team but especially so for the porters, struggling with their laden hods down the steep slope of Chevalier-Montrachet. Even the tractor was slithering and sliding as it manoeuvred a trailer of grapes along the edge of the vines.

I noticed that Louis Latour's pickers in the neighbouring vineyard were using the traditional Burgundian panniers to gather the grapes. These double baskets (plaited from willow, with a yoke in the middle) are ideal when harvesting at some distance from the winery because they can be loaded on to a flat trailer and transported back to the cellars without crushing the grapes. Designed to balance across one shoulder, such baskets are also somewhat easier to handle than the modern plastic boxes which were being used by the team harvesting below us, picking the Marquis de Laguiche's holding of Montrachet for Robert Drouhin at Beaune. The baskets have another advantage, which may be why Louis Latour had revived their use for this particular vintage: they don't hold water. If it rains during the harvest there is always a danger of dilution, but the porous panniers ensure that by the time the grapes reach the press, most of the unwanted moisture has trickled through the chinks in the wickerwork. Domaine Leflaive need not take such precautions. Their cellars are so close that a trailer-load of grapes can be transported there within five minutes, substantially uncrushed – and any surplus water is released from a sluice in the bottom of the trailer before the grapes are loaded into the press.

As Olivier lined out the mugs and bottles on a low wall at the bottom of the vineyard and called 'Casse-croûte, casse-croûte', up the hill, the pickers began to stream down towards us, most wearing the waterproof coats and trousers provided by the domaine as protection against the rain-soaked foliage of the vines. 'Self-service, Self-service,' shouted Olivier. They jostled and joked, forming a disorderly queue for coffee, soft drinks, wine and a baguette sandwich from the boot of the car. 'No plates?' asked one. 'We are the best,' asserted another. There was a sense of camaraderie and pride. Olivier had taken them out to a night-club at the weekend and had stood them all drinks – the sort of gesture which is exceedingly rare when working for other domaines.

About a third were locals, including full-time employees of the domaine and their families. Some were students or friends of the family and others were unemployed. Michel Thusseau, chef des vignes, was in charge. Head of the permanent gang of vineyard workers at the domaine, he is a compact man with an air of determination and competence. Beret on his head, secateurs in hand, he kept the team working without undue urgency but with a determination to get the job done. It was the second full week of the vintage and they'd reached the Grands Crus: the previous day was Bienvenues, now it was Chevalier, the next day Bâtard, followed by the Premiers Crus (Pucelles and Clavaillon) and then the young vines which are always left till last because they need more ripening to produce a decent amount of sugar in the grapes.

The daily routine is much the same for most domaines. The pickers are called at 6.30 for breakfast in the cantine, before leaving at 7.20 for the vineyards and the beginning of the day's work, ten minutes later. There is a break for the casse-croûte at ten, break again for lunch at noon, back to the vines at 1.20 and finish at 5.30, in time to wash, rest and change before the evening meal at 7.15. Leflaive's pickers are paid only slightly better than the official minimum rates but they are well housed, well fed, have decent wine to drink and free cigarettes. And when they leave, if they have worked well, they are given a ticket to any destination in France and a few bottles of wine. It's hard work, but everyone knows that Domaine Leflaive treats its team the best.

Most respond by working cheerfully and well, but occasionally an idler joins the team. I spotted this year's rotten apple immediately. As Michel Thusseau called the pickers back to work and they started to head up the hill after the brief break, one of them lingered behind and threw a full glass of wine down his throat before plodding reluctantly after the rest. Then he came back again, ostensibly looking for a match, and took the opportunity of pouring himself another drink. Red-faced and surly, with a slouching, untrustworthy manner, he pretended to busy himself with a few unnecessary tasks, lingering behind until he thought the coast was clear. Then he grabbed an unopened bottle of wine, pulled out the cork, took an enormous swig and finally heaved a hod over his shoulders and headed back to work.

The pickers jostled and joked, forming a disorderly queue for coffee, soft drinks, wine and a baguette sandwich from the boot of the car.

He was passed by the stalwart of the team, a truck-driver from Besançon, coming downhill with his already-laden hod to empty it into one of the small blue trailers which stood in the rutted track where we had just been resting. Weighed down by the considerable load of grapes on his back, the porter climbed a small ladder which was hooked to the edge of the trailer and then leant over quickly at the top, with a twist to the plastic hod which sent its load of grapes shooting smoothly over his shoulder into the trailer. He paused briefly to spread the piled grapes evenly with a curled, four-pronged fork and then it was up the hill again to stand braced against the slope as full buckets of grapes were passed across the rows from one picker to the next, and emptied into the long funnel-shaped hod which was strapped to his broad back. Porters normally work with groups of five or six pickers, keeping pace with their rate of harvesting, and need to be physically strong. They often get paid a small premium but there's a widely held opinion that it's harder work being a picker, having to crouch all day long at the level of the bunches on the vine, with aching knees and backs, snipping away with the secateurs among the wet leaves or, when it is hot, brushing away the wasps and insects who are lured by the ripe juice.

Olivier was half-way up the hill, keeping the line of pickers moving evenly together down the rows. He noticed the slacker as he finally took his place with the rest but said nothing for the moment. Everyone had been expecting the sun to come out as the morning wore on but instead the mist was getting thicker and the damp air was cold and clammy. The village was invisible, though only half a mile away down the hill. A tractor headed off to the cuverie with another trailer-load of grapes and disappeared gradually into the mist. Olivier, too, decided to follow it down, satisfied that the pickers had resumed their rhythm after the break. It was time to check how things were going in his own cellars, where Jean-Marc Boillot was supervising the reception and processing of juice and grapes from the dozens of small growers and the few big domaines which supply the négociant business of Olivier Leflaive Frères.

This year they expected to make about six hundred casks of wine and their biggest problem was persuading the growers not to pick too early. 'Most other pickers have finished in Puligny, except those from the négociant houses in Beaune, but we always take the risk of harvesting late,' said Olivier, as his muddy foot slipped on the accelerator of the car. We arrived to hear that Dominique Lafon had just telephoned from Meursault to offer them a couple of *pièces* (casks) of Meursault Premier Cru Goutte d'Or. Jean-Marc was suspicious because there was an intermediary involved in this transaction, a broker he distrusted. 'He'll go by his own place when he delivers the wine, swap it for a couple of casks of good Aligoté and bring them here. If I go to Lafon's cellars and pick it up myself it might be OK.' But as a native Burgundian familiar with the habits of his neighbours, Jean-Marc wondered why Lafon should wish to sell these two *pièces* if they were up to the usual standard of the domaine. It's a problem which always confronts the négociant when buying from a renowned producer with whom he doesn't have a regular contract for supply.

During lunch at the domaine, Olivier's secretary Ghislaine went round the tables noting details of each harvester for administrative purposes – address, date of birth etc. – all the bureaucratic necessities of the state. The pickers were relaxed and in good spirits; I began to get to know them. Sitting next to me was a young Dutch couple, Frank and Sylvia, who had come to work for Gérard Boudot at Domaine Sauzet. When Boudot had finished his harvest the previous week they had done a few days' work for two other growers in the village before ending up with Leflaive. 'It's by far the best food here,' said Frank, and I could believe him. We started with a salad of lettuce, tomato and tuna and then enjoyed a dish of pork and potatoes, then cheese, fruit and yoghurt, coffee. And plenty of decent wine, both white and red. No wonder everyone seemed so happy.

It was a cosmopolitan mix. At my table there were a German, three Frenchmen from the viticultural school at Montpellier, the Dutch couple, Olivier and his cousin Anne-Claude. Nearby sat two more Germans (wine merchants on holiday), an English boy, an American and the cheerful porter, Jacky Tisserand, a truck-driver who delivers goods throughout the EC. He told me proudly that it was his fifth vintage with Leflaive and that he was here with his girlfriend Josiane Fournier: 'On vie en concubinage.' She smiled shyly as she was introduced, the quiet, patient partner of her exuberant man. He called her 'La Biche', but it was evidently a term of endearment. Jacky also admitted that it was he who had placed the bunch of grapes in the boot, intending it as a trick on Olivier, and apologized that I had been the unintended victim. His neighbour, Nicholas Georges, had just time to tell me that this was his seventh year doing the vintage with the domaine before Olivier

'It's by far the best food here.' Bruno the cook and three of the harvesters: Jacky Tisserand, Josiane Fournier, Patrick from Idaho.

was on his feet, calling the pickers back to work. Everyone piled into the Hertz vans and set off back to the vineyards.

We took a small unsurfaced road up to Le Murger (the little hill of stones) which is the old name for the top half of Chevalier. Miraculously the sun had come out and the day was transformed. Jacky persuaded 'Petit Louis' – smallest of the men, a ringer for Astérix the Gaul – to climb into his hod and then charged down the hill with Louis riding like a monkey on his back. Half-way down Louis tumbled out, fell on his head and staggered to his feet, blood streaming from his scalp. No one seemed much perturbed, least of all Petit Louis, but Olivier insisted that he should climb up the hill again to be carted off for treatment.

It had suddenly turned into a wonderful afternoon, the atmosphere among the pickers was lively and there was a cheerful murmur of conversation along the line. I sat on a pile of rocks, remnants of the Murger, and watched as they moved steadily and swiftly up the hill; human locusts, droning merrily. It was hot now and they began to strip off their outer layers of jerseys and waterproofs as they gathered the healthy, tightly clustered grapes.

One pretty girl with greying hair tied in a rough pigtail had enticing eyes – during lunch I had gazed at her, sitting at the table opposite. Afterwards, before going out to the picking, she had put on lipstick and now she looked up from time to time, smiling at me as she crouched at her task. I felt the quick tug of vintage madness, the urge to hurl myself headlong into her alluring glance.

The map of the vineyards was clear, stretching down the hill to the village, clustered around its church, and then onwards into the plain. The rows of vines generally run downhill, west to east, but their direction varies slightly with each vineyard, forming a pattern of cross-hatching which identifies the boundaries of every appellation. Only at the Chassagne end of Montrachet itself is there a complete change of orientation, with the rows running north-east to south-west as the slope of the hill curves round towards Puligny's neighbour, enabling the grapes to gain maximum exposure to the afternoon sun. On this bright October day the leaves had only just begun to turn colour – a green striation of vines rippled over the contours, describing every fold and every wrinkle of the hillside in the cartography of well-ordered cultivation.

Below us was the line of stones, piled into a wall, which divides Le

Murger from the lower part of Chevalier. Then there was another wall, little better than a heap of rubble, forming the upper boundary of the long strip of Montrachet, stretching around the hill to my right. I could see Drouhin's team down there, harvesting the famous parcel which belongs to the Marquis de Laguiche. The lower wall of Montrachet had recently been rebuilt at its northern end, to my left as I looked down-hill, but was much decayed in the middle. Towards Chassagne, the wall was in a somewhat better state and punctuated at intervals by a series of grand stone gates. And beyond, far over to the right, the highest vine-yards of Chassagne could be seen, at an altitude which always means a late harvest. The vintage had not begun there – elsewhere it was nearly over. Below Montrachet itself, I could distinguish Bâtard and Bienve-nues. A tractor fitted with mechanical foliage-cutters straddled a row of vines in Bâtard, preparing the way for Leflaive's pickers on the mor-row. In a neighbouring section of the vineyard half a dozen pickers, a small grower and his family, gathered the harvest from his tiny plot.

A single tree stood on the boundary of Les Pucelles, a few scrub oaks struggled for survival among the stones of Le Murger and others in the pile of rocks at the southern boundary of Chevalier, over to my right. Above me were more rocks, more scrub, gorse and wild roses (covered in red hips), small sapling oaks, thistles and box bushes and tiny wild flowers scattered in the crannies as the hill climbed towards a scrawny wood.

The heat had brought the insects out – lots of midges and then a small and beautiful butterfly, buff-grey with pale violet and orange mark-ings, which settled briefly on my hand. The muddy track was drying out and becoming crumbly.

The day was so clear and lovely, the air so delicious that I felt I could leap off the hill and float through the thermals above the vines, drift-ing like a bird across the plain. Then a couple of Mirage fighter planes roared up the valley, flying low, and shattered the peace as they passed.

An old lady (a tough old girl, evidently a local) climbed the hill in front of me, in her faded flowered dress, to deliver the last bucket of grapes. There were still a few stragglers coming up behind her but most were finished and slumped to the ground, lighting cigarettes. There was a deal of badinage and good humour. One of the girls, originally from Laos but married to a local Frenchman, had a round beaming face like a brown moon and spoke in a shrill piping voice. Her name, Lune, seemed wonderfully appropriate and she was teased affectionately by the others. 'Lune, La Lune,' a high and loony cry floated across the hillside. She smiled happily.

Michel Thusseau was anxious to push on to the last section of Chevalier. He and Olivier chivvied the pickers to their feet again and organized the line, arguing about how many pickers there should be to each porter. Today they had fifty pickers and nine porters – it was a record. Normally they work with forty-eight pickers. The porters were visibly tiring – it's very hard work, climbing up the hill in such heat, with a full hod on the back. All the porters were men but the pickers seemed fairly evenly split between the sexes – perhaps a few more girls.

Petit Louis was back in action, with a bright green and white woolly cap perched on his now bandaged head, above his curling hair and huge moustache. He seemed indomitable, a small energetic reproach to the porter who had drunk so heavily this morning and was now sweating profusely, arguing with Michel and Olivier, reluctant to work. He trudged lopsidedly up the hill, and was overtaken by the stalwart Jacky, cheerful and persistent, who emptied his hod quickly into the trailer and hastened back for more. Michel Thusseau had had enough of the drunkard and ordered him to take the secateurs instead and give his hod to another. He protested, but Thusseau brooked no argument. The girl with the alluring eyes hummed a mocking little song and glanced up at me with a grin. Her name, I had discovered, was Cécile.

In the sunshine the wasps came out, buzzing above the heaped grapes in the trailer and hovering aggravatingly close to the pickers' hands. It was hot on the top of the hill and the drunk started protesting again to Olivier, who curtly ordered him to get on with his work. Michel came over to encourage Louis: 'Ah, mon Grand Louis,' he said approvingly. Petit Louis smiled briefly and bent again to his task. Several of the girls were singing – it had the atmosphere of a real harvest, a festival, but a hard-working one.

The tractor arrived with an empty trailer, backing it carefully along the rutted track. Having manoeuvred it into place, the driver rapidly hitched up with a full load and headed back to the press house. Michel oversaw the changeover and then paused beside me for a moment, surveying the scene. He explained that the younger vines had suffered most this year from the drought in July and August because their roots don't go down far enough – so they lacked sap and the grapes were less plump and less ripe as a result. 'There are plenty of grapes but they have often dried out, like figs. With these older vines the grapes are much better.'

No sooner was one section finished than the pickers started on the next, with longer rows of vines, even more arduous. But eventually it was over, row by row completed, and the pickers stood around resting or flopped on the ground as the stragglers completed their task. Chrétien, the drunk, was the first to finish and the old lady in the print dress was the last, except for Michel, still working in the vines, gathering a few precious grapes which had been missed. He called for a porter, emptied his bucket, and it was finished. One of the pickers squeezed a bunch of grapes between his fingers, rubbing in the cool juice to soothe his aching palms.

'C'est dur, Chevalier,' said Olivier. The slope is steeper here than in any other major appellation of Puligny, the physical difficulties of the harvest more acute. But the rewards are commensurately greater, because this exceptional vineyard produces Leflaive's finest and most sought-after wine.

There was a brief rest, then down the hill we went, to make a start on the Bâtard. The leaves here were beginning to turn, more noticeably than in Chevalier, because at this lower altitude the vines are more sheltered, gain more benefit from the sun, mature earlier – and in consequence produce some of the richest, most powerful wines of Puligny; grand stuff, if lacking the elegance which distinguishes a good bottle of Chevalier.

The changing colour of the leaves was always taken as a sign that it was time to harvest, in the days before the growers were capable of the sophisticated analysis of sugars and acids which they now increasingly insist on before deciding on the picking date. But nowadays it seems that well-cared-for vines retain their green foliage later than they used, for here we were near the end of the vintage and it was only now that the first signs of red and yellow indicated the autumn. 'Another two days of this weather and we shall be saved,' said Olivier. 'All the Grands Crus will be harvested.'

The vines of Bâtard run up to the ancient road (now a narrow lane) which divides this appellation from its neighbour, Montrachet itself. I climbed up the hill and peered over the wall to watch the harvest of the most valuable grapes in Burgundy. Robert Drouhin's team had been bussed in from Beaune to pick the Marquis de Laguiche's section of

Montrachet, the largest single holding in this fabled vineyard. Laguiche grows the grapes, Drouhin makes and markets the wine. It's an arrangement which seems surprising for such a renowned domaine but it evidently suits both parties. Laguiche is an absentee landowner and Drouhin is widely acknowledged to be one of the most sophisticated winemakers in Burgundy, as well as running a négociant business of uncompromising quality.

But the team had less cohesion than Leflaive's, and seemed less well disciplined. It included pickers from England and Australia who had no idea what they were harvesting. 'Montrachet, what's that?' was the general reaction, and when I proffered a sketchy explanation they laughed. 'Well the way we've been eating the grapes we must have consumed a huge value!' I glanced along the slope at the thin, lugubrious figure of the Marquis de Laguiche's son, who followed with his bucket in the pickers' wake, anxious to gather any precious grapes that they might have missed. The boss and his team seemed to be working at odds with one another.

In another section of Montrachet, already harvested by its owner, a middle-aged couple were going through the vines with even greater care than Laguiche's son, intent on spotting every single grape that had been left behind. The owner of this patch had evidently given them the right of *grappiage*, to gather the gleanings. Perhaps it was the local policeman, Monsieur Degrave, taking a day off with his wife to pick what they could for themselves. They were unlikely to find more than a bucket or two in Montrachet but they would add this meagre harvest to what they'd managed to glean from other vineyards of the village and perhaps end up making a single cask of wine, a mélange of the finest vineyards in Burgundy. Such a 'cuvée personelle' can be delicious, but it's rare to find it.

Further along the slope, in the Chassagne end of Montrachet, Aubert de Villaine and his father were examining the Domaine de la Romanée-Conti's vines, still unharvested. 'We'll pick tomorrow,' said Aubert. 'I've never seen such healthy grapes – there's no sign of rot, it's perfect. And it looks like we'll get a good-sized crop.' I asked whether there was any damage from the deluge of the previous afternoon. Aubert smiled with delight. 'None at all. I was harvesting down at Bouzeron and we could see the rain coming from the south. The cloud divided in two before it reached Montrachet and the rain fell on Santenay and Chalon. It was as though Montrachet was blessed.'

The afternoon sun was casting long shadows down the rows, the gleaners climbed into their battered Citroën 2CV and headed off home and Leflaive's team realized with relief that they had come to the end of another day in the vineyards. It was back to Puligny for a shower, a change of clothes and supper.

Vignerons and Virgins

Wednesday, 5 October. The day started with rain which then eased off sufficiently for the team to resume work in Bâtard but it remained overcast and cool. The pickers wore their waterproofs and seemed generally despondent – it's miserable work picking when the grapes are wet and the leaves drip chilly rivulets down your neck or into your cuff. Bouchard Père et Fils had a team working in Montrachet but there was little sign of life elsewhere on the slope. Most of the other growers had already finished and were rejoicing that they had gathered their harvest before the weather turned. The air was wet and more rain was forecast. I decided to spend the morning gathering opinions, not grapes.

So I walked through the vineyards to Chassagne and met André Ramonet wandering towards his cellars in a state of indescribable shabbiness – ten days' growth of grizzled stubble on his chin, an old flecked jersey, out at elbows, trousers of indeterminate colour and a pair of carpet slippers. Son of Pierre (patriarch of his village and founder of one of the most remarkable domaines in Burgundy) and father of a pair of energetic sons who now run that domaine with vigorous competence, André has a reputation for being the easy-going member of his family, hopeless but charming, too fond of the wine. If you were to encounter Pierre on any day except Sunday (when he puts on his suit) you would think the old man was a retired peasant vigneron, a proud man who hardly had two centimes to call his own. Seeing his grandson Noël at work in the cellars, wearing a dirty set of blue overalls, you would be reminded of a fairground hustler, quick with his fists. Meeting André is like running into an amiable tramp.

But each is worth a fortune – and André, seemingly the most eccentric and feckless, is an engagingly gentle man, always happy to stop and talk, peering up sideways with a look of innocent slyness and smiling guilelessly at complete strangers. He was amazed when I told him that Leflaive was still harvesting, stopped dead in his tracks and shook his finger with sudden seriousness.

'It's a mistake, this year. Sometimes those who harvest late can gain a bit but this year you can lose a degree with the rain; *lose* not gain. It's a mistake, it's a mistake.'

At Ramonet's they finished on the Monday morning, just before the big storm, and brought in their reds at an average of 11.5°, their whites at around 12°. In Montrachet they achieved 12.7°. It seemed that the wines would need no more than a degree of chaptalization.

I said goodbye just as Noël appeared, looking as dynamic as he must have done when he was stopped for speeding by a local gendarme. They say that it was late at night and the policeman not unreasonably assumed that Noël might have been drinking, so asked him to take a breath test. Noël's response was to punch the policeman on the nose. They took away his licence.

Back in Puligny I dropped into Carillon's cellars and discovered that they had harvested earlier still, beginning on Monday, 19 and finishing on Tuesday, 27 September. Their reds came in at degrees ranging from 11° for a basic Bourgogne to 12° for a Chassagne Rouge. The whites were a little higher – up to about 12.5° at best. Loulou Carillon was pleased with the quality – the grapes were very healthy and the fermentations were going well – indeed so tumultuously that the wines were overflowing the casks. There seemed every prospect of good concentration.

Opposite the entrance to Domaine Sauzet an Alsatian barked ferociously at me as I passed and tried to burrow under his master's gate in his eagerness to attack. This was evidently the fixed intention of the animal's life, judging by the deep trench he had scraped in the hard-packed gravel. One day soon he would escape and some innocent wine merchant would meet an untimely end.

In Sauzet's cellars there was a sense of calm tranquillity – the hurly burly of the vintage over and the new wine fermenting away in the barrels. Gérard Boudot had started picking on 23 September and finished on Sunday, 2 October. 'On Thursday afternoon and on Friday last week the rain was a problem but we only lost half a day's picking. When the grapes arrived at the cellar I let the juice from the trailer run off into the gutter because it was mostly rainwater, and I prefer to work with juice than water. Fortunately, we had finished before Monday's storm.' He seemed happy with the quality, without making any extravagant claims for the vintage. 'It was a very good year, right from the beginning. The flowering of the Chardonnay went perfectly and lots of large bunches formed on the vine. The Pinot Noir flowered a bit later and it didn't go so well so we didn't get such a big harvest but the quality is very good, as it is for the Aligoté which produced a rather smaller crop than usual. But here at our domaine we got a very good quantity in general, sixty hectolitres per hectare, with no rot at all. It was a bit smaller crop than in 1982 but pretty much the same style. I think we'll make wines which will be quite supple and relatively early maturing, because the acidity is fairly low.'

I found Vincent Leflaive in his office at the domaine and asked whether he regretted harvesting so late. 'We had intended to start on the 24th but we didn't think the grapes were fully mature so we held off until the 26th. In any case the forecast from the meteorological station at Beaune was that we were going to have unsettled weather until last Thursday [29 September] and then it was going to clear up and we would enjoy a steady period of sunshine. Actually it turned out the reverse – we've had terrible weather from Thursday onwards. But the grapes are extremely healthy, there's been no rot at all. We could do with just a bit more sunshine, like yesterday afternoon.'

Leflaive's Belgian importers arrived and we went to taste a range of the domaine's '86s in the cellars. Then, after suitably flowery compliments all round, they headed for their lunch in the hotel restaurant, clutching the remains of a bottle of Chevalier-Montrachet, while Vincent and I crossed the yard to the cantine. The team was just back from the morning's work. Jacky had rolled down his socks into puffy knots and was hobbling around claiming that he had swollen ankles and should go at once to the doctor. 'It's a serious malady – it comes from carrying two men.' His burden, Petit Louis, looked up with a smile – seemingly none the worse for the tumble on his head.

Sylvie Guillemaud (the girl who had crashed her car on the evening of my arrival in Puligny) was engaged in a provocative tussle with two of the men, vying for her favours. A tall, rangy extrovert, and one of the clowns of the team, Sylvie worked for a grower in the Côte Chalonnaise during the rest of the year, coming regularly to Leflaive for the vintage. She gave Vincent a cheerful hello as he passed and he responded with equal good humour.

We went in to lunch and Jacky beckoned me over to the table in the corner where he and Josiane sat surrounded by a gang of friends. 'You can be président of the table – you get the wine, the bread, you clear the plates!' Olivier Michou (generally known by his surname, to distinguish him from Olivier Leflaive, in whose band he played guitar) was looking decidedly haggard from too many 'nuits blanches' with Natalie, a full-time employee of the domaine, who worked in the kitchen. His mood was aggravated by the caustic comments of his neighbour Berangère, a comfortably hard-bitten girl who was studying to be an antique dealer. The circle was completed by Patrick from Idaho (complete with a degree in industrial engineering, specializing in the application of computers), and Petit Louis, who (like Jacky) was living in Besançon but was originally from the Herault, down south in the Languedoc.

Big Bruno, the cheerful moustachioed cook (who also joined the team when needed as a porter, smoking expensive Havana cigars as he worked), had produced a salad to start with, then a tremendous dish of choucroute, bursting with pork, ham and charcuterie, then fromage frais with cream, fruit and coffee. No wonder everyone was singing his praises.

'You've eaten well?' was Louis Thusseau's greeting as I met him in the yard after lunch. Father of Michel, our taskmaster in the vineyards, old Louis worked forty-four years for the domaine and retired in 1985, at the age of sixty-seven. Michel succeeded him as chef des vignes. 'I now work when I feel like it. They're good bosses – if they weren't I wouldn't come, I'm not obliged to.' His cheerful face was one of the inspirations for the rest of the team, who treated him with affection and played small practical jokes on him. He and Petit Louis were natural mates – the old man recognizing in the younger the same straightforward good-humoured appetite for an honourable day's work.

They had finished picking Bâtard in the morning so this afternoon it was off to Les Pucelles (the Virgins). This Premier Cru vineyard lies just across the road to the north of Bâtard-Montrachet and is capable of producing wine very close to the quality of its Grand Cru neighbour. A solitary walnut tree stands at the top of the vineyard just beside the patch which the Leflaive team was about to harvest. It marks one of those mysterious boundaries, familiar to locals but found in none of the standard reference works, which subdivides Les Pucelles into Petites Pucelles and Grandes Pucelles, otherwise known as Pucelles Fosses. The Little Virgins and Great Virgins suggested some confusion with the bib-

His cheerful face was one of the inspirations for the rest of the team. Louis Thusseau.

lical parable of the wise and foolish until I remembered that neighbouring Montrachet was once similarly divided, and that Grand Montrachet designated the best bit, the real thing.

The Leflaive domaine includes vines in each section of the vineyard.
Those in Petites Pucelles are a good twenty-five years old, and those in
Grandes Pucelles are not much less, so Michel Thusseau was expecting
a concentrated harvest, with around 13° of sugar. In recent years Les
Pucelles has regularly produced one of the best wines from the domaine,
the most seductive of its Premiers Crus.

The vines they were about to pick had the neat, well-trimmed appearance which follows the passage of the foliage-cutter, a simple but
extremely useful machine which Jean-Claude Bidault (son-in-law of
Bebel Bachelet who runs the épicerie) was manoeuvring slowly up a row
in Clos des Meix – the walled enclave which forms the lower part of Les
Pucelles. He was driving a tractor which straddled the vines and was fitted with two vertical discs – rotary cutters which trimmed the branch-
ing foliage, making it much easier for the pickers to work and enabling
them to spot every bunch of grapes, some of which might otherwise be
missed among the leaves. Leflaive is one of only two domaines in Puligny to operate such a system – most smallholders would find it hard
to justify the additional expense.

'Form your teams,' called Michel. 'We are fifty this afternoon,' he
muttered. 'I thought it was going to be forty-seven. I sacked Chrétien
yesterday [the drunk porter, reluctant to work] but we seem to have collected another three.' Methodically he checked the names of those present into his notebook, recording whether they were carrying or cutting, so that Ghislaine would be able to calculate their pay correctly at
the end of the week. 'We can count on three hours, perhaps three and
a half for this bit.'

Once again it was a fine afternoon, sunny and warm. As the porters
came down the slope towards the line of pickers, the latter began to
sing. A good lunch, a glass or two of wine and the sunshine had restored
everyone's flagging spirits. Michou, Petit Louis and Louis the elder
tossed grapes at each other across the rows and there was a good deal of
joking and fooling around. Michel Thusseau ignored this, simply urg-
ing the team to keep up and keep in line – the work goes much better
when everyone maintains a steady pace.

Immediately above us, across a small road which meandered up the

hill to our right towards the hamlet of Blagny, there was the large vineyard of Le Cailleret, the major part of which is a fine walled clos belonging exclusively to Domaine Chartron. It's very good, stony land,
at almost the same altitude as Montrachet but oriented very slightly
more to the east, fractionally less well exposed to the sun. Such minute
differences divide this potentially fine Premier Cru from the altogether
more exalted quality of the Grand Cru from which it is separated by
the width of a narrow track. Above again is a vineyard which was originally included in the appellation of Le Cailleret but reclassified in 1974
as part of the much grander Chevalier. A small green lane, dotted at this
season with flowers of comfrey and white campion, marks the boundary between the original section of Chevalier and its upstart neighbour.

The owner of this plot, Jean-René Chartron, had come up to see his
team of twenty-five pickers gathering the last of the crop and was now
standing in the road, chatting to a couple of passers-by. He looked
pleased and greeted me cheerfully when I joined him to ask how the
vintage was going. 'I'm hurrying to finish now in this good weather. It
looks like we'll harvest a fairly big crop, about the size of 1982, but with
the quality of '86 perhaps. A rare combination.'

Leflaive's team suddenly finished Petites Pucelles, a bit quicker than
expected, and everyone climbed into the rented Hertz vans, an empty
trailer and various cars for the short journey across the hill to Les Combettes, which lies directly below Blagny, adjacent to the village boundary with Meursault at the northern limit of the Puligny appellations.
The soil is richer here and the wines somewhat fatter, but lacking the
elegance of the finest Puligny. There was a short pause for coffee or soft
drinks after they unloaded, but Michel was anxious to get them working again in order to finish this relatively small patch before the end of
the day. First into the field were the two old local ladies who worked
for the domaine throughout the year; last was Cécile crying, 'Five minutes, Michel, I haven't yet had my cigarette.'

I left them to it and drove up to Blagny to enjoy the view. I could see
for miles across the vineyards of the Côte d'Or, downhill to the village
and over the plain towards the distant mountains. The slanting golden
light of late afternoon threw strong shadows, casting the details of the
landscape into high relief. The hamlet of Blagny itself was completely
still, becalmed in a timeless reverie, like a classical landscape by Poussin
or Claude Lorrain.

Late that night Olivier decided to rehearse with his band in preparation for the paulée at the end of the vintage. I followed the muffled beat of the drums through the deserted village streets until I found myself in a room above Olivier's cellars which was being used as a dormitory for some of the pickers. There was a clutter of wires and microphones, speakers perched on cupboards and behind beds, red lights and a haze of cigarette smoke: the necessary paraphernalia of every sixties rock band. OLF launched into a repertoire of old favourites, from 'The Midnight Hour' to a strange version of 'Eleanor Rigby', which meandered in and out of the Pink Panther theme; a never-ending medley of rock's archaeology. As Ellen Cartsonis said to me the next day, 'The trouble with French rock music is that they have no sub-culture.' Petit Louis dozed on one bed, waiting patiently for the band to finish so that he could sleep, and Nathalie sat on another, waiting less patiently to grab Michou. I left them still playing at midnight.

In the Cellars

Thursday, 6 October. It was raining again when I woke, not heavily but with a dreary persistence which suggested it had set that way for the day. As I lingered over my breakfast I pitied the pickers. The rain was not heavy enough to stop the harvest but sufficient to make life uncomfortable. It seemed a good day to spend in the cellars.

First I went up to the vineyards, to Clos des Meix where the team was working on the rows which had been trimmed by the foliage-cutter on the previous day. The rain had ceased, against all expectation, but it was grey, damp and dispiriting. As I watched the water dripping from the vines I remembered the stories that the pickers had been telling me about life in the cuverie – how the cellarmen mixed young, partially fermented wine with fiery marc, distilled from the skins, to make ratafia – a potent and invigorating drink which they drank when old Virot wasn't looking. Apparently they kept it in a bottle behind a plank in the back yard and would run out for a swig at every opportunity. Heaven knows how much Grand Cru Puligny had been syphoned off over the years to make this ratafia – it was time to investigate.

Jean-Paul Bachey was backing another trailer load of grapes into the yard when I arrived – it was a tight fit getting the tractor in under the arch which leads into the cuverie yard from the narrow street. With inches to spare, the trailer was reversed into the open door of the press house, where two Bucher pneumatic presses stood side by side. The finest presses available, these subtle machines produce the clearest juice by exerting the gentlest pressure. An inflatable tube runs down the centre of the stainless steel cylinder which forms the body of the horizontal press. This cylinder is pierced by thin slots, through which the juice runs out into a deep tray beneath, as the tube fills with compressed air and crushes the grapes against the steel walls. The entire cylinder can rotate and its operation is computer-controlled: Swiss engineering at its best.

One of the presses at Leflaive's cellars was midway through its task, the other had been emptied and hosed down and was now wheeled quickly into place by the press men, Dominique Cornu and Jean-François Royer. They connected an electric cable to the motor of the Archimedes screw (running lengthwise down the base of the trough-shaped trailer full of grapes) and signalled the tractor driver to raise the trailer on its hydraulic stilts and back it into position over the press. A switch was flicked, the screw began to turn and there was a gush of juice and grapes into the open tube. This first juice, which flowed freely through the cylinder before any pressure was applied, was collected in the tray underneath, sieved through stainless steel basket filters to scoop off any stray pips and skins and pumped to a stainless steel tank. Within ten minutes the trailer was empty and lowered to the ground, hydraulics and electrics uncoupled, and the trailer given a thorough washdown before being taken back to the vineyards to be refilled. It took five men to manhandle the fully laden press towards the back of the room so that the cellar floor could also be washed down and all made ready for the next load. The sliding plates on the side of the press were closed, the machine was switched on and at the first gentle pressure juice flowed rapidly again from the bottom, brownish in colour – very far removed from the brilliant green-gold clarity of the final wine. As the pressure increased the sluggish flow accelerated again until the desired pressure was reached (1.5 Bar), the motor cut out and all I could hear was the juice running out, like the sound of a fast-running brook in the rain. Then the motor re-started for a few seconds to maintain the pressure and so the cycle continued automatically, intermittently, for somewhere between an hour and a half and two hours. Eventually the press was emptied and the *marc* of skins, pips and stems discharged into a growing pile out the back, whence it would be taken to Distillerie Alexon, on the outskirts of Beaune, for distillation during the winter into a fiery spirit, some of which could eventually find its way back into the cellars as a constituent for the next vintage's ratafia.

The freshly pressed juice was pumped into decantation tanks, where it was allowed to settle for twenty-four hours at a controlled low temperature before chaptalization and fermentation. Michel Mourlin, the voluble head cellarman, took out his tastevin to give me a taste of the decanted juice, almost clear now that it had been 'racked' from its sediment. He told me that as well as letting settle all the solids in the juice, the dirt from the fields and any particles which had been picked up from the various treatments used in the vineyard, the period of settlement also effected a selection of the natural yeast cells, whereby the feeble perished and the strong survived.

Vincent Leflaive arrived to watch the work, and stood chatting to me for a few minutes while Jean Virot, the retiring régisseur, helped one of the cellarmen to move a dozen new oak casks from the barrel store just inside the entrance to the yard. They tumbled the casks end over end through the doorway and then rolled them expertly on their rims into the inner cellar. I tried to do likewise and found my cask heading out of control into the wall.

I followed Virot through a sliding door into the fermentation cellars, where Michel Mourlin was running to and fro on his short legs, talking to himself all the time as he connected and disconnected pipes, adjusted a pump, and checked that all was well before filling a row of casks from a tank of unfermented juice. 'That's good, and that; there's something else – ah, that's it.' He collected a box and trotted down the row of casks, collecting the bungs. One was stuck so he went to look for his cellarman's hammer, gave the bung a tap to knock it out and then contemplated the row of new oak barrels with some satisfaction. Each one was stamped with the name of its maker, DAMY, and the year, '88.

Michel's short, busy, bespectacled figure provided an entertaining contrast to the tall, pedantic solemnity of Jean Virot, who appeared at that moment from an inner cellar. In his slow and laboured way he told Michel not to close the door into the room from which he had just emerged – 'I want it kept open, so that the temperature may remain constant here' – and then he chided me for leaving another door open and letting in a draught from the press room. The thermostat on the air-conditioning system was set at maximum (25°C) and all the little shutters between the various cellars were open to allow the warm air to circulate and encourage the fermentation to get going.

For both Jean Virot and Michel Mourlin this was their last vintage – each was due to retire. Virot's job as régisseur was being taken over by Pierre Morey, a highly respected viticulteur from Meursault who had cultivated several of the Lafon vineyards *en fermage* until the lease came to an end and Dominique Lafon decided to take them back under full family control. Mourlin's successor was to be Jean Jafflin, whose house in Beaune was fortuitously situated just opposite Distillerie Alexon.

I found him standing by the sugar mixer, chatting to Gilbert Magnien as they supervised the chaptalization of a batch of Chevalier-Montrachet. Jafflin looked like a burly version of Lenin as he heaved fifty-kilogram sacks of sugar on to a stainless steel rack which bridged one end of the portable mixing tank. Almost clear juice flowed into the tank, where it was mixed by a paddle system with the sugar before being pumped back into the cuve from which it had come. It took seven minutes to dissolve each sack and four sacks were required for the fifty hectolitres of Chevalier-Montrachet. At the rate of four kilograms per hectolitre that would translate into 2.35° of alcohol. I must have miscounted somehow.

The process of sugaring wine to make good the deficiencies of nature is named after Count Chaptal, who regularized a much older habit by his decree of 1800. The merits of this practice are debatable, particularly when low natural degrees are the result of excessive yields rather than a lack of sunshine, but Burgundians are adamant in believing that 13° of alcohol is the necessary minimum for Chardonnay. So most vintages are chaptalized by a degree or two.

Michel Mourlin was finally ready to fill the casks with freshly fermenting wine. I followed him down the line as each barrel was connected to the racking head and filled to about three-quarters full. Michel took good care to leave plenty of headspace in every cask and the bung-holes open, to allow for the tumultuous upheavals of the first few days of the fermentation. As he worked I asked him about the drinking habits of the cellarmen. Michel winked discreetly, told me nothing but conceded that it was possible I might find a bottle or two in the fridge in the sugar store, just inside the front gate, and another behind a plank in the yard at the back.

He busied himself about his tasks with the familiarity of long practice, glancing up now and then through his spectacles with the smile of a trusting child, absorbed in his play. 'I was born in Buxy but I've lived in Puligny since I was four months old. My wife came to the village in 1963. Now we live right here, next to the cellars. I'm the guardian.' From a window at the back of the cellar I could see the little kitchen garden where he grew his vegetables, with a chicken hut in one corner. 'I don't know where we'll go when I retire. We've got no children – and although half the houses in the village are empty most of them belong to growers who prefer to keep them available to lodge their pickers during the vintage. And most people hang on to these houses for fear of not having somewhere in difficult times. They say that thirty years ago France had sufficient houses to lodge a quarter more than the entire population today.' But I sensed no fear of the future or nostalgia for the past. Here was a man living cheerfully in the moment.

Back in the vineyards, Leflaive's team was in good spirits, despite the dreary weather. A few grapes tossed across the rows led to a sudden skirmish and Sylvie Guillemaud fell backward into the vines under the onslaught of one of the men. Olivier ignored them – this patch of Clos des Meix was nearly finished – and he opened the sluice of the trailer to let the accumulated rainwater gush to the ground. It was beginning to get a lot wetter. 'Olivier, it's raining,' one of the pickers complained. 'No, it's sprinkling,' he replied. As the last grapes were gathered Dutch Frank challenged English Nicholas to a race down the hill, carrying their half-loaded hods to the trailer. The Dutchman won easily, to general acclaim. It was 11.45, not worth starting on another vineyard, so the team stopped for lunch.

In the courtyard at the domaine, the clan was gathering. Olivier's nephews Guy and Thibaud (sons of his brother Patrick) had come for the fun of the vintage. His older cousin Ludovic de Noue (a bulky man of about sixty) had the air of a man keeping an eye on his inheritance. He was wandering around in flip-flops, his bare turtle-like toes covered in mud, with an expression of slightly uncertain mateyness. Another cousin, more evidently welcome, was Anne-Claude, who seemed on excellent terms with the pickers, most of whom she knew by name, swapping jokes and cigarettes with them as they stood around in the yard before lunch. Vincent appeared, had a word for all the girls and for one or two of the faithful regulars among the men, and shepherded his guests into lunch – Philippe de Magenta and his latest wife, an English girl twenty-five years his junior. The Duc de Magenta is the last of an old

Franco-Irish family, the McMahons, and has a reputation for wit, superb manners and an amorously light heart. Exceedingly slim (partly the result of debilitating illness), this renowned proprietor of a splendid domaine had recently concluded an agreement with Louis Jadot, the Beaune négociant, whereby Jadot would farm the Magenta vineyards, make and market the wine. Magenta seemed to relish the absence of care which this agreement had brought him.

I sat at the back of the room with a subdued bunch of pickers. Michou explained that after playing music until past midnight they had all gone with Bruno the cook to the Casino at Santenay, where they had stayed until 4 a.m. He lost, they all lost – 'We lost with a smile.' Bruno, too, looked shattered as he placed a tremendous dish of beef and carrots on our table, but it didn't seem to have affected his excellent cooking. Michou told me that at the end of the night, Nathalie had promised him a candlelit dinner for two and an evening at a night-club. She had even written the promise on his cigarette packet. Remembering the long hours of repetitive practice as Jacky rehearsed his song for the paulée, Berangère asked Josiane how she could stand his singing. 'Because I love him,' said Josiane, smiling ruefully as Jacky caressed her neck.

Ghislaine went round each table explaining to each of the pickers that when they were paid they could either take all their pay by cheque or could have up to five hundred francs of what was owed to them paid in cash. Which did they want? Most, surprisingly, opted for a cheque to cover everything.

After the cheese, before the coffee, when Bruno appeared in the passage from the kitchen, everyone broke into the traditional Chant Bourgignon, hands twisting in the air and then clapping in time, to honour him and thank him for his cooking during the previous two weeks. Then Sylvie produced from under her T-shirt, with sexy exaggeration, his present from the team – a box of Monte Cristo cigars. Bruno was startled and clearly much pleased, standing holding the box with a huge grin on his face before bowing his way backwards through the door.

As I went out to the yard, I noticed the menu pinned on the board. It was headed 'Jeudi 6 Octobre. St Bruno – Bonne Fête Chef.'

The team headed for Le Clavaillon – I spent the afternoon at the village school.

A Bow in the Sky

Friday, 7 October. It was a bright clear morning and the pickers began work in Le Clavaillon with an air of festive expectation, certain that they were near the end of the vintage. Leflaive's team was the last on the slope, a cluster of colour, movement and cheerful voices calling across the rows, alone in the otherwise still and empty panorama of the vineyards.

Le Clavaillon lies immediately to the north of Les Pucelles and at approximately the same elevation but produces lighter, less assertive if perhaps occasionally more elegant wines. The differences, so marked in the flavour, are hard to discern on the ground. Perhaps the vineyard slips a little lower down the hill than its neighbour, is marginally less well drained, less sheltered or less well exposed to the sun, but such things are scarcely perceptible. It may be at least as important that the vines in Leflaive's holding (which accounts for eighty per cent of this Premier Cru appellation) are younger than those in Les Pucelles.

Clouds arrived with the casse-croûte and the weather lost its early sparkle but the pickers chewed their baguettes with relish and joked happily with Olivier. They could see that they would be finished by lunchtime. Michel Thusseau had lost his usual air of preoccupation and was able to join in the general levity, laughing at a wisecrack from Jacky and embracing a willing Cécile as he chivvied his charges back to work.

Shortly after eleven-thirty it was over. Within a few minutes all the pickers had emerged smiling from the final rows to toss their part-full buckets of grapes into the trailer. Last out of the vineyard was American Patrick, from Idaho. As he neared the trailer there was a conspiratorial chuckling from a huddle of porters clustered around Jacky Tisserand. Patrick tossed in his grapes and then found himself seized by arms and ankles, swung in the air with much raucous cheering from the rest and hurled into the trailer to land with a sticky squelch on the last of the harvest.

The exuberance was suddenly unstoppable. Some rushed to tear branches off the vines to decorate the vans and tractors, others pelted each other with grapes, others hurled buckets and hods into the trailers before seizing bottles of wine which were passed from hand to hand and throat to throat as with embraces and shouts the team piled on to or into every available vehicle for the triumphant procession back to the village. With headlights flashing, horns blaring and pickers hanging on precariously to the sides as they hurled fistfuls of grapes at any unwary

It was a bright, clear morning and the pickers began work in Le Clavaillon.

passers-by, the vans, cars and tractors roared down the hill towards the cuverie, where cheering cellarworkers sprayed them with the hose as they arrived. The tractor and its load were left in the yard and the rest of the procession continued with a noisy lap of honour round the Place du Monument before heading up past the hotel to the domaine. The cellarmen (forewarned by the approaching racket) aimed their hoses on the exuberant pickers as they tumbled out of the vehicles into the court-yard. There was a brief battle for control of the hoses, which were turned first on the domaine workers and then at the men from the cuverie as they arrived to join in the fun. Olivier produced a few bottles of cham-pagne, there was an explosion of popping corks, embraces and laugh-ter as the team celebrated the harvest home.

Lunch was a rowdy affair, with numerous choruses of the Chant Bour-guignon to honour Bruno and the cuverie team and anyone else whose name caught the pickers' fancy. Olivier was cheered as he stood up to announce that the harvest supper, the paulée, would take place that evening at 7 p.m. in the Salle des Fêtes. But there was still work to be done that afternoon. The men were to wash down the wagons and hods and waterproofs, clean and put away the secateurs, tidy their rooms. A third of the girls were to clean the dining-room and lay up for break-fast, a third to clean the dormitories and a third to clean the kitchen and washing areas. Everyone would be paid the following morning after an inspection of their rooms and those who were not in a hurry to de-part were invited to stay for a picnic lunch.

'It's difficult, the end of the vintage, because everyone wants to relax and finish,' said Olivier. 'But they're paid for the whole day today, even though they may only work an hour or so this afternoon.' He got them quickly organized after the meal, before the momentum flagged, but the air of festivity continued as the pickers joked and reminisced and splashed each other while they worked.

Everyone was keen on a photo. They persuaded French Patrick, 'le roi des emmerdeurs' (kingsize pain in the neck) – a lumbering, phleg-matic man – to pose with his friend Marcel, 'la poupée de Patrick'. The trainee architect, Marie-Paule Gautier, stood smiling sweetly beside Vin-cent Leflaive, his arm draped around her shoulder with fond affection. Michel Thusseau and Cécile embraced rather more warmly, Michel tak-ing advantage of the moment for an amorous fondle of her breasts.

Small explosions of anarchic mayhem punctuated the afternoon. The redoubtable Colette Imbert, cleaner and cook, burst from her kitchen with good-humoured wrath and chased the young scallywag Ivan (a male nurse from Rouen) across the yard with her broom. Squeals from the first-floor windows of the girls' dormitories were echoed by sudden scuffles and shouts in the yard below, as the pickers provoked or pursued one another with exuberant mischief. A pale, quiet Frenchman arrived in his little Renault and stepped out looking somewhat nonplussed by the general air of carnival. It was Lune's husband, come to take her home. She seemed sad to leave and the others gave her a boisterous farewell, leaning out of windows or lining up by the gate to wave her on her way. For the last time of the vintage the singsong call of 'Lune, Lune, La Lune' leaped through the air, to the apparent dismay of her husband and her own quite evident delight.

I drove up the vineyards towards Chassagne, through sunshine and showers. As I looked back towards Puligny a tremendous rainbow, wide and low, arced across the sky – one end springing from the village, the other in the hills; a reminder at the end of another harvest of God's promise to Noah, the first vigneron, never again to drown the world or obliterate the vintage in a deluge.

14 | St Vincent

Procession

An empty hangar in an abandoned quarry, before dawn on one of the coldest mornings of the winter, seemed an unlikely place and time to throw a party. As I trudged the last few yards up the hill a figure at my elbow announced in a gruff voice that it was minus nine degrees and the clouds of his breath added to the dank enveloping fog, through which the lights of cars and torches appeared as pale haloes in the dark. Further down the hill a huge and faintly glowing shape – the marquee – was already illumined in preparation for the great banquet of St Vincent (scheduled for that afternoon) but here, in the lee of Bernard Clerc's house just below the hamlet of Blagny, the crowds of converging Burgundians met in the shadows and the mist, like the ghosts of Hades.

But these were very substantial ghosts and they had brought their saints. There were dozens of them, patrons of the village confréries, crowded on to the long, frost-rimed trestles which had been set up outside the hangar, and more were arriving every minute. A man would appear out of the darkness with a carved wooden figure unceremoniously bundled under one arm and a folding carrier under the other. The carrier would be spread across the trestles, the figure placed carefully on top and perhaps decorated with elaborate garlands of foliage and artificial flowers before its guardian hurried inside the doorway ahead of us, to the party. Ranged in haphazard order, side by side, these wooden saints formed a strange and agreeable throng, brought here from as far north as Chablis and as far south as the extremities of the Côte Chalonnaise. Some were finely carved and had the baroque flamboyance of the St Vincent from Morey St-Denis, three or four feet tall; others were simple, rough-hewn and unadorned, like the tiny figure (no more than nine inches high) which had made the journey from the diminutive village of Orches, up in the hills of the Hautes Côtes de Beaune.

Most were representations of St Vincent, an obscure Spaniard martyred at Valence in 304 who has come to be the patron of winegrowers because of the symbolic echoes of his name (vin, sang: the sacrament of the Last Supper) rather than for any particular affinities with the story of his life or death. But some village confréries have chosen other saints, for reasons which range from the obvious (St Aubin, name of both village and patron) to the patriotic (Monthélie's choice of St Louis) to the obscure: Volnay is curiously represented by a gay, gilded cherub in a perspex case, labelled St Cyr. Puligny's confrérie, one of the earliest to be founded (in 1826), is dedicated to the great Cistercian, St Bernard – a native Burgundian whose monks did more than anyone else to establish viticulture on the slopes of the Côte d'Or and who gave their name to the road, Chemin des Moines, by which we had ascended the hill to Blagny.

For well over a century it has been customary in each of the wine villages of Burgundy to celebrate the Feast of St Vincent on 22 January by taking the confrérie's saint on a tour of the village. He is carried in procession to the church for mass and thence to the house of a family of vignerons who will have the honour of looking after him for the succeeding year. The new hosts naturally welcome the other villagers to their cellars for a glass of wine, after which everyone sits down for a splendid feast. Thus the saint 'turns' from house to house every year, as the honoured guest of each confrère in succession.

In 1938 the Chevaliers du Tastevin organized the St Vincent Tournante as an event on a much grander scale, hosted in turn by a different wine village on the first Saturday after 22 January. This celebration has grown bigger year by year and it has become customary for each village to try to outdo its predecessor in the scale and splendour of the decorations, the magnificence of the feasts and the size of the crowds. In 1991 it was Puligny's turn. For over two years this tiny community of five hundred inhabitants had been preparing to welcome a hundred and fifty thousand visitors within the space of two days. But the real celebration, more important than all the razzmatazz for the tourists, began with this party at dawn for the confrères, the saint-bearers from all over Burgundy.

Inside the hangar (which normally houses the tractors and mechanical harvesters of Bernard Clerc) approximately fifty wooden barrels stood on end, one for every confrérie, each identified by a card bearing the village name. On top of every barrel was a magnum of the Cuvée St Vincent (a blend of Puligny-Montrachet made with wine contributed by the growers of the village), a ring of glasses and a pile of bread; and around these essential supplies were clustered the representatives of each village, cheerful red-faced men and women, well wrapped against the cold. Some wore tastevins on silver chains, some sported curious caps or sashes or badges of office. Various bands were warming up in the corners of this cavernous hangar, with squeaks of pipes, clatter of drums and the deep burp of enormous tubas, whose fat serpentine coils wound their way around stout bandsmen, wearing uniforms which ranged from the full-dress absurdity of potentates from the land of Babar (complete with white spats) to a simple blue peaked cap, tilted casually over one ear. Louis Carillon, président of Puligny's confrérie and therefore host for this occasion, stood with an air of cheerful self-importance, surrounded by his confrères, as new arrivals pushed through the throng to shake him by the hand, greeting him grandly as 'Monsieur le Président'. A film crew conducted interviews, under the blaze of portable arc lights, and local pressmen pointed flashguns at all the pretty girls. Towards the edges of this heterogeneous crowd were several knots of people who seemed to have found their way to this gathering from the bleak fastnesses of a more primitive age. My attention was caught by a particularly wild-eyed bunch from St-Romain: gleeful, angular men (all elbows and knees) and big, voracious women, wearing clothes so roughly cut, from such thick material, that they might have been chopped with an axe from felt wadding and elephant hide.

Each village is expected to send two representatives (rewarded for their presence by a dinner at Clos Vougeot as guests of the Chevaliers du Tastevin), but most had come in parties of six or eight. Several hundred people were crowded into the quarry and the first arrivals had been drinking since before seven; a cloud of cigarette smoke hung in the air and the noise was deafening.

As the darkness faded into a grey dawn there were calls on the loudspeaker for everyone to form up outside in the designated order of pro-

Cheerful red-faced men, well wrapped against the cold, at the feast of St Vincent.

cession. Two men from each village shouldered the little wooden stretchers on which the saints were carried, another took charge of each confrérie's banner (richly embroidered with a pair of clasped hands or similar device, symbol of the mutual assistance which the confrères are sworn to provide one another in times of sickness or misfortune) and everyone else fell into place along the route. It was all remarkably well organized, with stakes at regular intervals along the first couple of hundred yards, adorned with the name and coat of arms of each village, and with several stewards armed with walkie-talkies coordinating the formation and departure of this great procession and ensuring that the four or five bands were stationed at sufficient distance from one another to minimize the clash of different tunes. A black squirrel raced up the pine tree beside me and suddenly we were off.

It was a cold morning; misty air, frost on every branch and vine, a chill smokiness that muted colour and softened every sound. A quiet murmuring of cheerful conversation ran along the lengthening line, a droning continuo beneath the music of the bands, but many remained silent and self-absorbed. Imperceptibly I became aware that whatever the promotional trappings of the rest of the weekend's festivities there had survived in this procession an unexpected devotional camaraderie, a sense of pilgrimage and penance, celebration and thanksgiving. As the banners and the bands, the people and their saints flowed down the hill and through the vineyards, time flickered. This was the Journey of the Magi, illuminated in the winter landscape of a medieval Book of Hours, or a nineteenth-century Mission of the Cross, painted by Courbet; and every face had been viewed through the lens of Marcel Carnet or Cartier Bresson. Whether mobile, melancholy and down at heel or jaunty and sharp, alluring or dowdy, stiffly gaunt or bonhomously well-fed, each was unmistakably, indefinably and timelessly French.

Ahead of me the band fell silent, save for the rattle of the drums. The white-gloved hands of the uniformed bandsmen dropped by their sides, swinging loosely as they marched, but the right hand of one brushed the left hand of another, then caught and twined together across the narrow gap that separated a spotty, lovelorn boy from his mischievous girlfriend. She turned to him and smiled, then their hands parted and they raised their cornets with the rest, for an exuberant fanfare that blared through the morning mists like the risen sun.

But the sun itself stayed hidden as the procession curled down the

The white-gloved hands of the uniformed bandsmen.

lane above Clos de la Garenne and turned right across the hillside between the low walls of the ancient track which leads to the Cross of
Montrachet. Here, at the junction that separates the Premier Cru vineyards of Le Cailleret and Les Pucelles from the Grands Crus of Montrachet and Bâtard, the marchers turned left, to the east, towards the
village. The entire route, like all those leading to Puligny, was lined with
scraggy Christmas trees which were embellished with colourful paper
flowers and bows of blue and silver foil, and as we approached the first
houses the decorations grew more lavish. Green arches spanned the road,
there were flags above our heads and every bush and branch sprouted
flowers, hundreds and thousands of them, a startling paper counterfeit
of spring.

Crowds awaited our coming at the entrance to the village and the procession slowed almost to a standstill. Many of the throng were already
clutching glasses of wine and the noise was of bubbling excitement. The
frozen fingers of the bandsmen seemed to find life again, the drummers
beat a rhythm that echoed from wall to wall across the narrow streets
and we pressed on in triumph into Puligny, with the saints swaying above
our shoulders, the banners of the confréries raised to meet those that
sagged across the road and the urge to dance lifting the heels of the light-
hearted as they linked arms in anticipation of the evening.

The procession pushed through a dense hubbub of onlookers down
the Rue de Poiseul and erupted into Place Johannisberg where more
crowds were awaiting us, clustered around an absurd but spectacular set
piece: two vast prancing horses, twenty or thirty feet high, mounted by
knights in cardboard armour whose stuffing was packed in lumpy legs
like drooping sausages and whose shields bore the arms of Puligny. Other
figures were propped on balconies and grouped in courtyards around
old wine presses or sitting astride ancient tractors: figures of monks and
knights and maidens in medieval dress, and vignerons in smocks and
berets, with straw poking out from beneath their hats or behind their
masks or with the stiff elongated fingers on rigid limbs which betrayed
their transformation from shop window dummies. At intervals across
every street hung blue banners emblazoned in gold letters with the names
of Puligny's vineyards, from the glory of Montrachet to the humblest
lieux-dits of the village. And everywhere the flowers.

A line of cherry trees had burst into vivid pink blossom along a pavement in Place des Marronniers and the windowboxes of the Hôtel Le

Montrachet dripped with pink and purple sweet peas, so real you could almost smell them. Yellow roses climbed in profusion up the wall of their neighbour's house, above a bed planted with giant irises in every possible and improbable colour. Pale purple wisteria dripped from one balcony, cascades of laburnum from another. There were pots of pink geraniums, tubs of hydrangeas, baskets of azaleas and dahlias; tulips sprouted from the pavement and a magnificent *Magnolia soulangiana* spread its white flowers over the angle of a wall. As we processed down La Grande Rue, turned left down a narrow alley and wound our way slowly around the edge of the village to return to the Place du Monument, we passed hedges bright with paper petals and huge opulent bushes of gaudy roses, pushing their improbable blossoms through the bars of an old railing. In a small walled kitchen garden the leafless branches of a dozen willow bushes sprang from the bare red earth, apparently covered in tiny white catkins. Above a nearby fence erupted the long stems of winter-flowering jasmine, streams of yellow against the grey sky.

With the bands blaring and the marchers stamping their feet and slapping their hands against the penetrating cold, with breath rising like the steam from Monsieur Champion's still, the sheer surreal splendour of it all made the head spin. Halted momentarily in a side street as the procession squeezed its way towards the square, I noticed a bush of yellow forsythia, no more than four feet tall, and it occurred to me to count the tiny flowers. A rough calculation showed that this single bush was covered in at least three hundred yellow paper flowers, each individually made, each individually wired to its slender shoot or branch. Multiply that figure by the hundreds of bushes and trees, the hedgerows and the gardens, the tubs and pots and baskets and bouquets and garlands of flowers which decorated midwinter Puligny and you begin to get some idea of the extraordinary scale of the preparations which had occupied the villagers for the previous two years.

And so, finally, we arrived at the Place du Monument, already seething with people. The stewards with their walkie-talkies struggled to manoeuvre the bands and the saints into their allotted positions near the centre of the square, where a gaggle of small children dressed in traditional Burgundian costume chatted and nudged one another at the feet of the red-robed dignitaries clustered near the war memorial, the officers of the Chevaliers du Tastevin. Their standard bearer was a benev-

A gaggle of small children dressed in traditional Burgundian costume.

olent old duffer who beamed through his spectacles at the children, while his colleagues stood around in their quasi-historical splendour, mimicking the characterful profiles of early Renaissance portraits. They were attended by half a dozen lean, booted men in red coats, white stocks and riding caps, with hunting horns curled around their shoulders and faces like foxes, sniffing the crisp morning air. There, too, was the mayor of Puligny, Monsieur Lafond, with a tricolor sash slung slantwise across his overcoat, and the Sub-prefect of Burgundy, and the gendarmes, and of course the pressmen who obligingly snapped their shutters as the Sub-prefect, an experienced politician, made agreeable small talk with the mayor.

The band struck up a drum-roll, the mayor laid a wreath on the war memorial and there was one of those brief unexpected silences, perfectly timed (like a ripple of wind across a field of standing barley) before it was hats off for the Marseillaise. As this hymn of the revolution lifted over the crowd, lifting our hearts with it irresistibly, I thought of that fevered night of brandy and inspiration in Strasbourg, when Rouget de Lisle scribbled music and words in a frenzy of patriotic exhilaration, with the sure, show-stopping instinct of Rodgers and Hammerstein.

Then everyone was smiling and chatting again and the guardians of the saints from all the other villages of the Côte d'Or packed up their charges and furled their banners and raced home for their own celebration of the feast day, while the bands began to play and the men of Puligny lifted the little figure of St Bernard and started on another circuit of the streets, and we all headed for the church.

Ceremonies

There was an agreeable mixture of protocol and chance about who got into the church. The nave was reserved for dignitaries of the Confrérie de St Bernard, the Chevaliers du Tastevin, the Mayor, the Sub-prefect, various elderly vignerons of Puligny and others who had managed to wangle themselves a place, in diminishing order of precedence from altar to porch. It was guarded from the throng by several politely determined ladies of the village, who ushered the invited to their appointed seats and directed everyone else to the aisles. Here it was a matter of forethought and elbows, of getting to the church ahead of the rest and of pushing through the crowds at the door to find a seat. Soon there was standing room only and those of us who were safely ensconced in the aisles looked around at one another with an air of gentle self-congratulation, as others less fortunate retired to a crush at the back or the even greater crush in the little square outside. At which point only the photographers and television crews continued to force their way into the church, taking no heed of protests as they clambered on to anything that would give them a sightline or pushed one another up the narrow spiral staircase leading to the organ loft.

After a long, chattering wait there was a sudden commotion at the porch, the main doors of the church were thrown open, the organ burst from placid meanderings into triumphal chords and the choir began to sing a hymn of welcome. In came a procession of priests and bishops, culminating in Monseigneur Coloni, Bishop of Dijon, a short, cheerful figure wearing a mitre which appeared to be made of sackcloth and flourishing a sturdy wooden staff that looked more like a quarter stave than a crozier. 'Man is the image of God,' sang the choir, but the Bishop seemed more like a benign version of the American general then commanding the allied armies in the Gulf; the Church Militant, perhaps.

When all the ecclesiastical grandees had settled into their places around the altar the parish priest, Père Menestrier, gave a short speech of welcome. He referred to the ideals of solidarity and fraternity expressed by the Confrérie de St Bernard but he alluded with sadness to the war which had recently started in the Middle East and which had already claimed one casualty from Puligny's festivities; Monseigneur François Garnier, Bishop of Luçon, whose grief at the war had the force of close personal experience from his days as a missionary in that region, and who felt unable to attend as he had hoped, to give the sermon of celebration.

Those twin themes, of rejoicing and regret, gave peculiar force and poignancy to what might otherwise have been a ceremonial interlude of no great moment. The reading from the Gospel was St John's account of the miracle of Cana, when Jesus saved the wedding feast by turning water into wine. Everyone smiled in satisfaction. But the sturdy Bishop, speaking in place of his absent colleague, reminded the congregation that war was the world's sin, and all bowed their heads in penitence. Children of the village carried bread and wine to be blessed at the altar as the organ burst into exuberant voice, but most of the congregation went to receive communion with eyes lowered and an air of sombre meditation.

'Let us bless the Lord, Amen, Alleluia,' sang the choir and everyone rushed for the doors, surging outside into the tiny square which was already densely packed with visitors, waiting for the mass to be over. It was like opening a sluice gate: the force of the crowd pent up inside the church gushed in turbulent currents into the flood-swollen pool of the square. There was the statue of St Bernard, bobbing above the human waves, and there the bright red caps of the Chevaliers du Tastevin, separated one from another in the stream as the procession struggled to reform itself. The stewards tried to shield the oldest vignerons and vigneronnes from the torrent, piloting them to the cars which were to take them to the Château de Puligny (there to be enthroned as Chevaliers), but they were in danger of being carried off by the tide or dragged down by the undertow. Old Stephan Maroslavac staunchly pushed his way forward, an ancient St Christopher wading through the river, but his wife Katerina, confused and frail, lost her grip on his arm and was torn away, seeming close to drowning before she found a safe anchorage on the arm of another man, a family friend, who steered her through the flood to the shore.

The bands began to play and the procession moved forward inch by inch, shoulder to shoulder, through the narrow gorge to the Place du Monument and then flowed with increasing freedom down the Rue du But out of the village and along the stone wall which bounded the former park of the Château de Puligny, until we reached the yard of its modern cuverie. Here a large crowd was already gathered, held back by crush barriers from the stage which had been erected just inside the open doors of the high-tech building. I recognized the château's young winemaker, Jacques Montagnon, guarding the entrance to a privileged enclosure within the cuverie itself, reserved for invited dignitaries and the press. He gave me a cheerful wink and let me pass.

Three or four rows of chairs below the stage were filling up with a smartly dressed audience of important personages and local politicians but a much greater number of photographers, journalists, camera crews and other vultures had perched themselves precariously on gantries and ladders, stainless steel tanks and expensive wine presses, to the increasing but largely ineffective fury of the château's director, Monsieur Schneider. The stage itself was under attack from a particularly dangerous-looking gang, clad in black leather, black shades and unshaven black stubble, clutching cameras, microphones and portable arc lights.

They forced their way on to the steps beside the platform, ignored vociferous protests from others whose view they blocked and resolutely refused to be dislodged. On the stage itself, lost in the maelstrom and ignored by all who had supposedly come to honour them, the old vignerons and vigneronnes of Puligny sat in bemused wonder, waiting for their moment of glory.

Suddenly through the curtains at the back of the platform came the huntsmen, flourishing their curling horns. A wild fanfare, primitive and exhilarating, cut through the cackle like hounds giving tongue. They were followed on to the small stage by a gaggle of Chevaliers, the skirts of their red robes swirling and smothering the elderly villagers who were still seated meekly at the sides. Mayor Lafond took the microphone and made the obligatory speech of welcome to all the guests, thanks to all the organizers and summary of the history of Puligny, its Confrérie and its wines. The Commander of the Chevaliers followed him: more thanks, more history and a paeon in praise of Montrachet. All of which was well and entertainingly done. Then it was time for the 'intronisation'.

Despite the 'medieval' panoply of its ceremonials, the Confrérie des Chevaliers du Tastevin is not an ancient order nor is it in any way exclusive: anyone may join who has a few connections in the wine trade and can afford an expensive dinner at Clos Vougeot. Mostly that means foreigners and restaurateurs who like to frame the gaudy certificate of membership for the edification of their friends and customers. But as with the grand orders of chivalry, the Confrérie has different grades of membership and the higher ranks are reserved for those who have truly distinguished themselves and enhanced the renown of Burgundy. In addition, the Chevaliers du Tastevin are nominally responsible for organizing the St Vincent Tournante and they have established the tradition of honouring each year the oldest vignerons and vigneronnes of the host village. Hence the 'intronisation' at Puligny.

So the mayor was to be enrolled out of respect for his office, Loulou Carillon since it was his turn to be Président of Puligny's Confrérie du St Bernard, Vincent Leflaive as Président of the Syndicat des Vignerons, and ten octogenarians, because they were old. As each candidate was called to be honoured his or her merits were declaimed for the entertainment of the crowd which saluted them with varying degrees of enthusiasm while they were dubbed on each shoulder with a knobbly vine root and kissed on each cheek by the Grand Commander. Vincent

Leflaive, Stephan Maroslavac and Louis Thusseau got the most affectionately raucous welcome, the old Comtesse de Montlivaut (grande dame of Blagny) the most respectful.

Abruptly it was over. The arc lights were dowsed, the photographers scrambled down from their perches and the Chevaliers stood alone on the platform, faintly ridiculous in their dressing-gowns, as the audience swarmed outside. The ceremonies were concluded not with speeches or fanfares but by that most compelling of Burgundian instincts; the imperative inner rumble which declared that it was time for lunch.

Banquet

Lautrec would have loved her profile; the arched brows and the expressive line of her intelligent mouth and above all the nose; a nose of delicately exaggerated aquiline absurdity and wit, aristocratic in its elegance, pungently Parisian in the vivacity of its cut. The tip of this quite wonderful nose wrinkled in polite distaste as the Dutch journalist beside her lit another cigarette. His long dark hair hung in lank curtains beside a moustachioed face of squat self-importance. Beauty and the Beast.

They were sitting opposite me at a table immediately below the stage in the huge marquee which had been erected for the occasion, three-quarters of the way up the steep hill of Blagny. Outside was swirling fog and bitter cold, with ice riming the frozen land; stems, leaves and the filaments of cobwebs were petrified like delicate fossils from the Ice Age. Inside fifteen hundred guests were assembling for a six-course banquet, shedding coats and scarves to a line of fast-moving cloakroom girls at the counter near the entrance and gossiping in a gathering roar as friends found their tables and the aperitif was poured.

Few people would have chosen to spend their fiftieth birthday preparing a feast for such a crowd in such a place. Even the experienced Jean Crotet, chef of the Hôtellerie de Levernois, must occasionally have quailed as he calculated his profits and organized his team for the great day. The logistics alone were terrifying. Every piece of equipment (stoves and fridges, preparation tables and warm plates, saucepans, cutlery, crockery and glasses) had to be transported there; nearly fifty thousand separate items to be listed and counted and cleaned and counted again, minus the breakages. Plus hundreds of various fishes, vast quantities of lobsters, ten thousand snails, a truckload of hams and another of cheeses, morilles and marrons and chocolate cake and custard and coffee in mind-

Lautrec would have loved her profile.

boggling profusion. And the wine.

Which, alas, was the least interesting part of the feast. Monsieur Crotet managed miraculously to serve six interesting and well-cooked courses to this enormous throng (fish terrine with sauce verte, snails, sole mousse with lobster florentine, chicken and morilles, cheese, chocolate gâteau and marrons glacés) but the vignerons of Puligny provided for this banquet a selection of lack-lustre wines which did little to enhance the reputation of their village. Disguised by the special label which had been designed for the Committee of the St Vincent Tournante, the bottles preserved the anonymity of their producers; no one had an opportunity for personal glory, so none did more than avoid collective shame. The apéritif was a 1988 Puligny, a respectable if unexciting example which also accompanied the first course. Next came a 1986, oxidized and dull, and then an '86 Bâtard-Montrachet which should have been splendid but owed rather more to expensive new oak casks than exemplary winemaking. The chicken was served with a 1985 Puligny Premier Cru Les Combettes, decent if rather dull. By this time everyone was longing for some good red wine, so it was just as well that the '87 Clos du Cailleret Rouge listed on the menu (stewed taste, rather nasty) was accompanied by a simple 1987 Blagny, unannounced, which turned out in its modest straightforward way to be one of the most agreeable wines of that afternoon. A forgettable Crémant de Bourgogne was poured with the dessert.

Jean-François Bazin (Deputy Mayor of Dijon, journalist and author of a book on Montrachet) presided over the feast and made a confused but convivial speech in honour of Puligny, St Vincent and the Burgundian way of life. Loulou Carillon proposed the health of the chef and Vincent Leflaive told his well-known fable about Montrachet and his son the Chevalier and the Bâtard and Les Pucelles (the Virgins) and the unexpected arrival of the Bienvenues. All of which has been told many times before and was familiar to most of his audience but was received with great good humour both for Vincent's manner of telling it and because he is so universally loved. And every now and then Les Joyeaux Bourguignons sang incomprehensible drinking songs and led their audience in yet another rendition of the Chant Bourguignon; hands twisting in the air and clapping in rhythm in honour of one or another of the more distinguished guests or just for the sake of punctuation, between courses.

Throughout which the old Comtesse de Montlivaut, seated diago-
nally across the table from me, preserved a bird-like insouciance and
good humour, showing no sign of fatigue despite her considerable age.
This remarkable octogenarian lives in solitary splendour in the only
grand house of Blagny and is a major proprietor in most of the best
vineyards of this hamlet. 'Une vraie Bourguignonne,' whispered the
neighbour on my right. I nodded but immediately regretted having
done so because this brief gesture of comprehension was sufficient to
launch him on a lengthy exposition of his family history, his connection by cousinage to an important local domaine and the splendour of
the day's events. As it soon became apparent that nothing further was
demanded of me than the occasional nondescript exclamation, I glanced
at the old Countess with respect, listened with half-conscious polite-
ness to the gently agreeable chatter of her daughter-in-law, on my left,
and reserved all my attention for the niece sitting opposite, or rather
for the curve of her superlative nose. It lifted like the fin of a young
shark, cutting through the babble of self-satisfaction, and beside it an
eyelid was lowered in a palpable wink, the long lashes brushing away
cobwebs of boredom. We began a bantering conversation, an intermit-
tent game of mutual recognition which punctuated the ripple of gossip that lapped me from one side and the perfectly formed paragraphs
of prose which flooded me from the other. She raised an eyebrow,
wearily; I muttered a few dark words to provoke a smile and the corners of her expressive mouth pulled downwards with mischievous
amusement as she leaned across the table to deliver her so clearly enun-
ciated retort. In another time, another place, we might have linked these
fragments of compatibility into some tactile and continuing relationship, but the table was between us, the air filled with a suffocating fog
of respectability and all the pleasure was in riposte, not conjunction.

I forget how the feast proceeded but remember the skulking silhou-
ettes of the black-clad film crews, looming over the revellers with cameras and microphones. I remember, too, the brisk professionalism of the
waiters, serving and clearing, clearing and pouring and finally clearing
again the remnants of the long festivity; at which point, without further prompting, we left. Albert Franck's band began to play and 'Les
Miss Mediterranée' started to strut their stuff, a trailer for the evening's
entertainment, but nobody was in the mood for plastic rock. I collected
my coat, wrapped my scarf tight and headed into the darkness.

Outside the marquee the cold made me gasp. It was a world invisible. Accumulated social warmth and alcohol provided some sort of brief blanket but icicles relentlessly pierced the bones. Stumbling down the hill, jostled by unseen figures and bumping into stone walls and parked cars, I found myself constantly having to clamber out of the way as another pair of pale headlights flared through the thick layers of darkness. To escape this clogged stream of cars and lurching revellers I turned off the road into a path through the vines, uncertain of the direction but relishing the sudden solitude, hugging the cold and the stillness of the frozen slope, repeating silently to myself like an invocation the names of the Grands Crus, Premiers Crus and Village vineyards through which I groped my way, a litany of the appellations which seemed crudely to correspond to the actual invisible maze. Downhill had to be approximately the right direction and eventually I did indeed emerge from the vines on the north-west corner of the village.

Fuzzily against the faint lights of Puligny, visions of the night loomed eerily out of the fog, swaying groups of figures lurching along the roads, some singing, some silent. There were sudden scuffles and the sound of smashing glass, curses and contempt, attempts at restraint. Men were pissing in courtyards and against the walls, defiantly, and others pale, semi-conscious, were supported by their friends who half carried, half dragged them down the road. Girls cackled drunkenly, arm-in-arm, taunting the boys, and older couples huddled close to the walls for protection as they hurried timidly home, fearful of the brawling youths. The streets were littered with broken glass, plastic cups, paper wrappers and a scarf or a glove dropped in a fight, already rimed with frost and trampled by the feet of passers-by whose breath seemed to solidify in clouds of steam which froze in the icy air. The yellow beams of headlights, turning through the fog, silhouetted the figures of gendarmes standing at the intersections as drivers circled the village, looking for the Ball. And faintly from up the hill could be heard the beat of the band as Albert Franck squealed his trumpet at the throng of dancers now crowding the immense marquee.

The Morning After

I was awakened at first light by the grinding buzz of a small mechanical street-sweeper being pushed slowly around the pavements of Puligny. The accumulated litter of the night vanished into its innards but the

Sunday sky was dirty grey (dull, lifeless, with an unfulfilled hint of snow), the air dank and penetratingly cold, the expectant exhilaration of the previous dawn altogether vanished.

By breakfast time the squares were already filling with apparently aimless clusters of people, wandering from caveau to caveau, clutching the St Vincent glasses which they had purchased for twenty-five francs apiece from stalls on the periphery of the village and which entitled them to a taste of indifferent wine (the same in each cellar) served them by weary villagers for whom the thought of the evening and some rest outweighed all sense of celebration. Yesterday there had been the feeling that we were all participants in a truly local feast, as the saints and bands from the neighbouring villages had squeezed through the narrow streets and the exultant crowds. Now Puligny was selling itself, more or less comfortably, to a world which must pay and be ill rewarded. And the trippers from Germany, Belgium, Spain and Switzerland, from Japan and Paris and England and the youths from Beaune and Dijon drifted through a series of scenarios which might have blazed with colour and naïve delight if only the sun had shone but which seemed instead like the Christmas decorations of a previous year, reappearing one time too often, dusty and tawdry in the cold light of morning. Puligny had the air of an abandoned film set; just cardboard and stuffing and all the sad mechanisms of momentary illusion. The magic was over.

I breakfasted late, visited a display of cask-making manned by students from the viticultural school at Beaune, and dropped into the Mairie to witness the International Concours of Cadets-Sommeliers. The contest was taking place in the old schoolroom (redecorated for the occasion in vivid pink), which was packed with a crowd of onlookers, many of whom seemed to have come in to escape from the cold. On a small dais at the front of the room, the four judges sat around a table, laid with cutlery and glasses as if for a meal. Serious men for the most part (plus the slightly less lugubrious figure of Jean-Claude Wallerand, sommelier of Le Montrachet), they listened impassively as a young contestant tasted a 1988 Auxey-Duresses and then tried to describe it. He spoke haltingly, using phraseology familiar from the wine magazines, hackneyed words which could as aptly have been applied to almost any wine. But the judges seemed well enough pleased and summoned the next candidate. She was dressed, like the others, in a black cutaway jacket and black apron, with a cluster of gilded grapes at her lapel, symbol of her profession. The judges consulted an imaginary menu and ordered lunch, then asked the girl to recommend wines for each course.

She began boldly, suggesting a Bourgogne Aligoté de Bouzeron with the fish, a young wine with sufficient acidity to enliven the palate at the start of a meal. It seemed to me an excellent choice but the judges were in no mood for such a modest wine and firmly steered the poor girl in the direction of something more substantial. Rashly she forgot which village she was in and proffered a Meursault, from Puligny's neighbour and rival. The judges snorted and insisted on Montrachet. Nothing but the best was clearly their motto on this occasion, however inappropriate the balance and sequence might be. Curbing her intelligence, the girl followed their lead, suggesting a '78 Gevrey-Chambertin with the meat and a fabulously expensive La Romanée with the cheese, but she slipped up badly by proferring a Marc de Bourgogne with the coffee. I wanted to applaud this decisive recommendation for clearing the palate but the judges thought it much too rustic a digestif for their distinguished tastebuds and bullied the girl into endorsing their own choice of Armagnac. Close to tears, she retired from the fray and I, disconsolate, left the room.

Two things were evident throughout the contest. One was the regional chauvinism of all concerned (nobody thought to suggest a wine from Bordeaux, let alone from Italy or Australia), and the other the extraordinary conservatism of the judges, whose taste embalmed the gastronomic preferences of the nineteenth century. Luxury was all. Originality of choice, true discrimination, witty combination of flavours, vivacity and eclecticism were clearly regarded as defects. The job of the sommelier, in the eyes of these judges, was to uphold the greater glory of Burgundian wine and to flatter the self-esteem of their customers by proposing wines of obvious renown, which none of them could normally have afforded.

And so the day drifted by, with cars parked on the verges of all the roads for miles in every direction around the village and the crowds continuing to pack the streets. The decorations had lost their freshness and the weather was awful, but still the visitors came and each one contributed to the staggering statistics of that weekend. One hundred and ten thousand of the specially decorated St Vincent glasses were sold, at considerable profit to the village, plus large numbers of posters and pens and aprons and other souvenirs of the festivities. Twenty-nine thousand bottles of the Cuvée St-Vincent were consumed, at very little cost to the growers (most of it was excess production which should officially have gone for distillation). The commune of Puligny made a profit of more than half a million francs. Forty-three visitors were found semi-comatose in the streets on Sunday night and thirty-three on Saturday. All in all, there was cause for congratulations.

The Year Begins Again

The next day I climbed to a point high above Blagny, to the prow of Mont Rachet near the boundary with St-Aubin, where the orientation of the vineyards changes abruptly from south-east to south-west and where they lie exposed to the chill winds coming down the valley from the north. Perched on a half-ruined wall, I looked back towards Puligny, far below. Already they had cleared away the lines of Christmas trees which had stretched up the hillside from the village; the landscape was returned to its midwinter bareness and the vignerons were back at work, pruning their vines. Grey smoke from their bonfires drifted along the slope to mingle with the mist and the low-lying clouds. The smell of those fires and of the damp red earth, the stinging cold and the hard angularity of the rock on which I sat combined to lift my heart suddenly out of the dumps. The mad, crowded weekend was over and all was well. All remnants of the uncomfortable, long-drawn-out unease of the second day of those celebrations vanished in the air as Puligny and its vines resumed the unhurried rhythms of daily life, familiar, steady and by now much loved.

After years of listening and watching and asking questions, trying to locate the heart of village life, I realized the essence of Puligny is stillness, not social activity, that the spirit of the place is dispersed in the land, not focused on a building or institution, and that a cold, grey, rainy day in January scouring the heart's malaise, is more expressive of the constant renewal of rural life than anything which has ever been spoken or written about the place and its people.

Sitting on the cold hillside, breathing the scents of mist and smoke, and imagining that I could smell the rising sap of the new year at every cut of the pruning knife, I remembered that each vintage is the harvest of a thousand smells, accumulated imperceptibly during the slow ripening of the vine and that this accumulation continues afterwards, until the wine is bottled. When made honourably, without unnecessary artifice, a mature vintage from one of the great vineyards of Puligny-Montrachet can evoke the full cycle of the seasons: winter sharpness and the spark of broken flint under the plough steel; budburst and sap of early spring; lush leafiness and the faint honeyed scents of pollen; drowsy summer heat, baked earth, wilting wildflowers; the astringency of grape skins and stalks and the juicy sweetness of pulpy fruit; yeasts and fermentation; oak staves and autumn bonfires; the cool, damp fern and limestone smells of a dark cellar. All these scents and more are refined with time into an intense but elusive testimony to the place. Savouring such a wine is like listening to a vigorous old man, grand and immensely civilized but born a peasant, telling the tales of his long and varied life. Taste is memory distilled.

APPENDICES

APPENDIX I

Appellations

The Grands Crus

The five Grands Crus of Montrachet are clustered together at the southern end of the hill, on the border between Chassagne and Puligny. French troops marching down the Route Nationale used to salute Montrachet as they passed, but nothing now announces to the visitor that he is walking through some of the most remarkable vineyards in the world. Their walls are neglected, their gateways are open; the very anonymity of these irregular patches of vines is their only protection from trampling tourists.

Chassagne claims one of these Grands Crus exclusively (Criots-Bâtard-Montrachet, a tiny vineyard of one and a half hectares) and has a half share in two others: Montrachet itself and Bâtard. The other halves of these appellations, plus the whole of Chevalier and Bienvenues, lie within the boundaries of Puligny.

Montrachet is long but narrow, eight hectares of exceedingly precious land which begins in a rough terrace, immediately above the track that marks its boundary with the Chassagne Premier Cru of Blanchot Dessus. At this end of the vineyard, climbing up the narrow road which divides Montrachet from Bâtard, you pass four or five rather grand gateways set with incongruous pretension into a low stone wall; all that remains of the head-high structure which must once have surrounded this renowned site. Each gate belongs to one of the domaines which own segments of this appellation and most are inscribed with the nineteenth-century form of its name: Grand Montrachet. From the different coloured tags which identify ownership of rows and part rows of vines it is equally clear that Chassagne's half of Montrachet is divided between a great many growers. In fact an area of just under four hectares is shared between a dozen proprietors. The largest portion (just under two hectares) belongs to Domaine Thenard, of Givry, but the most renowned is the tiny patch which produces the fabulously expensive Montrachet of the Domaine de la Romanée-Conti. Perhaps in future that fame will be matched by Leflaive's recently acquired morsel, but their holding is so small that few will ever have the chance to taste the end result.

In Puligny's half of the vineyard there are few gateways and fewer proprietors. Four domaines share the land. Two hectares belong to the Marquis de Laguiche, an absentee landowner whose wine is made by the respected firm of Drouhin, in Beaune. One hectare belongs to another Beaune négociant, Bouchard Père et Fils, a quarter-hectare to the Ramonets of Chassagne, and three-quarters of a

The Grands Crus of Montrachet are clustered together at the southern end of the hill.

hectare is divided between the numerous heirs to the Domaine Boillerault de Chauvigny, most of whom live in Paris. Their grapes are sold to some of the top négociants. It is a sad but longstanding fact that not a single square metre of Puligny's most famous vineyard is owned by an inhabitant of the village.

What of the often reported qualitative difference between the two halves of Montrachet? There are certainly some quite evident physical variations. The Chassagne end of the vineyard falls lower down the hill and turns slightly but noticeably to the south. Perhaps because of this the rows of vines are planted on a north-south axis, so that the sunlight slants down the alleys for most of the day. In the rest of the vineyard, as in all the other vineyards of Puligny, the rows are oriented east–west, reflecting the fact that the land itself is tilted more to the east. It is also arguable that the soil in the lowest part of Chassagne's portion of Montrachet is marginally richer than that at the Puligny end. All of which would probably be sufficient to account for the wines being slightly richer from Chassagne, slightly more elegant from Puligny.

That is what many have asserted and continue to affirm, but the evidence is extremely confusing. Since no proprietor owns vines in both sections of Montrachet it is impossible to compare like with like; we may easily attribute to the soil what are in fact stylistic differences that reflect the character and preferences of individual winemakers. My own tastings suggest that there are three pre-eminent producers of Montrachet, all bottling very different wines. That made by Drouhin for the Marquis de Laguiche is the most elegant, while Ramonet's Montrachet has superlative spicy complexity: both are from the Puligny end of the vineyard. Somewhat between the two, with an initial reserve which can develop into great splendour, is the wine of Domaine de la Romanée-Conti, from Chassagne. None of the other growers makes a Montrachet which has quite the overwhelming exhilaration of a good vintage from one of these three and there are some who disgrace the vineyard's reputation (and their own) by what they sell under this label. Montrachet can be so extraordinarily good that you forget about the outrageous price, but it can equally be so disappointing that you are left with a sad feeling of having been conned.

Chevalier-Montrachet climbs up the hill above Montrachet itself and is only slightly smaller (seven point three hectares) but falls entirely within Puligny. The slope of the hill is considerably steeper and particularly at its southern end the vineyard is much broken up by 'murgers', the piles of rocks which provide such vivid testimony to the back-breaking labour of those who originally cleared this land. Its outline is somewhat irregular towards its upper limits and there is evidence that formerly the vines climbed higher up the hill, but erosion has put paid to those fringes. It is clear that the soil is extremely poor and has a higher proportion of lime mixed in it than you find in Montrachet; consequently the wine tends to be somewhat lighter, emphasizing finesse rather than power.

Since the introduction of Appellation Contrôlée, Chevalier has gained two significant chunks from neighbouring vineyards, both the subject of some

The soil is extremely poor and has a higher proportion of lime mixed in it than you find in Montrachet.

controversy. In 1939 a hectare of vines in Le Cailleret was officially granted the appellation of Chevalier at the request of its owners, the Beaune négociants Louis Latour and Louis Jadot, who referred to this parcel as Les Demoiselles. Their application was fiercely resisted by Joseph Leflaive and the other growers of Puligny but somehow the commission was persuaded. Les Demoiselles was promoted from Premier Cru to Grand Cru status. In 1955 Jean Chartron (mayor of Puligny) requested that another parcel of Le Cailleret belonging to his family be re-classified in similar fashion, to add to the large segment of Chevalier which he already owned. In 1974 that request was finally granted and Chevalier was further enlarged, this time by a quarter of a hectare.

Whether or not these extensions of the appellation were fully justified remains a matter of some debate, but there is no doubt that the traditional heart of the vineyard is capable of producing great wine, fully worthy of its Grand Cru classification; better than all but the very finest wines from Montrachet itself. Subtlety, elegance and seductive charm are the characteristics of a fine Chevalier — indeed the wine is often so delicious when young that it is tempting not to wait. But there should also be underlying structure, sufficient to enable Chevalier from a good vintage to benefit from at least a decade of bottle age.

The best example, without any question at all, comes from the Domaine Leflaive, which owns nearly two hectares of this appellation. Bouchard Père et Fils of Beaune have a slightly larger share of the vineyard but their Chevalier has never excited me to the same degree. Nor have the wines from those other growers whom I have mentioned. But there is greater consistency of quality in the production of Chevalier than of Montrachet itself; I have regularly been disappointed by only one producer, Jacques Prieur.

Bâtard-Montrachet is the largest of the Grands Crus (nearly twelve hectares, just under half of which lies in Chassagne) and the most fragmented. The land is divided between more than thirty-five owners. The most important (Domaine Leflaive) controls nearly two hectares, but the vast majority of the growers have less than a quarter-hectare and the smallest holding of all (three ares seventy centiares) is just sufficient to make half a cask of wine. As a result of this division of ownership (and because most of the larger proprietors have holdings which are split between both villages) it is impossible to distinguish a typically 'Chassagne' or 'Puligny' taste to the wines of Bâtard. But there is a clear family resemblance between the wines of this vineyard, even those from the least distinguished of producers. They have a richness of flavour, a weight, which is unlike most of the other Grands or Premiers Crus, and tasters are often reminded of toasted bread, nuts and honey.

These characteristics result from the vineyard's situation. Lying across the road from Montrachet, Bâtard starts several feet lower down than its neighbour and descends in a very gentle slope towards the village. The soil is deep, rich, and has a high proportion of clay, hence the amplitude and longevity of the wines. The 1860 classification put the top third of the vineyard (that section closest to

Montrachet) into the Premières Cuvées while the rest was relegated to the Deuxièmes Cuvées. Many growers would agree with this assessment today but it is not a distinction recognized by the appellation nor one that can be identified from the labels.

Because of the tiny landholdings, much of the wine is sold to the négociants but there are still numerous growers' labels to choose from. Of these, the finest quality comes from Ramonet of Chassagne (whose holding lies within the Puligny section of the vineyard) and from Domaines Leflaive and Sauzet of Puligny, whose holdings lie in both villages. Several other proprietors come close to this level and in my experience it is relatively unusual to find a poor bottle of Bâtard, though rustic vigour can sometimes be more evident than complexity or finesse.

Bienvenues-Bâtard-Montrachet is a roughly rectangular block of 3.68 hectares which fills what would otherwise be the north-east corner of Bâtard, at the lowest end of the vineyard. The boundaries are partially defined by the remnants of low walls but for the most part you have to look very closely to notice a break in the rows of vines, or a slight change of direction, which marks the change of appellation from Bâtard to Bienvenues. Because it is at the bottom end of the slope, having fractionally less satisfactory exposure and worse drainage, Bienvenues produces wines which tend to be lighter, less long-lived and which never quite achieve the quality of the best examples from its neighbour, but the style is extremely similar and differences of taste are more often the reflection of the aptitudes of different producers than of the soil. The finest producers are the same as for Bâtard (plus Carillon) and of these the largest proprietor is again Leflaive, with nearly a third of the appellation.

The name, meaning 'welcome', has an ancient association with land farmed *en métayage*, by tenants who themselves undertook the labour of cultivation but shared the crop with their lord. But various local growers will readily weave you an engaging 'historical' fable which twines together the names of Montrachet, Chevalier, Bâtard, Bienvenues and Les Pucelles (the Virgins, perhaps the best of the Premiers Crus). It's fun, very French and complete nonsense.

Puligny Premier Cru

The Premiers Crus of Puligny lie north of the Grands Crus and west (i.e. uphill) of the basic 'Village' vineyards, from which they are separated by Le Sentier de Couches, reputedly the old Roman road from Meursault to Santenay. The best vineyards are those situated at opposite ends of the slope: south, adjacent to Montrachet, and north, on the boundary with Meursault's finest Cru, Les Perrières.

That much is certain, but there is considerable ambiguity about names, numbers and even location of these Premiers Crus of Puligny. You can reckon on somewhere between thirteen and twenty-four vineyards, depending on how you count them, and there appears to be a good deal of latitude in determining which designations are permitted by the laws of appellation. Some proprietors choose to sell their wine under the name of the 'lieu-dit', some under the name of the 'climat', and none of the maps mark all the options. I have listed the main appellations in common use and indicated where possible the alternative names which may sometimes be employed.

Les Demoiselles presents me with the first and most serious problem: where is it? I have already mentioned the vineyard of this name which lies above Le Cailleret and adjacent to the Grand Cru of Chevalier, of which it is now legally counted a part. There is, apparently, another section which is classified as a Premier Cru, unmarked on the most authoritative maps and unrecognized as a distinctive appellation. Several writers refer to Les Demoiselles as the finest of the Premiers Crus, state its size as just under a hectare and suggest that it is bounded by Chevalier on one side, Montrachet on another, and that it lies at the southern end of Le Cailleret. All of which seems clear enough except that Domaine Chartron claims the whole of Le Cailleret as its exclusive property, designated as Clos du Cailleret. And they produce a map of the domaine's holdings which leaves no room to sandwich a hectare of vineyard in the narrow lane which separates Clos du Cailleret from Montrachet. As for the land above Le Cailleret, one slice is owned by Chartron and the rest is entitled to the appellation of neighbouring Chevalier. It's all a bit of a mystery, but two producers bottle wines with the appellation Les Demoiselles Premier Cru (Guy Amiot and Michel Colin, both of Chassagne) and those who have tasted them shower praise on that from Colin. I plead ignorance.

Le Cailleret is, or should be, the finest of the Premiers Crus since it is effectively a continuation of Montrachet to the north. Of comparable shape, size (just under four hectares) and altitude to Puligny's half of Montrachet, it appears from the map to deserve Grand Cru status and it was indeed classified in the first rank on the Agricultural Commission's map of 1860. But there are differences between Le Cailleret and its famous neighbour. Its soil is very stony (hence its name) and it slips slightly lower down the hill. Perhaps more important, it catches less of the afternoon sun and is less well sheltered by vineyards above; indeed part of it abuts on to barren rock and would suffer badly from erosion were it not protected by a wall.

This wall surrounds the appellation on three sides (the fourth being the road which leads to Blagny) and justifies its title as Clos du Cailleret, the name given it by its owners, Domaine Chartron. Chartron used to be contracted to supply the whole of the harvest to the house of Drouhin, who made an excellent wine from it. Now the wine is made and sold by Chartron themselves. My impression is that recent vintages of Clos du Cailleret are well balanced and 'correct', but lack the excitement which one might expect from so well-sited a vineyard. Curiously enough I prefer the lean but characterful Pinot Noir which comes from a small strip that divides Le Cailleret in two, producing the only red Premier Cru within the commune of Puligny.

Les Pucelles is to Le Cailleret as Bâtard is to Montrachet; in other words it lies immediately downhill of its neighbour and produces wines which are rather fatter, more immediate in their appeal. The southern boundary of Les Pucelles is divided only by a road from Bâtard and Bienvenues; its wines have a similar character, on a smaller scale. Seductively scented, softly textured, more poule de luxe than virginal, Les Pucelles mature fast but can be irresistible. The best example comes from Domaine Leflaive, which owns nearly three hectares out of the six and three-quarters hectares which constitute this appellation. Their holding is in two blocks, one of which lies within the southern third of the vineyard, traditionally known as Grandes Pucelles and classified in the nineteenth century at a higher rank than the rest. Les Pucelles contains within its boundaries a section called Clos des Meix (occasionally sold as a separate appellation) and, confusingly, another *clos* (Clos de la Pucelle) which is the exclusivity of Domaine Chartron. Just over a hectare in extent, this *Clos* incorporates parts of Petites Pucelles and Clos des Meix, on the northern boundary of the *climat*. Other proprietors include Pernot, Maroslavac, Chavy and Moroni from Puligny, Marc Morey from Chassagne and Boillot from Volnay. The name of the vineyard has a more prosaic origin than many would wish: 'Poucelles' or 'Parcelles', meaning land which is much divided between its proprietors.

Les Folatières is by far the biggest of the Premiers Crus (over seventeen and a half hectares) and incorporates the largest number of individually named 'lieux-dits': Ez Folatières, En la Richarde, Peux Bois and Au Chaniot. It is a steep vineyard, much subject to erosion which washes away the soil, hence its name (Folle-Terre). The fact that the ground is so stony and difficult to cultivate meant that most of this vineyard was not planted until 1959, with the help of a good deal of dynamite. But the results certainly justified the labour, because the combination of excellent exposure and lime-rich soil produces wines which can seem austere when young but have the structure for long ageing. A mature bottle of Folatières often has very considerable finesse, and sometimes an attractive nuttiness on the palate, elegant and graceful.

A big slice of the vineyard belongs to Pernot, who sells most of his grapes to the négociant firm of Drouhin. Their wine I know to be excellent and Pernot's own production also has a good reputation, but I have not tasted it. The other substantial proprietor of Folatières is Domaine Chartron, and various smaller fractions are owned by Leflaive, Meney, Pascal, Clerc and Gérard Chavy (all from Puligny) plus one or two growers in Meursault.

Clavaillon, by contrast, has only two owners: Domaine Leflaive (with five hectares) and Gérard Chavy (half a hectare). It lies immediately to the south of Folatières, lower down the slope and on richer, deeper soil. Apparently it was once renowned for its red wine, but now produces a white which is surprisingly elegant but also has some of the substance and structure which you might expect from its situation. Never a great wine, the Clavaillon from Leflaive is nonetheless exceedingly well balanced and often (by Puligny standards) good value for money. The vineyard's name is derived from that of a thirteenth-century seigneur of Puligny.

Champ Gain is the highest of the Puligny Premiérs Crus (up to three hundred and sixty metres) and one of the most recently planted. Ten point seven hectares in extent, it lies above Les Folatières, from which it is divided by an irregular patch of barren rock and woods. The soil is meagre, much mingled with limestone, and the upper third of the vineyard was nothing but scrub and stones until the seventies, when Stephan Maroslavac brought in a huge machine to break up the rock and reclaim for the vine what had lain uncultivated since the arrival of phylloxera, a century earlier. The name Champ Gain (Meadow Reclaimed) suggests that the whole of this appellation was thus laboriously won for cultivation from the unyielding hill. Maroslavac's three hectares produce a characteristic Champ Gain, the initial impression of ripe fruit giving way to a sappy astringency, but with good length of flavour. Other proprietors include Joly (who sells his harvest to the négoces) and the firm of Olivier Leflaive, which makes the best wine of this appellation.

La Truffière, as its name implies, was formerly the place where you would go to hunt for truffles, suggesting that it must then have been shaded by beech trees or oaks. The present vineyard is divided by an old quarry and is one of the smallest (two and a half hectares) and least known of the Premiers Crus. Most of the production is sold to the négoces and blended with that from other Premiers Crus of the village. The exception was the small quantity produced by Domaine Sauzet from their quarter hectare of La Truffière, but this is an exception which makes me regret the disappearance of the rest into the négociant's soup. Sauzet's wine had, somehow, a scent of truffles and its elegant structure was overlaid with enticing fruit. The past tense is indicative, because the division of the family inheritance means that La Truffière now belongs to Jean-Marc Boillot of Volnay, an extremely capable vigneron who should continue to produce a good wine.

Les Chalumeaux lies north along the slope from La Truffière and abuts the boundary with Meursault. Its five and three-quarters hectares includes the *lieu-dit* of Sous le Courthil, just below the Comtesse de Montlivant's tennis court at Blagny, and is bounded by old quarries and scrawny woods. The name implies tubes or spouts, perhaps suggesting the crannies in the rock which abound hereabouts, and the soil is an extremely porous mixture of gravel and limestone. Together with its aspect (which is distinctly more to the east than most of the other Premiers Crus) this results in wines which are relatively light and quick-maturing, but which can have considerable finesse. A good Chalumeaux is produced by Pascal of Puligny and there are said to be honourable examples from some of the Meursault growers, including Pitoiset-Urena and Matrot — I have not tasted them.

Champ Canet (five and a half hectares) incorporates two other *lieux-dits*, La Jacquelotte and Clos de la Garenne. I've never seen the former on a label, but

Clos de la Garenne is a fine walled vineyard, most of which belongs to the Duc de Magenta and is now farmed by the renowned Beaune négociants, Louis Jadot. Lying below Les Chalumeaux, the rock of Champ Canet is also deeply fissured, so the roots of the vines can burrow deep enough to survive the drought which tends to afflict this scanty soil. There is perhaps more lime here and the wines can vary from the relatively substantial example from Domaine Sauzet (a marvellous wine) to the generally lighter specimens which are typical of most other producers. Carillon makes a fine Champ Canet and Meney's is said to be good. I have not been able to discover the authentic origin of the vineyard's name, so I persist in my illusion that this once was a meadow grazed by ducks.

Les Perrières. We have come back down the hill, below Clos de la Garenne, alongside Clavaillon. In fact this end of the vineyard is a four-hectare *clos* (out of the total for Les Perrières of eight and a half hectares) called Clos de la Mouchère, the exclusive property of Domaine Boillot of Volnay. The walled *clos* gains its name from the bees ('mouches à miel') which used to swarm there, whereas the name of the *climat* as a whole recalls the quarries which were excavated just above the present vines. Exceedingly well-balanced soil, rich but not too heavy, with plenty of pebbles, streaks of iron oxide, marl and lime; Les Perrières is not dissimilar in this respect from Montrachet itself, but the altitude is lower, the aspect more southerly and the wines less grand. It used to be known for its red wines but now entirely produces whites, which can be a little heavy but are long-lived and generous. The best comes from the old vines of Sauzet and I have tasted excellent examples from Carillon and Gérard Chavy.

Les Referts (five and a half hectares) is effectively a continuation of Les Perrières along the slope to the north and is often counted as the *climat* of which Les Perrières is part. Drainage and aspect are very similar, the soil perhaps a little heavier, with a fair amount of clay. The result is a rich wine, sometimes lacking finesse, reminding me of Meursault more than Puligny; not surprising since the vineyard's northern boundary is that of the neighbouring village. Sauzet and Carillon make the best wines of this vineyard, which is split between several proprietors, including Maroslavac.

Les Combettes. The name refers to the combes or deep crannies in the otherwise dense rock which underlies this vineyard. Nearly seven hectares in extent, Les Combettes is above Referts, below Champ Canet and on the border with Meursault. Its soil ranges from a high proportion of limestone at the top of the vineyard to a fair amount of clay at the bottom, and the character of its wines should ideally be balanced between the typical characteristics of both: combining elegance with power. At its best, Les Combettes does indeed exhibit this refined splendour, with a nuttiness and 'sweetness' of aroma which is characteristic of Meursault. Balancing the austerity of Cailleret at the other end of the slope, Les Combettes is the most generous of the great Premiers Crus of Puligny. Leflaive and Sauzet challenge each other to make the best wine of this appellation, followed by Carillon and Clerc. Ampeau of Meursault owns a good chunk of the vineyard and makes a fine wine, as do other smaller owners, but a fair amount of Combettes is sold to the négoces.

Blagny

The octogenarian Comtesse de Montlivaut, a small, alert, bird-like Burgundian, lives alone in a rambling house of no great architectural distinction but splendid views, high above Puligny in the hamlet of Blagny. Her near neighbour is Monsieur Matrot (a well-known vigneron of Meursault), and a short way down the hill is the hideous Swiss chalet of Bernard Clerc. Otherwise there are a few barns, the old chapel of the monks from Maizières, and two or three cottages which appear locked and deserted. This tiny settlement falls within the boundaries of the commune of Puligny, as do half its vineyards. The other half, on the northern side of the hill, belong to Meursault.

Partly as a result of this division between the two communes, partly because Blagny is still noted for its red wines almost as much as for its whites, the system of appellations is somewhat confusing. Most of the vineyards on Puligny's side of the hill are entitled to the appellation Puligny Premeir Cru if the wine is white, or Blagny Premier Cru if the wine is red. One vineyard, above the rest, is simply entitled to the village appellation of Puligny or Blagny, depending on the colour of the wine. In Meursault, by contrast, the majority of the vineyards retain the right to the appellation Blagny Premeir Cru for the reds but can claim only the village appellation of Meursault for the whites. I shall confine my remarks to Puligny's side of the hill but it is worth noting that my favourite red Blagny, from Domaine Leflaive, comes from vineyards which lie just within Meursault.

Hameau de Blagny. About four and a quarter hectares lying immediately below the houses of Blagny and above La Truffière, this vineyard has quite rich, deep gravelly soil which might be better suited to the production of Pinot Noir than the Chardonnay which is more generally grown there. As with most of the Blagny vineyards, the Comtesse de Montlivaut is the major proprietor but her estate is farmed by a number of tenants, including Clerc. The whites are supposed to be aromatic, elegant and capable of modest maturation. I have not tasted any which particularly excited me.

La Garenne is a long strip of a vineyard (nearly ten hectares) which stretches from Blagny to the borders of St-Aubin, immediately above Champ Gain. The soil is similar to Hameau de Blagny but the ground seems a bit rockier and the exposure is more southerly. Altitude (and therefore a cooler microclimate) necessarily means that the wines rely more on finesse than force of character, but those from La Garenne can have greater substance than others from Blagny. Producers include a number of growers from St-Aubin and Domaine Baudrand, from Corpeau, but one of the best examples comes from the négociant firm of Drouhin.

Sous le Puits. Above Blagny, adjacent to the border with Meursault, this vineyard is high, fairly exposed and decidedly richer in limestone (i.e. having a more impoverished soil) than either La Garenne or Hameau de Blagny. The combination of cold winds and thin soil means the vines ripen late and can thereby attain an agreeable aromatic complexity, but seldom have much weight. The best wine is unquestionably the white which comes from Jean-Claude Bachelet of St-Aubin, one of the great characters of Burgundy, utterly wedded to the traditional ways. The vineyard's name comes from the old well ('puits') at the top of the hill, which still supplies water to Blagny.

Le Trezin. Above La Garenne, south of Sous le Puits, this is the least favoured vineyard of Blagny, entitled only to the simple village appellation.

Puligny-Montrachet (Village)

The basic village appellation covers one hundred and fourteen hectares of vines which lie below Le Sentier de Couches (the road from Meursault to Chassagne) and above and around Puligny itself. In general these vineyards have rather heavy soil, poorly drained, and lie on the gentlest of slopes. Some are clearly much better situated than others (particularly Les Enseignères, which lies immediately below Bâtard-Montrachet and Les Charmes, on the border with Meursault below Les Referts), but it is exceedingly rare to find a vineyard name on the label and thus impossible for the consumer to identify the exact origin of his wine. In any case, most proprietors have small holdings in several different *lieux-dits*, which they blend together to make a uniform wine, so the question of vineyard name is largely irrelevant. One exception to this is L'Enclos du Château of Maroslavac, which comes from a sheltered vineyard surrounded by a high stone wall, immediately adjacent to the Vieux Château in which he lives.

Given the considerable variation in potential of the different village vineyards, the difficulty of identifying the precise origin of a Puligny-Montrachet from the label alone and the exceedingly depressing quality of some wines from this appellation, you have to rely on the name of the producer when choosing. Reliable Puligny can be had from most of the domaines mentioned in this book's section on the growers (Chapters nine to twelve); my favourites are those from Sauzet, Domaine Leflaive and Carillon.

Approximately four-fifths of the village production is sold to the négociants. The results are generally undistinguished wines, offering very poor value for money.

Bourgogne

Below the village, on flat land which stretches as far east as the Paris-Lyon railway line, nearly two hundred and fifty hectares of vines come within the communal boundaries but outside the appellation of Puligny. The wines are sold as Bourgogne (which can be either red Pinot or white Chardonnay), Bourgogne Aligoté (exclusively from that refreshingly appetizing white grape) or Bourgogne Passe-

Tout-Grains — an appellation rarely seen now, being a blend of Gamay and Pinot which normally obliterates the character of each grape variety. A good Bourgogne Blanc or Bourgogne Aligoté, from a reputable producer, can offer far better value for money than a Puligny-Montrachet Village, and may sometimes be of better quality. Here again, it's a question of choosing your wine from the most reputable domaines. Some vineyard names occasionally appear on labels: look out for Champ Perrier, Les Femelottes, Les Houillères and Les Setilles.

APPENDIX II

Vintages

The great years for red burgundy rarely coincide with the best vintages of the white wines because Pinot Noir and Chardonnay respond in quite different ways to varying weather conditions. Of particular importance is Pinot's relative tardiness in terms of ripening date; Chardonnay grapes are always ready for picking between a week and a fortnight earlier, which can make a big difference to final quality. The weather is often very changeable around the autumn equinox. An extended Indian summer may save the vintage after months of grey skies, or torrential rain can bring dilution and rot, washing away the expectations engendered by a heatwave in August. As it happens, many of the best red vintages during the past decade have been made by a burst of late sunshine, whereas Chardonnay has seldom found the perfect balance of sun and rain to bring ripeness without serious loss of acidity. It's a delicate balance, easily missed, and we have had to content ourselves with a series of good vintages but hardly any which were truly great.

Caveat. Vintage notes are generalizations; each wine is different. What follows is necessarily a simplification of conditions over the past twenty years.

1991   Cold weather in June caused an uneven flowering, with a fair amount of *millerandage* (a condition when some or all of the grapes in a cluster remain hard and small). A hot, dry summer promised a great year until a solid week of rain in September, just before the harvest, caused a good deal of dilution and some rot. The wines will be agreeable but rather light, perhaps comparable in style to 1982.

1990   June was cold and wet but the summer was hot and there was just the right amount of rain in September before a fine vintage. The size of the harvest seems to be all that prevented this being a great year. The grapes were ripe, acidity rather low and the wines charming but generally rather soft in style, unlikely to be notable keepers. From old vines and vigorously pruned vineyards, some much more substantial wines were made.

1989   A marvellous summer ripened the grapes rapidly for a very early vintage. A big crop was harvested, of generous wines, low in acidity but unexpectedly well balanced nonetheless. There were signs of overripeness and botrytis, producing rich and bizarre flavours in some of the late-picked grapes, but the best wines of the vintage have surprising concentration and will benefit from several years' maturity in bottle.

1988   A fine spring, summer and autumn produced a big, healthy crop, weakened only by its size. The structural elements of a great vintage were there, but diluted among too many grapes. The best wines have real character, good acidity and length of flavour and will keep for a long time; but these are the exceptions.

1987   September was cold and rainy, ruining the effects of a good summer. Many wines were light, meagre and dilute but the crop was small and the best (notably those picked early) have lasted well and are still enjoyable, in a minor key.

1986   Fine weather throughout the spring and summer produced a big crop, but there was rain before the vintage which added rot and dilution to the problems of over-production. Nonetheless this was a year which produced many delicious wines with the acidity to keep them fresh and with considerable elegance of flavour. Most were best enjoyed young.

1985   A mediocre summer ended in a spectacular autumn, producing an unexpectedly large crop of magnificent reds and fine whites. The latter are more marked by power than by elegance and some seem to lack grace. But the finest should be kept and will be magnificent.

1984   A cold, wet year ending in a foul vintage produced unripe grapes, high in acidity and low in natural sugar. The best were harvested late and have developed surprisingly well with bottle age, but most are now past their peak.

1983   A wet July was followed by exceptionally hot (and occasionally rainy) weather in August and September. Botrytis spread rapidly through the vineyards, enabling a few growers to make sweet wines, in the style of Sauternes! For most, however, the results were bizarre, alcoholic, overripe wines, rich and impressive at first but ageing very quickly. There are few memorable exceptions.

1982   A huge crop was the result of marvellous weather during the spring and summer which was thoroughly diluted by heavy rains at the vintage. Not wines for keeping, for the most part, but some who picked early and who managed to restrict their yields made exceptional bottles which are still evolving.

1981   After a good spring and early autumn, rain arrived with the vintage, doing less damage to the whites than the reds but the summer had not been sufficiently hot to ripen the grapes early and the result was somewhat austere wines, occasionally very good. Most are now past their best.

1980 A cool spring and early summer resulted in the late flowering of a rather small crop, and hence a late vintage. August and September were sunny but there was rain, and some rot, during the harvest in mid-October. The best wines lacked substance but had considerable elegance. Few remain interesting now.

1979 A very big crop which needed considerable chaptalization after a cool summer, but the whites were surprisingly agreeable. Their charm has faded and they now look rather tired.

1978 A cold spring produced a small crop, which struggled to ripen in a cold summer. The vintage was saved by a remarkable autumn which produced some concentrated long-lived wines of real stamina and class. These are only now beginning to show their full potential.

1977 Big crop, wet summer, decent autumn. An 'off-year' which turned out surprisingly well for the best wines because they had acidity to keep them fresh as they aged. These were the exceptions in a vintage which was generally mediocre.

1976 A large crop ripened in exceptionally hot and dry conditions during the summer, resulting in a very early harvest. Rather high levels of alcohol and low acidity marked wines which aged rapidly. Interesting for a few years, but most examples now well past their best.

1975 A good deal of rain in August and September ruined the prospects of this year, producing wines which were generally meagre and often rotten. Not recommended now.

1974 Medium-sized crop harvested in miserable, wet conditions. Generally dismissed at the time as an 'off-year' but some whites had the acidity to give long life and are now unexpectedly good.

1973 A huge crop, further diluted by summer rain, produced wines which had some initial appeal but never the stamina, ripeness or acidity to last for more than a few years. Flabby.

1972 A large crop struggled to reach maturity in a cold summer and the results, particularly for the white wines, were generally disappointing. Very rarely you can find a bottle from low-yielding old vines which is still delicious.

1971   Cold, wet weather in June ensured a small crop, further damaged by hailstorms in the summer. The September harvest took place in fine weather and the surviving wines can have real concentration.

1970   A successful flowering produced a big crop of grapes, generally ripe but lacking the acidity or concentration to make wines for long ageing. Most are well past their best.

APPENDIX III

Tastings

In addition to my regular tastings in the growers' cellars and elsewhere, I have over the past few years organized a series of blind tastings of the Grands Crus of Puligny and Chassagne in three good vintages: 1985, 1986 and 1988. In each case the wines were tasted between two and three years after the harvest, in the company of other wine enthusiasts so that opinions could be shared. Some clear patterns of winemaking competence began to emerge.

But there are a number of cautions. In the first place, such wines are hideously expensive and often very difficult to obtain; it was not possible to assemble a complete succession of samples in each vintage, from every producer. Second, these judgements are highly subjective. Although discussed with others of great experience, the opinions are entirely my own. The reader should also bear in mind that the quality of winemaking at these domaines and négociants can change quite suddenly (for better or worse) when a new generation succeeds the old.

Finally I should mention that reading other people's tasting notes on past vintages of unobtainable wines has always struck me as a pastime for oenophile voyeurs. It is far better to enjoy the real thing.

1985

Bienvenues-Bâtard-Montrachet   The best example was from Ramonet, whose wine reminded me of a rich quince and apple pie, complete with cloves. It had a delicious, spicy concentration. Leflaive's wine, almost on the same level of quality, was utterly different, emphasizing a clear elegance of structure, balancing fruit and oak with great subtlety. Somewhat less exciting were the four-square Bienvenues from Carillon and the rather old-fashioned wine from Remoissenet. Henri Clerc's example was decidedly dull.

Bâtard-Montrachet   My preferred wine of those available came from Gagnard-Delagrange; grand, rather serious, fine oak, rich fruit, lots of promise. Leflaive's Bâtard was more closed at this stage, even tough, but also suggested that it would evolve splendidly. The rest were a long way behind: a good but unexciting wine from Louis Latour; an over-sulphured example from Fontaine-Gagnard; antiseptic from Chartron & Trebuchet; cheesy from Albert Morey; oxidized from Henri Clerc.

Chevalier-Montrachet   Leflaive's wine was head and shoulders above the rest, still closed but quite evidently grand, serious and fine. Perhaps less immediate charm than in some vintages. There were two samples from Chartron. One was English-bottled and tasted of dishcloths and sulphur; the other (French-bottled) was corked.

Montrachet   We had another corked bottle in this section of the tasting (from Baron Thenard) plus a badly oxidized sample from Louis Latour and a slightly less oxidized bottle from Chartron & Trebuchet. That left a rather odd wine from Gagnard-Delagrange (smelling of spent fireworks, but suggesting some latent potential), an assertively old-fashioned wine from Lafon (not my taste, but it had its fans) and a better-balanced example from Remoissenet which was entirely honourable but failed to excite. All in all, a disappointing showing of one of the world's most sought-after appellations. Nearly three years later I tasted Baron Thenard's wine again. It suggested brioches and pâté, not unpleasantly, and had considerable length of flavour. But it was not fine. On the same occasion I enjoyed the faultless splendour of a Montrachet from the Domaine de la Romanée-Conti. Still very closed, and rather strongly marked by oak, it nonetheless was wonderfully balanced between power and elegance, with complexities which could still only be guessed at, needing years of bottle age to reveal its full potential. A magnificent wine.

1986

Criots-Bâtard-Montrachet   Only one sample of this tiny vineyard, an impressive wine from Louis Latour: greengages and straw, old-fashioned, good length of flavour.

Bienvenues-Bâtard-Montrachet   Again, only one sample in this tasting: Remoissenet's. A good wine, worthy rather than exciting. On other occasions I have tasted excellent examples from Leflaive, Sauzet and Carillon.

Bâtard-Montrachet   Four good wines. The best, for me, was from Louis Latour. This had real life and character, a tropical opulence of fruit flavours balanced by toasty oak and excellent acidity; great balance, great potential. Utterly different, but almost as fine, were the elegant, charming wine from Bachelet-Ramonet and the generous, complex and vivid example from Drouhin. A little way behind, somewhat understated, was the Bâtard of Olivier Leflaive. I have also tasted splendid Bâtards from Domaines Leflaive and Sauzet.

Chevalier-Montrachet   A dreadful wine from Jacques Prieur and a dreary one from Chartron were offset by a moderately exciting bottle from Bouchard Père et Fils and a magnificent one from Louis Latour: buttery, rich, opulent and alluring, but balanced by really elegant structure. Domaine Leflaive (more subtlety, less grandeur) had a hard job to win this race by a nose.

Montrachet Three samples, none of the very finest quality. Bouchard's was concentrated and closed, perhaps with more potential than it showed; Louis Latour's Montrachet was clearly less exciting than his Chevalier and Gagnard-Delagrange's likewise lacked the spark of greatness.

1988
Criots-Bâtard-Montrachet A single sample, from Olivier Leflaive, which seemed overwhelmed by oak.

Bienvenues-Bâtard-Montrachet Two excellent samples. Carillon's had a hint of grilled goat's cheese on toast on the nose but was discreetly elegant on the palate, with firm structure and good acidity; perhaps picked just a little too early. Sauzet's was spicy, characterful and long, pungent but elegant.

Bâtard-Montrachet By far the most exciting wine came from Ramonet. Biscuits, vanilla and oak at first, restrained, even reserved; then an explosion of rich, opulent complexity and splendour. Sauzet's wine on this occasion seemed less fine than his Bienvenues, though I have received the contrary impression on other occasions. Gagnard-Delagrange's Bâtard was somewhat dull, undefined, even a bit stewed. Leflaive's Bâtard (tasted later) was marvellous, but not a match for Ramonet.

Chevalier-Montrachet Discreet elegance, a light fragrance of spring wild-flowers, a touch of oak, sappy persistence and subtlety of flavour: Domaine Leflaive. Chartron, by contrast, made a wine which lacked real exhilaration and left a suggestion of boiled sweets. Bouchard (tasted later) seemed limp, and rather cardboardy.

Montrachet Baron Thenard's wine was fat and dull, Bouchard's substantial but unmemorable. Fortunately there were two great Montrachets, from Ramonet and Laguiche. Ramonet's Montrachet, like his Bâtard, was full of rich fruit flavours, entangled in complexity, and was deep, toasty and persistent: it seemed to go on for ever, growing more magnificent as it opened in the glass. Drouhin's version from the domaine of the Marquis de Laguiche provided a complete contrast. Scented of fresh cheese and straw, so discreet as to appear to lack substance at first, it too opened up in the glass to reveal hidden splendours. But its hallmark was the refinement of power by civilization, whereas Ramonet's retained all the character of its vivid Burgundian patois.

APPENDIX IV

Producers

This list includes the names of all the growers and négociants of Puligny who registered with the Syndicat Viticole of the village in order to obtain a certificate of appellation for the wines which they had harvested during the 1990 vintage.

Growers

Bavard, Jean-Paul
21190 Puligny-Montrachet

Bavard, Paul
21190 Puligny-Montrachet

Belicard, Bernard
21190 Puligny-Montrachet

Bidault, Jean-Claude
21190 Puligny-Montrachet

Bidault, Patrick
21190 Puligny-Montrachet

Boudot-Boillot, Gérard
21190 Puligny-Montrachet

Bzicot, Stanislas
21190 Puligny-Montrachet

Chavy, Christian (Mme)
21190 Puligny-Montrachet

Chavy, Gérard
21190 Puligny-Montrachet

Chavy-Chouet, Hubert
21190 Puligny-Montrachet

Chavy-Ropiteau, Albert
21190 Puligny-Montrachet

Chifflot, Rémy
21169 Couchey

Courreaux, Bernard
21190 Puligny-Montrachet

David, Camille
21190 Puligny-Montrachet

Desfêtes, Renée
21190 Puligny-Montrachet

Deveze, Bernard
21190 Puligny-Montrachet

Deveze, Marcel
21190 Puligny-Montrachet

Dubuisson, Didier
21190 Puligny-Montrachet

Dubuisson, Jean-Michel
21190 Puligny-Montrachet

Dubuisson, Thierry
21190 Puligny-Montrachet

Dureuil, Michel
21190 Puligny-Montrachet

Gaçon-Moingeon, Yveline
21190 Puligny-Montrachet

Guérin, Gérard
21190 Puligny-Montrachet

Henry, Marcel
21190 Puligny-Montrachet

Joly, Albert
21190 Puligny-Montrachet

Joly, Daniel
21190 Puligny-Montrachet

Llorca, François
21190 Puligny-Montrachet

Llorca, Gérard
21190 Puligny-Montrachet

Maroslavac-Kovacevic,
Stephan Père
21190 Puligny-Montrachet

Maroslavac-Leger, Roland
21190 Puligny-Montrachet

Maroslavac-Tremeau,
Stephan
21190 Puligny-Montrachet

Martinerie, Rémy
21190 Puligny-Montrachet

Meney, Georges
21190 Puligny-Montrachet

Mignot, Gaston
21190 Puligny-Montrachet

Monnot, Jean-Pierre
21190 Puligny-Montrachet

Montlivault, Louise de
Blagny
21190 Puligny-Montrachet

Morin, Roland
21190 Puligny-Montrachet

Pagand, Claire
21190 Puligny-Montrachet

Pascal, René
21190 Puligny-Montrachet

Pernot, Jean-Marc
21190 Puligny-Montrachet

Ponelle, Daniel
21190 Puligny-Montrachet

Ponelle, Jean
21190 Puligny-Montrachet

Ponelle, Jean-François
21190 Puligny-Montrachet

Potier, Léon
21190 Puligny-Montrachet

Riger, Jacky
21190 Puligny-Montrachet

Roze, Paulette
21190 Puligny-Montrachet

Roze-Thomas, Germaine
21190 Puligny-Montrachet

Savry, Marcel
21190 Puligny-Montrachet

Thomas, Pierre
21190 Puligny-Montrachet

Thusseau, Louis
21190 Puligny-Montrachet

Thusseau, Michel
21190 Puligny-Montrachet

Vallot, Guy
21190 Puligny-Montrachet

**Domaine Louis Carillon &
Fils**
21190 Puligny-Montrachet

Domain Jean Chartron
21190 Puligny-Montrachet

Domaine Henri Clerc & Fils
21190 Puligny-Montrachet

**Domaine Château de
Puligny-Montrachet Scea**
21190 Puligny-Montrachet

Domaine Leflaive
21190 Puligny-Montrachet

Domaine Jean Pascal & Fils
21190 Puligny-Montrachet

Domaine Paul Pernot & Fils
21190 Puligny-Montrachet

Domaine Etienne Sauzet
21190 Puligny-Montrachet

Négociants

Chartron et Trebuchet
21190 Puligny-Montrachet

Olivier Leflaive Frères
Place du Monument
21190 Puligny-Montrachet

INDEX

Index

305

306

A Note on the Type

This book was set in a type face called Garamond. Jean Jannon has been identified as the designer of this face, which is based on Garamond's original models but is much lighter and more open. The italic is taken from a font of Granjon, which appeared in the repratory of the Imprimerie Royale and was probably cut in the middle of the sixteenth century.

Composed in Great Britain

Printed and bound by Arcata Graphics/Martinsburg,
Martinsburg, West Virginia

Scale 1:20,000

SAINT-AUBIN

Chassagne-Montrachet

SANTENAY

Les Baudines

Les Embazées

Bois de Chassagne

La Grande Montagne

400

300

En Virondot

Les Combards

Pot Bois

Le Parterre

Chassagne du Clos Saint-Jean

Clos Saint-Jean

En Pimont

Clos Pitois

Francemont

Tête du Clos

La Romanée

Les Grandes Ruchottes

La Grande Montagne

En Cailleret

Vigne Derrière

Les Murées

Les Rebichets

Les Grands Clos

Les Petits Clos

Les Petites Fairendes

Les Fairendes

Les Champs Gain

La Matroie

Chassagne

Macherelle

SANTENAY

La Grande Borne

La Cardeuse

Les Brussonnes

Morgeot

Morgeot

Vigne Blanche

Morgeot

La Boudriotte

Les Masures

La Canière

Ez Crets

Les Chênes

Les Places

Les

Clos Chareau

Les Boirette

La Chapelle

Ez Crottes

Guerchère

Les Chaumes

Champs Jendreau

Les Chaumes

Le Clos Réland

Les Essarts

Clos Bernot

Puits Merdreau

Minchottes

Les Voillenots Dessus

Clos Devant

REMIGNY

Les Barbaudes

Les Benoîtes

Champs de Morjot

En L'Ormeau

La Platière

La Goujonne

Les Morichots

Le Concis du Champs

Voillenot Dessous

Les Chambres

Champ Derrière

Dessous les Mues

SAÔNE-ET-LOIRE

Les Benoîtes

Champs de Morjot

La Platière

Les Lombardes

Le Poirier du Clos

La Corvée

Bouchon de Corvée

Sur Matronge

Dessous les Mues

La Tétière

Les Pierres

R.N. 6

CHAGNY

CORPEAU

BEAUNE

Montrachet
Chevalier-Montrachet
Bâtard-Montrachet
Bienvenues-Bâtard-Montrachet
Criots-Bâtard-Montrachet

Chassagne-Montrachet

Puligny-Montrachet premier cru
Chassagne-Montrachet premier cru

Puligny-Montrachet

Puligny-Montrachet premier cru (white)
Blagny premier cru (red)

Puligny-Montrachet (white)
Blagny (red)